MW01283148

Home, Uprooted

Home, Uprooted

Oral Histories of India's Partition

Devika Chawla

FORDHAM UNIVERSITY PRESS

NEW YORK 2014

Copyright © 2014 Fordham University Press

All rights reserved. No part of this publication may be repro-
duced, stored in a retrieval system, or transmitted in any form or
by any means—electronic, mechanical, photocopy, recording, or
any other—except for brief quotations in printed reviews,
without the prior permission of the publisher.

Fordham University Press has no responsibility for the persis-
tence or accuracy of URLs for external or third-party Internet
websites referred to in this publication and does not guarantee
that any content on such websites is, or will remain, accurate or
appropriate.

Fordham University Press also publishes its books in a variety of
electronic formats. Some content that appears in print may not
be available in electronic books.

Library of Congress Cataloging-in-Publication Data

Chawla, Devika.
    Home, uprooted : oral histories of India's partition /
Devika Chawla.
        pages cm
    Includes bibliographical references and index.
    ISBN 978-0-8232-5643-3 (hardback) —
ISBN 978-0-8232-5644-0 (paper)
    1. India—History—Partition, 1947—Personal narratives.
    2. Refugees—India—Biography.   I. Title.
    DS480.842.C43 2014
    954.04'2—dc23
                                                        2013048882

Printed in the United States of America

16 15 14   5 4 3 2 1

First edition

CONTENTS

ILLUSTRATIONS

ACKNOWLEDGMENTS

There can be no story without interlocutors. There would be no stories here, but for the generosity of Delhi Partition refugees and their families who humored my entry into their homes with my father, Papa, in tow. Your stories and your willingness to tell them have made *Home, Uprooted* a possibility.

The field-homework for this book began informally in June 2007 in Delhi, the city where I was born in 1974, the city that will always *feel* like home to me, but also the city that I have lived away from for almost seventeen years. I salute both her and her inhabitants.

My fieldwork travels were supported by two Ohio University funding sources—the Ohio University Research Council (2009) and the Provost's Summer Award for Research and Creativity (2008). Colleagues in the School of Communication Studies remained consistently supportive of my research endeavors. They endorsed a one-year-long faculty fellowship sabbatical, which allowed me the time to write this book. In particular, I thank Austin Babrow, Benjamin Bates, and Judith Yaross Lee. My former dean, Gregory J. Shepherd, was enthusiastic about this project right from its inception, and for that I owe him a great debt. Marina Peterson, a friend and colleague in the School of Interdisciplinary Arts, read many portions of the proposal and opening chapters; her critiques and guidance continue to energize my thinking. Gillian Berchowitz, Director of the Ohio University Press, counseled me on important aspects of the proposal and review process. Graduate research assistants Courtney Cole, Karen Greiner, Mumba Mumba, and Lindsay Rose were conscientious and timely in completing the many tasks I requested of them. Thinking along with my graduate and undergraduate students in the Postcolonial Studies, Critical Ethnography, and Performance Studies seminars has, over the years, enriched and influenced many of the ideas that I work through in this book.

Colleagues and friends at other institutions were unreserved in their generosity. Myrdene Anderson at Purdue University, ongoing mentor and fellow ethnographer, read and reread drafts, sometimes at very short notice. Amardo Rodriguez at Syracuse University continues to "drop everything" to attend to my writing, conversations, and miscellaneous matters. I thank Caryn E. Medved at Baruch College for her personal and intellectual friendship. Craig Gingrich-Philbrook at Southern Illinois University, my sabbatical twin and kindred spirit, I value both our virtual and real conversations.

Fredric Nachbaur, director of Fordham University Press, has been a generous, thoughtful, and accessible editor. I am grateful to him for making the process seamless. I thank Eric Newman, the managing editor, for all his assistance. I could not have asked for a more meticulous, careful, and engaged copy editor than Ann Miller. I thank Lawrence Marotta for creating the index. I thank Stacy Holman Jones from California State University, Northridge and the second reviewer for their important critiques and necessary suggestions, which have sharpened the conceptual focus of the book.

I wrote *Home, Uprooted* in its entirety here in Ohio, in the little college town of Athens that houses Ohio University—the place that, for now, I call home. The sedentary and lonely activity of staying put and just simply writing has taught me something about the human desire for fixed spaces, what some call home.

I thank my family and friends both near and far—Samarth Chawla, Abha Chawla, Ira Lakshmi Chawla, Anuradha Ruhil Barua, Abhay Kashalkar, Preeti Kohli, Erik Garrett, and Suraksha and Yogesh Gajwani.

I am indebted to my parents, Bindu and Sudhakar Chawla, for the home(s) that you have given me. Going home still means going home to *you*. This book would not exist without Papa—my informant, my interlocutor, my participant, but most important, my father. Not only were you present at every stage of the project, but your presence is palpable in every page of this book. I hope the last chapter, "My Father, My Interlocutor," does justice to your irreplaceable role in this work.

My spouse, Anirudh V. Ruhil, lived my field-homework, listened to me talk of these stories, and unselfishly read every single page, even when the statistician in him felt discombobulated by the humanist tenor of the research and writing. He continues to be its (and my) champion.

Home, Uprooted

ONE

Beginnings—in Headnotes

> To work and suffer is to be at home.
> All else is scenery.
>
> —ADRIENNE RICH, *"The Tourist and the Town"*

Stories begin in memories. This one has its origins in a walking history, if there is such a thing. It finds its start in the early 1980s when I was seven years old. We lived in a small North Indian town called Moga, just thirty kilometers from the border with Pakistan. My grandfather had recently died, and Biji, my grandma, had come to live with us. She and I were forced to share a room and developed the love-hate relationship that inevitably ensues when a child finds herself rooming with a seventy-five-year-old grandparent.[1]

Biji had many rituals—waking up at 4:00 A.M. to recite the Gayatri Mantra and portions of the Gita; cleaning her dentures as she whispered *hai ram* (invoking the Lord Rama) for the next hour; oiling her hair with coconut oil; eating her *isabgol* with warm water—*isabgol* is a traditional, Ayurvedic stomach cleanser, which everyone in generations previous to mine swears by. On weekdays, we held to a reluctant peace since I needed to wake up for school at 6:00 A.M. and with Biji around I was never going to be late. But during weekends, the room became a battle zone as I resisted getting out of

I

bed until 8:00 A.M.—a considerably late wake-up time in Biji's world. For Biji, every day was every day, and she lovingly nourished her routines.

After the first year we became used to this pattern. Weekend mornings were still unpleasant, but we had discovered a fondness for one another, a fondness that came from my childish realization that Biji's presence was beneficial to me. She had begun to help me tidy my room, and being a devout Hindu she would tell me stories from the Ramayana and Mahabharata before I slept. I have never taken to religion, yet because of Biji, I remain enthralled with the fantastical dimensions of most religious stories. And whatever I know about Hinduism comes from these bedtime tales. Biji bathed me before school, braided my hair, and even helped me with my Hindi homework. Born in 1908 in what is now Pakistan, Biji was my paternal grandmother. She never attended college, but had completed the highest-level examination in Hindi proficiency that women were allowed to take in the early 1900s. It was called the Prabhakar, and my parents tell me that it was then considered equivalent to a master's degree. It is only now that I realize how radical this education must have been for an Indian woman born in the early 1900s. I wish I had met her as a grown-up. Alas, grandparents are always presented to us in the autumn of their lives and we are able to garner mere remnants of their personalities.

In time, I stopped complaining about the morning rituals and would even help Biji oil her long white hair. Today, here in the United States, three decades later, a mere whiff of coconut oil still takes me back to my elderly roommate. Much to Amma's chagrin, I keep the product away from my own hair. Amma, my mother, constantly reminds me that the coconut oil was the secret behind my grandmother's tresses, which remained thick and long until she died. I have long black hair that Amma fusses over; "Take care of it, your Biji died with a full head of hair, it is the coconut oil." I buy it—Parachute is the brand—but it stands lonely and unused in my bathroom vanity. Sometimes when I miss Biji, I open the bottle and sniff it, and even though I detest the odor, it brings her closer to me.

One summer evening I was asked by Amma to begin going for walks with Biji. "Why do I have to do that, Amma?" I demanded. Yet another hour of my day was being given to my grandparent. Amma's only response was a frightening glare. I conceded. What option did I have? I often threatened to leave home because of such incidents, but my parents and Biji would laughingly cajole me to stay until the next morning, knowing sleep would turn my misery into memory overnight. At breakfast the next morning, Papa explained that Biji's evening walks had become unsafe. "How?" I growled. We lived in a compound that was enclosed within the Nestlé factory where my father was the personnel manager. Biji walked along the sidewalk adjacent to large eucalyptus trees that were apparently home to an army of crows. Since she was a diminutive woman, they'd fly close to her head and scare her. A crow had poked its beak at her skull a few evenings previously. When she complained, Papa and Amma thought a companion would help. I was asked to fling around my grandfather's walking stick if the crows came too close. The stick went with Biji wherever she traveled. Biji was a small woman and I probably stood barely four feet tall at the time; I have never grown over five feet tall anyway. Stick or no stick, we hardly made a daunting pair.

Her walk began a half hour after our regular afternoon tea, which was taken at 4:30 P.M. Not surprisingly, I was sullen when we started, and Biji humored me by telling me about the time when I was a toddler and fell into a shallow open ditch, full of dirty water, outside the family house in Delhi. "What happened? Did I drown?" I asked. "You would not be here, would you?" she grinned.

I think nothing is more fascinating for a child than to hear about her infant days. As I have grown older, childhood stories have taken on a mystical and mythical quality. They are a space that I long to know again, but as an adult. I also find this fascination with one's past, whether more immediate—as for a seven-year-old—or further on in time, sustains us, as one of the ways we meet our selves in the present and future. We are not our childhood, but that space shadows us, asking to be recalled.

When Biji and I reached the row of eucalyptus trees I realized that Papa had not been exaggerating. There were at least twenty crows perched on two of the trees and as soon as they saw Biji, they began crowing angrily. There were some men walking ahead of us, but the crows had their eyes on my tiny grandmother. I thanked all of Biji's Hindu gods that I was carrying the stick and waved it around angrily. Biji continued talking, and walking. And so began our daily walks that would last until I was ten and was sent to boarding school.

We were a curious pair—a small white-haired lady in a white cotton sari with her head covered and a little girl almost a foot shorter, in a frock, carrying her dead grandfather's walking stick. But we were fearless together. These walks and our room created a bond that otherwise would never have been forged. As the weeks, months, and three years went on, we talked of everything. She gave me my earliest memories of the Chawla family in Pakistan, about my maternal great-grandfather who was given the title of "Rai Sahib" during British rule, about my grandfather, Pitaji, who worked for the British railways until the Partition of India in 1947. I came to know that Biji had had a baby brother who died of an illness some months before his first birthday, leaving her an only child.

It was from her that I learned of the great Quetta earthquake—*Quette ka bhuchal*—of 1935, a seismic catastrophe that almost killed Pitaji's youngest brother Mahinder, who was then just nine years old. Mahinder was trapped under a large wooden wardrobe and was rescued by Pitaji, who was two decades older than he. This explained why Pitaji was so dear to my granduncle Mahinder, who from then on took care of my grandparents like a son. It was also from Biji that I first heard about the other catastrophe—the human-made one—the Batwara, her generation's name for the Partition of India. Now, here, with the luxury to indulgently retrospect, I think of *partition*, the English word for *batwara*, as too neutral, and an almost dispassionate translation for what *batwara* invokes, incites. *Batwara*, as I heard the word from Biji, felt more forceful, more emotional, and more intimate. Biji gave meaning to the word in stories of how my family were forced to leave our farmlands and our home. It was from her, and later from Papa, that I became aware of Pitaji's choice to stay behind in Pakistan in the hope that the communal riots would subside, and he could just remain home—a belief in the impermanence of the rupture that echoes in the pages that follow. I was the only grandchild among five who knew early on how my family lived as refugees in different localities in Delhi, and how my father and his siblings came to be educated amid deep economic hardship.

If I had not joined these walks to stave off these *kumbakht* (irritating) birds, as Biji called the crows in Urdu, there would have been none of these early stories—memories in words—of that other place that was Biji's home. I could not have known then that these walking-talking-listening-imagining strolls would become the earliest impetus to the work of home that speaks from these pages. In these walks I learned to listen and see, in step with the field/the body of memories that was my Biji. Walks—my first encounter with the field of/as memory—at home. A kind of peripatetic learning about how to do homework.

Sometimes when her stories disturbed and frightened me, I'd naively urge Biji to forget them and not be so unhappy. I am ashamed to admit it, but I often demanded that she stop: *"Aap koi aur baat kyon nahi karte, itna boring hai yai"* (why don't you talk of something else, this is boring). She would sigh and say the following words, which I repeat here in her mix of Hindi and Urdu because I must resurrect some sense of her in her vernacular:

> *Desh to hame mil gayaa angrezoon sey, par humara ghar chala gaya. Bhoolana aasaan nahi hai. Aur jub aadmi buzurg ho jata hai, to bas zyada dukh hota hai. Kaise batoun tumhe, beta. Angrezi mein iske liye shabd hota hain*—melancholy—*nahi jaati wo.*

> [We got our country from the British, but we lost our home. That is difficult to forget. And when you grow old, you are just sad, I cannot explain it, there is a word in English for it—*melancholy*—it does not go away.]

The memories of my cruel words to her and my writing them here give me remorse, making me mourn more deeply for this widowed refugee who was also my grandmother. Grief remains an unknown place until one has encountered it.

Our evening jaunts ended when my parents decided to send me to Waverly, an all-girls Catholic boarding school in Mussoorie, which is a small North Indian hill station nestled in the foothills of the Himalayas. My older brother Samarth had left for boarding school a few years before me, and with no grandchild in the house, Biji decided to return to living with her older son, my father's older brother. As an adult, I've come to understand how important this moment of departure really was because after it, Biji and I would never again live together under the same roof. Now we only met at extended family gatherings and crowded family vacations.

At the age of twenty-three, in 1997, I left for graduate studies in the United States, never to see her again. I was in the United States when Biji passed away. She died on a cold December day in 1999, three days before I was to arrive home for winter break. It was a sad entourage that came to meet me at the Delhi airport. On the thirteenth day after her cremation, as is customary, there was a celebration in our neighborhood temple—a small *havan*, high tea for the extended family, and the singing of *bhajans*, devotional songs. Afterwards we congregated at my parents' home for dinner—we had not been together like this for almost ten years. Not surprisingly, the talk turned to Biji, who I was told had been very worried when I had moved away to the United States. She'd blamed my father for letting me go and told him, "This child is now lost to you, she will not return." I think she saw my leaving the country as a betrayal of all that was homely, secure, familiar—all that was home. *Wahaan* (there) is what she called America in Urdu, and it was *yahaan* (here) that she wanted me to belong.

My father's older brother, Bade Papa, addressing me by my family nickname, asked, "Gudia, you were her favorite, you know?" I shook my head, "Oh no, she loved Samarth the most, she treated him like a son." Samarth had been almost entirely raised by Biji because when he was born my Amma held a full-time job. Biji became his day mother and Amma his night mother. My cousins and I always knew that he was special to her. We did not feel unloved by her, we just knew.

Bade Papa walked over to his briefcase, popped it open, and took out a picture of me from when I was sixteen, an old modeling shot that a professional photographer friend of the family had taken. I'd mailed Biji that picture because after she moved away we only met once a year, and I wanted her to keep up with how I was changing. I wanted to show off and let her know that I was almost an adult and that I was pretty. She replied with a letter written in her very proper mix of Urdu and Hindi. In it she admitted that I was turning into a beautiful girl, but she cautioned me to cultivate modesty. Instead of taking pride in my appearance, I was to worry more about school and making something of myself, she instructed. After she died, my uncle and aunt discovered the photograph inside her Gita; behind it she had written in Hindi, "Gudia, *meri poti*," my granddaughter. Bade Papa said she inevitably displayed the picture to all her visitors, proudly announcing that I was living and studying for a doctorate in the United States. She never failed to mention that I had taken care of her by being her guard during her evening walks and saved her from the wicked crows. The moral of this story, according to my uncle, was simple—if I could fend off Indian crows, I was brave enough to live alone in the United States. There were shouts of laughter around the table with my older cousins improvising a rhyme, "Gudia can fend off crows, so Gudia is brave, so she can live alone—there—in the United States."

I tearfully joined in the laughter, silently acknowledging that our walks were an enduring memory when she was dying. Maybe Biji was right, maybe staving off the crows was brave, maybe it taught me to be unafraid. Our walks remain my *only* memories of Biji's lost home in Pakistan—a bridge between the country of *her* childhood, the India of *my* childhood, and this new country, the United States, that I now call home. I will always regret not having seen her before she died. There is nothing to be done, no dramas to be staged, no memorials to be built, and no eulogies to be read. There are only memories. And words.

In *Home, Uprooted* I tread forward with the weight of Biji's lost homes on my back. She is the first reason for this quest, for this homework. Here.

TWO

Fieldwork/Homework

Anilji and I have spent two hours combing every corner of his retirement flat. The birth certificate must be found, because "we must begin at the beginning," says Anilji.[1] We eventually find it well preserved between two old photographs from Karachi. It establishes Anil Vohra as a "British Subject" born in Karachi in 1930. "Why is it important?" I naively ask this seventy-seven-year-old man. He says it's not important, but it establishes where he's from. He wasn't born in Pakistan; there was no Pakistan, he was Indian, and a British subject. Home can be about origins.

Kiranji, an eighty-seven-year-old refugee, also returns to origins. She says, "It's very heartrending, you've left your birthplace. We are Indian citizens, there is no doubt about that, but it's the birthplace you always think about." Home is the mother, Kiranji tells me; "The real mother is where you are born. . . . It is like losing a limb . . . like you've lost a life that you would love to live over again. . . . But, would I be where I am or be *what* I am, had I not lost this home? I don't know the answer to that." Home—

coterminous with the body. An almost umbilical link. Its material loss can be a gain.

I am late for every meeting with Dadaji (granddad), a ninety-two-year-old once-famous radio artist from Lahore. Dadaji chides me about my lateness during every visit. "The traffic has become awful, Dadaji," I apologize after every late arrival. Dadaji's days are regimented; he awakens at 5:00 A.M., takes his morning walk at 5:30, and brews chai for the entire household by 6:15 A.M. Today he is in a mood to recite *shairi* (Urdu sonnets) sung by him and aired on All India Radio in the 1930s. After a few hours when I am ready to leave, Dadaji asks his daughter-in-law to look for the invitation from the Queen. "Of England?" I ask. "Yes, of course," he replies. His son, a surgeon who lives in England, is being named a Member of the Most Excellent Order of the British Empire for his service to medicine. Dadaji, the sole surviving parent, has been invited. And he is flying to attend the ceremony. "Have you ever been to England?" I ask. "No, this will be my first time, I never saw the Queen when she ruled us, but I get to see her now," he announces proudly. I am both surprised and not. I think this is some sort of a homecoming.

"I went to Sibbi last night," Arjunji announces. I'm confused. Sibbi is his village in Pakistan. He laughs, his wife laughs, and they explain that every few days he "goes away" to his *ghar* (home) in Sibbi in his *sapne* (dreams). "I wake up and my wife and I discuss all the details of my dream, where I was playing, which room in the house I was in, and what we were doing—it's almost real," he smiles. Home can be visited in dreams, imagined. Sibbi lives.

Mrs. Chopra will not sit still. Every visit is a tour around her home in South Delhi. She is a sprightly eighty-three-year-old who does not stand on too much formality. One day she takes me on a tour of the bedrooms; "See this table and this cupboard, and this bed, they are so old, they're from Lahore, but my daughters—and none of them have even been to Pakistan, they were all born here—they won't let me throw these away." She laughs, "These are so old, I don't know why they like them." Nostalgia seeps into generations. And stays. You can miss home, even when it was not home.

Sheilaji will not return to her birth place. For her, there is nothing to see and there is nothing she wants to see. "Don't you want to visit your old home?" I ask. "No, my memories of that home are all about terror, it does not seem like home." People often invite Sheilaji to go with them to revisit

Lahore, but she keeps refusing; "The bad memories are more than the good ones, I don't want to see it." I ask curiously, "Your children? You don't want them to see where you are from?" "No, they don't need to see or know." Yet her grandson has joined a cricket club and travels to Pakistan to play the game. Sheilaji disapproves. Home can be about the terrors of belonging.

What is home and how do we encounter it? Is home about origins and place? Or is it a poetic space that unleashes the imagination? Can home be a state of becoming and unbecoming? Or is home a process that is coterminous with our minds and bodies? How is its material and emotional loss necessary to gain a semblance of self? Can homes persist in different spaces and across times? Are homes—as places, states, processes, and relationships—almost unnecessary and disposable?

Home, Uprooted is a storied contemplation on the conceptual nexus of home, travel, and identity in cross-generational oral histories of refugees of India's Partition. I meditate on this nexus, attending to it as a complex yet tenuous thematic that is comprised of a series of tensions along which home is often experienced—as a space/place/idea that is stayed in (here-native), traveled to (there-Other), inhabited (or colonized), domesticated (or subjugated), felt (or not felt), and arrived at (or departed from). I consider home as a spatial, discursive, poetic, and contradictory imaginary that enables (and is simultaneously enabled by) multiple narrations of individual and family identity. I address identity fluidly, as a narrative and communicative process, a story we tell about ourselves to both ourselves and to others.[2] And in telling stories we create selves, cultural understandings, and a world.[3] I hope to forward the idea that in telling, performing, and embodying versions and visions of un/home, India's Partition refugees reclaim old selves and invent new ones (and do not).[4] I am relying here on contemporary literature about home for my use of the term *un/home* because it includes "elsewhere spaces" and conditions that can be experienced as home.[5] I am suggesting that for these persons in these moments with this ethnographer, performing home—as sense, presence, absence—becomes an exercise in performing selves.

To enter the oral histories of the displaced is to inevitably enter the material loss of house and home, because the displaced "view home with a more urgent longing" than the secure.[6] In that sense my proposed thematic here is inevitable, natural, and unique. This is motivation enough to propose an idea, to pursue an object of study, to examine a tidy thematic. After all, refugees are persons without homes, so they are, by that definition, people residing in between geographies and nationalities—border people with border identities—Homi Bhabha's interstitial figures who live in between spaces.[7] Home for them/us is palpably absent. And (but) absences always gather presence. This thematic then is an unsurprising induction.

Yet, in my introduction here, I want to consider more and other, parallel motivations that move me into this thematic, this book, these stories. Because what I hope to perform here are checkered stories and homely narratives. Sometimes the stories, anecdotes, incidents, memories may seem like the *ordinary affects* that anthropologist Kathleen Stewart describes as "public feelings that begin and end in broad circulation," but that are "also the stuff that seemingly intimate lives are made of."[8] To notice, to take pause for ordinary affects is to pay attention to "things that happen," that

> happen in impulses, sensations, expectations, daydreams, encounters, and habit of relating, in strategies and their failures, in forms of persuasion, contagion, and compulsion, in modes of attention, attachment, and agency, and in publics and social worlds of all kinds that catch people up in things that feel like *something.*[9]

This book moves like an archive—of field, of home, of memory—attending to things remembered, things noted, and things that just came to be in conversation with this *native* ethnographer who has removed herself from and re-placed home. This is a book about the homes the ethnographer-I enacted with her own and with others in oral histories, so much so that home came to be the most likely thematic that would emerge. For my own family history seeps, leaks, and submerges with the stories I encountered both *here* and *there*—an archive of my own family memories. This book is a return home for this South Asian, Indian, naturalized American, second-generation "refugee" ethnographer, who went home to study her own—her own family of Partition refugees, made homeless by India's division.[10]

This is a book about traveling home and finding an ethnographic field. It is also about traveling to the ethnographic field and finding home. This book was taking form during a period when the ethnographer surrendered one citizenship for another, a period of residing in between national allegiances—India and the United States—complicating further the notion of home, of origins, of identity. It is a book about the uneasiness of identifying home. This is a book about leaving home to remember and remake home. An attempt to solve and unsolve the riddle that is—home. An attempt that is destined to both fail and succeed.

Homework/Fieldwork

It is the first image that greets visitors when they enter my home in Athens, Ohio. As paintings go, it is nothing spectacular. I purchased the print in 2005 for 80 rupees (about $2.00) at the National Gallery of Modern Art in New Delhi. It shows an old lady in a *salwar kameez*—the long shirt and trousers worn by Punjabi women—sitting sideways on a *charpoy* (a frame strung with rope, a bedstead),[11] knitting in the afternoon sun. Her expression is pensive, lonesome. A few black crows hover around the charpoy; some look away, others seem to inspect her mood. The artist Anjolie Ela Menon has entitled this work *Mataji* (Grandma). Even to strangers who don't know the story behind the portrait, Mataji's sorrow is palpable. The artist has portrayed Mataji as a refugee who daydreams of her home in Lahore, lost to her by India's Partition in 1947.[12]

Diagonally across from the painting, near a corner window in the living room, stands a small edge table that was originally meant to hold a houseplant. On it I have placed a small, hand-sized, rectangular trunk-shaped metal box that has seen better days. It belonged to Biji. Intricately decorated in maroon, black, and gold, it looks like an ornamental keepsake box that used to have a key for a built-in lock. A miniature Taj Mahal is etched on the lid, and can only be seen when peering at the box from the top. The bottom gives a clue to the box's origins, with the stamp "English Make."

When I became a first-time homeowner in 2005, I took my time deciding on the décor of the living room, but I knew, no matter what the style of the interior, *Mataji* and the box would have a place there. I did not yet own the print, and the box was with Amma, who welcomed my asking her for it; she says I had coveted it for a long time. It was left to Amma by Biji, who used it to store money for daily household purchases. No one knows how and when Biji came by it, and she herself did not remember its history—

A photograph of a reproduction of Anjolie Ela Menon's painting *Mataji* in the author's home in Athens, Ohio.

only that it traveled with her from Pakistan. All of the family's other belongings were lost when the train carrying them was looted in Lahore.

I've developed my own reading, a story if you will, for the box. The words *English Make* on the bottom clarify that it was manufactured in England

The lid of Biji's Taj Mahal "English Make" box.

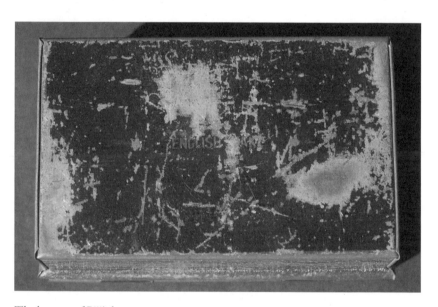

The bottom of Biji's box.

during the Raj. An inexpensive tourist trinket representing the Empire's length and breadth, it was probably sold with some pride within India and other British colonies. The Taj Mahal, a symbol of Moghul architectural splendor, is captured in miniature on the top of the box. The Taj's British ownership is stamped on the bottom, showing—symbolically and literally— that the imperial power owned this monument, and could mass-produce a symbol of Empire in any form it desired. Even as a child, I was not averse to the irony embedded in the object and its label. I think I wanted it then because the box had a lock and key, making it a potential holder of secrets and treasures. I wanted it because the English Make label made it a British object, and like all children who grew up in post-independence India, even though I was supposed to reject Britishness, I was also encouraged to embrace it in my speech and mannerisms. This object was *bona fide* English and made me feel a part of the Raj. Ultimately, as an adult I wanted it because it had belonged to Biji and is a material symbol of my family's politically impelled migrations.

The painting, on the other hand, does come with a story. My mother also bought the print at an exhibit because it reminded her of her in-laws who fled Pakistan. I think it also reminded her of her own displacements, which were smaller, but felt nonetheless. Amma, born and raised in Delhi in an independent India, has never experienced forced migration. But she married my father, whose life had been defined by his family's refugee status; he embraced effortlessly a nomadic sort of corporate life as a management professional, moving us from Indian state to Indian state for better prospects, new experiences. Even though Amma was a willing traveler, she longed to return to Delhi, where she was born and where she grew up. The years spent away from her birthplace—the 1970s and 1980s—were a hiatus, and she only came fully alive on her short visits home each year. It was from her that I learned to miss Delhi, just as it was from Biji that I learned to miss the old country—both of them places that I cannot rightfully claim as home. For Amma, the mataji in the painting represents Biji (and perhaps herself)—a benevolent matriarch and also a wife who remained helpless against the overwhelming melancholia that shrouded her owing to an enforced exile. After leaving Quetta, Biji never fully experienced at-homeness in the new country that came to house her; she was not unhappy, she just remained without anchor. In 1990, my father returned my mother and us to Delhi, and Amma remains there—happy, anchored. In 1997, fifty years after my family fled Pakistan, I left India, hoping to return; but here I am in 2013 a new citizen of the United States, anchored to an existential notion of home as an everywhere and nowhere place. Notwithstanding, bringing *Mataji* and the Taj Mahal box into my house in Ohio seemed crucial—a symbol of inherited filial longings.

Why hold on to these two objects? Some of the reasons are obvious. I have experienced my own share of childhood displacements—not living in the same home for longer than five years, moving from state to state with my father's jobs, living in boarding school for most of my adolescent life. These movements were involuntary, because my parents made those choices to move me. As an adult, as soon as I could, I chose my own consequential displacement—a move from India to the United States on an intellectual whim, aspiring for American higher education. So, my desire to retain these objects seems to contradict my desire for movement, my wanting to leave home behind. I find my fondness confusing. Even though I have willingly (and some say unsentimentally) left behind homes of the past, because homes can be prisons that restrict whomever we might become, yet these objects moor me in interesting ways by being familiar figures in my imaginings of home/s as conceptual and emotional spaces.

In *Family Frames*, Marianne Hirsch proposes the notion of *postmemory*, an idea that provides a compelling explanation for my fondness for these objects to which I am linked cross-generationally, but with whom I have no history of recollection. Postmemory, Hirsch notes,

> is a powerful and very particular form of memory because its connection to its object or source is mediated not through recollection but through imaginative investment and creation. . . . Postmemory characterizes the experiences of those who grow up dominated by narratives that preceded their birth, whose own belated stories are evacuated by the stories of the previous generations shaped by traumatic events that can be neither understood nor recreated.[13]

Even though Hirsch develops her understanding of postmemory in the context of family photographs and children of Holocaust survivors, the frame is useful in exploring other second-generation memories of cultural-collective trauma. In many ways, the work of homing and home-remembering, in this book, is the narrative work of memory and postmemory across generations.

For Hirsch, objects such as photographs are a medium that connects "first- and second-generation remembrance, memory and postmemory . . . they affirm the past's existence, and in their flat two-dimensionality, they signal its unbridgeable distance."[14]

At the same time, certain objects, Elizabeth Spelman notes, are "a scaffold for memory, in the sense that they provide a kind of platform through which memories are reached for, a guiding structure through which a past is recalled."[15] Such objects also tell us that home can be understood in terms of "belonging" and experienced via "belongings"—items and artifacts of material culture that we choose to carry with us. Katie Walsh states:

> Thinking about belonging through *belongings* is productive because it is empirically and theoretically attentive to the way in which the home is experienced simultaneously as both material and immaterial, lived and imagined, localized and (trans) national space of belonging.[16]

Even as I agree with such metaphors for belongings and memory, I want to also believe that these objects exist in my home because they are reminders of displacements and un/homes, and that they serve not only the task of holding the past, but also of unhinging both the past and home. They un/settle the meaning that home might have, signaling home as movement as much as finality.

Approaching Partition

The reasons for the box and *Mataji* were brought into relief in the process of my oral history fieldwork with Hindu refugees from Delhi who were forced to move from Pakistan to India owing to the British partitioning of the subcontinent (with the compliance of Indian political leaders at that time). While my entry into this research subject would seem obvious, in reality it was circuitous, even hesitant. Here in the United States, I completed two graduate programs, collecting academic credentials, writing a master's thesis and later a doctoral dissertation on identity, yet still not intellectually embracing my ancestral legacy of displacement. I must have been preparing myself unconsciously, however, because in the decade between 1997 and 2007, I read—intermittently yet incessantly—academic, fictional, and nonfictional literature on the Partition.

The Partition, commonly referred to as the *Batwara* by first-generation refugees, was India's bittersweet accompaniment to independence. It was the division of British India into the secular state of India and the Islamic state of Pakistan. Its human cost was the loss of about one million lives and the displacement of an estimated eighteen to twenty million people on both sides of the border.[17] Kathinka Sinha-Kerkhoff points out that the losses of Partition were such that, in India, the event is remembered as a catastrophe, and she further notes that while "most historical accounts welcome the departure of the British, Partition narratives also recount the extreme violence and massive transfers of populations as an anticlimax to *azadi* (independence), and recall the religious or communal character of the flows of Hindus and Muslims accompanied by horrific sectarian and often gendered violence."[18]

Scholars across disciplines agree that a confluence of historical, social, and political factors were responsible for the division of British India and the creation of Pakistan.[19] At the time of negotiations with Britain for an independent India, politicians from the All-India Muslim League put forth a "two-nation theory" (India and Pakistan) as a counterweight to the secular nationalism of the Indian National Congress, India's other main political body, because there was fear among Muslim political leaders that India's Muslim minority would be forced into political oblivion once the British left the country.[20] It is commonly agreed that Hindu revivalists were equally responsible for widening the chasm between Indian Muslims and Hindus because they resented the Muslims who had ruled over India for centuries before the British. Further, they were offended by some everyday Muslim norms such as the slaughter and consumption of cows, considered sacred among Hindus.[21] When India became free of British rule in 1947, the two main political and religious parties, the Congress Party and the Muslim League, agreed to partition the country along religious lines.

As a watershed event that reshaped the political and geographical topography of the subcontinent, the Partition and its sociopolitical and economic consequences have periodically drawn scholarly attention. I have perused the literature on Partition for some time, and I approach it in terms of three broad domains: (a) high politics or official literature, (b) fiction and film, and (c) everyday local history and nonfictional literature.

Studies within the high politics domain constitute "official history" and emphasize larger national dialogues about the historical, religious, and political aftermath of Partition.[22] *Official history*, a term used by Indian historian Ranajit Guha—a founding member of the Subaltern Studies group—expresses the idea that all academically produced histories of India are merely accounts of the evolution of the modern Indian nation-state and echo the statism that is entrenched in South Asian historiography.[23] Official history speaks in the commanding voice of the nation and presumes the historic for the citizenry, thereby muting the "small voice of history"—that of the oppressed, persecuted, subaltern, and, I would add, the ordinary.[24] In this body of work, historical subjects are discussed only from the standpoint of their rights as citizens and not as unique individuals.[25] Critiques of this literature notwithstanding, official historiography continues to provide valuable insights surrounding the two-nation theory, British colonization, postcolonial nationhood, religious fundamentalism, nationalism, the Indian National Congress, Mahatma Gandhi's role in state politics, the Muslim League, the Hindu-Muslim problem, and so on. In large part these studies deal with the causes, the consequences, and the political ramifications of the Partition.[26]

The second body of literature—what is popular and accessible—consists of fictional writing, film, and literary critiques of Partition fiction written in Urdu, Hindi, Punjabi, and English by both Indian and Pakistani writers. Works in this area take into consideration localized stories, incidents, and events. Indeed some very evocative and accessible narratives about the Partition on both sides of the India-Pakistan border have emerged in short stories, films, poetry, and plays by writers and artists who experienced the Partition and its aftermath.[27] It can be argued that this body of work has begun to take the place of public memory in the generation born three decades after the Partition.[28] However, it is also critiqued for its elite bias because writers, poets, and other artists addressing the Partition were a part of the bourgeois intelligentsia who remained more or less secure from pre- and post-Partition communal violence.[29]

The third domain of literature, one that has acquired momentum in recent decades and one in which I situate *Home, Uprooted* engages everyday, local narratives of ordinary persons displaced by this extraordinary watershed event.[30] This body of research serves as a counterfoil to official history, which often glazes over the human tragedy that was the Partition. This third domain is diverse in its methodological approaches and includes oral and life history work, testimonials, diaries, witness accounts, women's testimonies, and so on. In *Borders and Boundaries: Women in India's Partition*, Ritu Menon and Kamla Bhasin successfully attempt a feminist historiography or a "gendered social history" that shows us how the lives of "non-actors in the political realm are shaped by an epochal event."[31] They portray the particular impact of the Partition on women as they struggled to resurrect their lives. In life history interviews, conducted across North India, the authors explore how women rebuilt their place (or not) in the fragmented nation and home, what nationhood and religion meant to them, and how they experienced political freedom. Furrukh A. Khan's feminist historiography, "Speaking Partition: Pakistani Women's Narratives of Partition," focuses on the experiences of economically impoverished female refugees from Pakistan.[32] His emphasis is on how

> [t]he experience of trauma suffered during Partition represents a theoretical and political preoccupation with the lived and witnessed reality of women— the position to articulate them is constantly challenged not just by the community, their exclusion is institutionalized by the state. . . . [B]y expressing individual perspectives these women take the first tentative steps to bridge a hitherto missing link to the collective imaginary.[33]

Another resonating and influential work, *The Other Side of Silence* by Urvashi Butalia, broadly explores how the lives of ordinary persons were shaped by the watershed event that was Partition.[34] Butalia relies on interviews, diaries, letters, memoirs, and parliamentary documents to address how people on the margins—children, women, the lower castes, the untouchables— experienced this event. She accesses moments of her own Partition-scarred family before she begins the investigation of other experiences.[35]

In *Epicentre of Violence: Partition Voices and Memories from Amritsar*, Ian Talbot and Darshan Singh Tatla present twenty-five disparate first-hand accounts linked with Amritsar in the Indian side of Punjab, a city that was a major transit place for Partition refugees. Focusing on locality, Talbot and Tatla tell the stories of persons in one city, thus allowing for unique insights into processes of migration and resettlement. Moreover, they emphasize the differing experiences of the elite and subaltern classes during and after this turbulent event.[36] Even though the book focuses on the unique nature of each displacement, several themes unite the first-hand accounts—the suddenness of the uprooting; a belief that displacement would be temporary; a sense that the violence was motivated by politics, and not by culture or religion. These themes are consistently present in the accounts of *my* participants in the pages that follow, and show how oral histories, even as they provide singular accounts, are always imbricated in collective narratives.

Alok Bhalla's *Partition Dialogues: Memories of a Lost Home* is a narrative exploration, via interviews, of how six Pakistani and Indian writers and intellectuals, who experienced Partition and its aftermath, remember and resurrect home and boundaries in their memories of the event. The narratives presented in the book detail the litterateurs' memories of pre- and post-Partition days, their experiences of communal harmony among Hindus, Muslims, and Sikhs, their ideological shifts, and difficult moments of survival, and the event's impact on their writing and craft. Even though this book addresses a thematic somewhat complementary to what I am pursuing here, its scope is limited to litterateurs often considered part of an elite bourgeois intelligentsia.[37]

A more recent work, Ravinder Kaur's *Since 1947* is a narrative study of Punjabi migrants in Delhi (it is also a locality-based study) that broadly explores how "the past is employed to repair ruptures in people's ordinary lives."[38] The book focuses on the experiences of ordinary Punjabis who settled in three resettlement colonies in Delhi between 1947 and 1965. Kaur explores how memories of a past trauma are held close and remembered by refugees in order to sustain them in the present. And while they remember the trauma, they want to forget and even shun the refugee identity that came to define their being in the new India.[39] *Since 1947* illustrates how the past and its memories are employed, ambivalently, to reframe new refugee identities.

Much of the oral and life history work in this domain details the human tragedy of this event (and process) and how its repercussions continue to permeate people's daily lives. A crucial contribution of this area of storytelling and theorizing is that the ambivalence surrounding the figure of the refugee is consistently produced, or as Vazira Zamindar pointedly asks, "Where, indeed, is India? Where is Pakistan? Who is an Indian? Who is a Pakistani?" She argues that it was through "the making of the refugees as a governmental category, through refugee rehabilitation as a tool of planning, that new nations and the borders between them were made, and people, including families, were divided."[40] Indeed, as Zamindar notes, the making of the refugees was not merely a one-time event, but was "profoundly shaped by the two postcolonial states as they struggled to classify, enumerate, and manage these displacements."[41] In fact, much of the literature in this domain argues that the categories of *Hindu, Muslim,* and *Sikh* were a cause and consequence of the Partition—as the event and its process re-produced and fixed these communal identities.

Summer 2007 marked the sixtieth year of India's Partition (and independence). Temporal markers are significant for scholars and publishers, and both the Indian and international book market saw the release of new books, essays, and stories re-engaging Partition.[42] I was reading them all and wondering what was holding me back. Admittedly, I felt paralyzed by all the ways in which the Partition had already been addressed. Since I am neither a trained historian nor a political scientist, what would I add to the conversations? What could I say that had not already been said? And was it even necessary given the plethora of research that already exists? Unable to postpone it any longer and quite prepared to encounter redundancy, I made a decision to return home to attempt to understand how Partition *lives along with* and *in* family stories across three generations.

My academic training in the areas of literature, communication, and anthropology pushed me into a predictable course of action. I created a project wherein I would collect cross-generational oral histories from ten middle-class Sikh and Hindu Delhi refugee families to understand how ordinary people organize their lives and families—and therefore their identities—as a consequence of politically and communally motivated displacements. I wanted to consider how identity (individual and familial) is negotiated when political, economic, emotional, and social resources are either scarce or simply unavailable. I wanted to understand how everyday stories of Partition are lived on a daily basis, how they circulate (if at all) in (our) families, how we learn (or do not learn) to live with them, and what (if anything) ultimately becomes of these stories. Unsurprisingly, I encountered armies of memory and distinct and overlapping accounts that sketched Partition more numerously than I had either imagined or could fathom. My decade-long exercise in reading Partition literature had sensitized me to look for certain patterns—my goal at this time was to conduct a cross-generational analysis of participant stories, address how each generation reframed the event (or did not reframe it)—thereby filling a gap in the literature.

But fieldwork is never this simple. Quite often it resembles a wrestling match between academic training, experience, the ethnographer's history, and instinct. Something must give. Partition literature in the sphere of everyday history focuses heavily on the witness record, the survivor's tale, the nostalgic account, and the rehabilitation story. And in my fieldwork too, such accounts were a persisting presence. I was probing these accounts because they are undoubtedly integral to how the displaced story their lives. They are where such stories must begin. And while these expected redundancies were present, another plot was at work.

In the years between 2007 and 2010, following about twelve months of fieldwork and forty-five oral histories in the state of Delhi, I kept returning to a rather simple (or so I thought) observation—my participants' narrations of politically enforced displacements were complex narrations of home and identity. Even though an anticipated nostalgia for homes from the old country endures in my field discourses, my participants also seemed to be un/defining, longing for, rejecting, and sometimes finding home in other locales that were unfamiliar, unsettling, uncanny—un/home. The loss of home—spoken, experienced, and felt—was not always a cause of angst or anger and was also experienced as relief and reconfiguration. The loss, surprisingly, was not always a loss. Home was being crafted in broad and contradictory strokes, but one thing was clear: home was the center of these narrations.

This was the story my participants wanted to tell. This was the story I needed to note. This is the story I am telling. Here.

Addressing Home

In her recent foreword to *Women on the Verge of Home*, anthropologist Ruth Behar writes that in contemporary anthropology, owing to global geopolitical-economic shifts in the twentieth century—primary among them decolonization movements—no longer can there be a distinction between field and home, because the global equation upon which such a separation was based is moot.[43] Caren Kaplan reinforces this idea, stating, "For many of us there is no possibility of staying at home in the conventional sense—that is, the world has changed to a point that those domestic, national, or marked spaces no longer exist."[44] History, says Michael Jackson in *At Home in the World*, "has made go-betweens of us all . . . anthropology is itself a product of an age of trespass and travels."[45] Home in the traditional sense of the place that one lives and travels away from to other places has ceased to be a received idea. The breaking down of the home/field bifurcation has necessarily meant the melting away of others—subject/object, participant/researcher, native/other, interpretation/representation. In fact, as Arjun Appadurai notes, "natives, people confined to and by the places to which they belong, groups unsullied by contact with a larger world, have probably never existed."[46] Sociocultural anthropology's earlier construction of the primitive, along with its role in the consolidation of a native/Other binary, is no longer useful or relevant.

Navigating these relationships between self and other in anthropology—now neither new nor novel—addresses the condition of this ethnographer/I for whom home and field and native and other collapse, coincide, and coalesce.[47] My work here is both the homework and the fieldwork of an émigré sitting in the *now* in a distant land trying to fathom why and how home is so crucial to the subjectivities of her participants, trying to understand her self-imposed exile, trying to gather why she had to travel away to encounter home, and return home to find a field—in short, what does home, field, and travel mean to us in this/our contemporary moment?

The literature on home is vast and interdisciplinary. Home is viewed as a multidimensional theoretical concept that can have contradictory meanings wherein it may be considered space, place, feelings, practices, and an active state of being in the world.[48] Contemporaneously, discussions about home occur in the backdrop of travel.[49] Home, migration (forced or otherwise), and travel are no longer characterized as distinct conditions, and instead it is considered more constructive to interrogate how, "up/rootings and re-groundings are enacted—affectively, materially, and symbolically—in relation to one another.[50] Even so, a consistent thread that runs through contemporary cross-disciplinary thinking on home and travel is a modernist version of home whereby home is projected as "a stable center of safety and domestic virtue."[51] This notion of "home as haven" is predicated on the distinction between public and private, and the inside and the outside world. "According to this dichotomy," states Mallet,

[t]he inside or closed domain of the home represents a comfortable, secure, and safe space. . . . It is a confined space. Some say it is a feminine space, yet others dismiss this idea as simplistic. In contrast the outside is perceived as an imposing, if not threatening or dangerous space. It is more diffuse, less defined. Different performative expectations exist for people in this outside space.[52]

In these discussions, home connotes a safe (often feminine) sphere that can stand for "community; more problematically, it can elicit a nostalgia for a past golden age that never was, a nostalgia that elides exclusion, power relations, and difference."[53] From a traditional anthropological standpoint, home is the place of return and is always imagined in contrast to the field/other.[54] Home remains here (inside), and field is relegated to there (outside).

In his classic study *Home: A Short History of an Idea*, Witold Rybczynski traces an emotional and material genealogy of home, positioning home as both a physical place and as a state of being-at-home that embodies love, security, safety, and dwelling.[55] Elaborating upon Rybczynski's ideas, Mallet notes that "ideas about privacy, domesticity, intimacy and comfort emerged as organizing principles for the design and use of domestic spaces among the bourgeoisie, particularly in the Netherlands."[56] Of course, concepts such as privacy, intimacy, domesticity, and comfort continue to be recurring themes in contemporary discussions of home. It is also possible to trace the roots of these ideas to (among others) Martin Heidegger, in his classic rumination "Building Dwelling Thinking,"[57] and to the phenomenological commentary of Gaston Bachelard in *The Poetics of Space*,[58] wherein home is seen as familiar, as a physical location, as a state of being at home in the world, as a question of arriving at meaningful selfhood, and as a space of the imagination.

Heidegger proposes that humans build to dwell, and in dwelling may find traces of being human, or as he states, "I dwell, you dwell. The way in which we are and I am, the manner in which we are humans on earth, is *Buan*, dwelling."[59] His concern is to mystically explicate what it is to live and be at home in the world—a question of arriving at meaningful selfhood. Psychologists Daniel López and Tomás Sánchez-Criado have drawn on Heidegger's notion of dwelling as "the constitutive relationship through which space is opened up and subjectivity is comprised." As they remark, many scholars have noted that Heidegger's key contribution is to disassociate "dwelling" and "being-at-homeness" from a specific location or place, and have seen in his conception of dwelling "a revaluation of the study of home as a distinct human space in contrast with the spaces of mobility and labor." Under such an understanding, the concept of dwelling is seen "as a sort of ideological statement in favor of rigid and traditional identities against the total mobilization of the world."[60] Others, less sympathetic to this approach, refer to it as male-centered, dangerously nationalist, and overly romantic.[61]

The ideas proposed by Heidegger are complemented by Bachelard's ruminations on home, imagination, poetics, and space wherein he associates home and the house "as our corner of the world. As it has been said, it is our first universe, a real cosmos in every sense of the word."[62] From this viewpoint, *home* is used as a near-synonym of *family*.[63] Bachelard's conceptions differ (in degree) from Heidegger's, in that the former was more interested in a topoanalysis of the space that is the house. For Bachelard, this topography

> . . . shelters daydreaming, the house protects the dreamer, the house allows one to dream in peace. . . . [T]herefore the places in which we have *experienced daydreaming* reconstitute themselves into a new daydream, and it is because our memories of former dwelling-places of the past remain in us for all time.[64]

Undoubtedly, in both of these traditional iterations of home, home is not just a physical location, but also a space of the imagination. It is viewed as a space that offers freedom and control, creativity and regeneration, and intimacy and closeness. Such a home can survive its material loss because it can be imagined and poetically excavated. Moreover, homeowners and homemakers "constitute themselves as [their homes'] inhabitants" and define themselves through home, which is why "moving into another dwelling is a change of life."[65]

Such ideas about homely-homes are utopian, bourgeois, idealized, and indeed Eurocentric—a critique rightfully leveled at modernist understandings of the relationships of home, habit, and place with subjectivity.[66] Anthropologists who challenge the notion of home as haven often note that such portrayals were constructed by Western elites to position the non-Western as Other/not home and themselves as West/home. Still others critique this characterization of home as an idealized one that remains at odds with how a large percentage of women, children, and young persons experience home—as an unsafe place of terror, a site of fear and isolation, and often as a prison.[67] These scholars favor a phenomenological understanding of home that disregards the dichotomy between outside and inside suggesting that safety, comfort, security, and comfort might be found beyond home. And in this era of forced and continuous global migrations, we know that homemaking can also be experienced as destabilizing, terrifying, disabling, and disembodying.[68]

Broadly, from a feminist standpoint, home has often been conceptualized as both a haven and as a site of oppression, because on the one hand women are socialized to take on a nurturing role in the home—in fact, to create a home—and on the other hand they are consigned to a life of reproductive and domestic labor.[69] Hilde Heynen, for example, argues that in the West, specifically, there exists a certain complicity between modernity and domesticity.[70] At the same time, ideas about home as a space nurtured by women predates Western modernity. In Hindu thought, for instance, the Sanskrit word for home and hearth, *grihastha*, is the second of four necessary stages in the life cycle of Hindu men (in the Vedic ashram system). In fact, married Hindu women are often referred to as *householders*, those who keep, create, and nourish household activity. The Sanskrit word for wedding, *vivaha*, translates into the procurement and carrying away of a maiden from the house of her father to the house of her husband. The ancient Hindu version of home, household, and feminine domesticity aligns complementarily with the idealized home of Western modernity. Although feminist critiques of home are often perceived as controversial, primarily because of their focus on fixed and bounded notions of gender, sex, and sexuality, they do provide us with a constructive critique of the house-as-haven idea that dominates modernist understandings of home.

Such ideas share resonance with those held by transnational studies scholars who veer away from examining "home" and "away" as oppositional experiences. For instance, Sara Ahmed argues against a conceptualization of home as a fixed space, proposing instead that home can be experienced as both strange and familiar.[71] In fact, home may be experienced as *unhomely*, a strategic translation of Freud's notion of *unheimlich* (the uncanny) by postcolonial theorist Homi Bhabha, who astutely positions the unhomely as a postcolonial space that relates the "traumatic ambivalence of a personal, psychic history to the wider disjunctions of political existence."[72] The unhomely, notes Bhabha,

> captures something of the estranging sense of the relocation of home and the world in an unhallowed place. To be unhomed is not to be homeless, nor can the "unhomely" be easily accommodated in that familiar division of social life into public and private spheres . . . . The home does not remain the domain of domestic life, nor does the world become its social or historical counterpart. The unhomely is the shock of recognition of the world-in-the-home, the home-in-the-world.[73]

The unhomely reveals "the forgotten but familiar strangeness of home as a site that elicits enigmatic longing, control, or outright violence."[74] This "uncanny" nature of home and the "unhomely condition" can also be seen in Theodor Adorno's critique of bourgeois society in *Minima Moralia*,[75] wherein the private space of the conjugal family that cultivated subjectivity is now a nostalgic impossibility. A dwelling space is no longer the home of childhood memories, and to remain homeless is now one's home.[76] Home as a state of un/familiar strangeness is approached as the "foreignness within" by Julia Kristeva in her *Strangers to Ourselves*. Gilles Deleuze and Félix Guattari approach home from a subject position arguing that the presence and absence of home/feeling is actualized in the subversive figure of the nomad—a position contrary to the fixed nature of the modernist home.[77] However, with material homelessness on the rise as a global epidemic, Deleuze and Guattari's subversive homeless and rootless nomad is critiqued and often negated as a resistor.[78]

Clearly, in its postmodern, postcolonial, and transnational iterations home can be a space (or an idea) that is unfamiliar and unsettling, and it embodies the potential to provoke intimate terrors. Home may never have been home, yet it continues to be intricately linked to our subjectivity in its un/homeliness and absence. What remains "is the necessity and inevitability of a desire for a 'home' in an inhospitable world, the accompanying dangers of the desire, and the continuing need to create 'homes' for ourselves."[79] And home and being at home are "a matter, at least in part, of affect or feeling—as the presence or absence of particular feelings."[80] Transnational renderings of home usefully theorize it as the lived experience of locality;

a/the locality enters the self through the senses (sound, smell, touch), and the self penetrates locality in equally sensual ways—thereby making the boundaries between home and away and between inside and outside both permeable and flexible.[81]

Any fieldwork with displaced populations in this globalized world necessitates an engagement with how losses of home are enacted, positioned, and incorporated by transposed subjects. In *Home, Uprooted*, I focus on home as *the* unit of analysis from which these particular displaced persons story their lives in these particular moments spent with this ethnographer. The stories told here, those of one set of persons in the Indian subcontinent, where geopolitical displacements remain and indeed continue to fester, provide the basis of a sustained analysis of home. Analyses of home vis-à-vis housing, resettlement, and property have been rigorously addressed in previous works on the Partition such as Kaur's *Since 1947* and Zamindar's. *The Long Partition*, wherein the authors focus on the minutiae of rehabilitation efforts. They include such matters as the Muslim and Hindu exodus between Karachi and Delhi, its unevenness, and the disparate ways in which Muslims from Delhi who moved to Karachi became embroiled, not of their choosing, in conflicts and were positioned as separatists (Mujahirs) by the ethnic Sindhis, while on the other hand, Hindus and Sikhs resettled in Delhi without any "noticeable local-refugee conflicts."[82]

Even as I assimilate these historical insights, in making home the locus for my explorations in this book I am taking seriously the call of contemporary social researchers who note that it is crucial, even necessary, that marginalized (displaced) persons craft home (discursively and materially) outside of the modernist imagination.[83] For if home is so central to these (our) stories and if our stories are a means for "claiming the space of home," then perhaps crafting home can enable newer capacities for self-making.[84] In short, I attend to home less in its materiality than as a metaphor for the *homing self*.

A brief caveat seems necessary here. Even as I present this book in stories guided by some theory and some analysis, in its simplest description the book is "what I saw" and heard, what I experienced, and, more importantly, what I chose to note. In his classic work *Let Us Now Praise Famous Men*, James Agee wrote carefully of his endeavors in speaking for the sharecroppers of the American Deep South, saying, "I can tell you of him only what I saw, only so accurately as in my terms I know how."[85] What *I* tell here are some liminal moments of understanding between that space "there," where I met my participants, and this space "here," where I revisit them/us in memories and writing, in between fieldwork and homework. It is a space that most ethnographers are used to inhabiting, a discursive terrain that neither fully coheres nor completely bodies the ethnographic moment. It is a terrain quite like that of the novel, which Bakhtin introduces to us, in the *The Dialogic Imagination*, as a complex discursive space where many voices compete for expression, wanting to be included, seeking a space in the center, and searching for a mode of textual production that adheres to dialogism and polyphony as text that is heteroglot.

There is neither a prescribed measure nor an evocative formula for heteroglossia, what Bakhtin describes as "the situation of a subject surrounded by the myriad responses he or she might make at any particular point, but any one of which must be framed in a specific discourse selected from the teeming thousands available,"[86] yet it is a mode of representation that remains an aspiration here—"a plurality of relations, not a cacophony of different voices."[87] An aspiration that cancels itself out—repeatedly—because I choose, I edit, I remove, and thus I contain the messiness of the field, of home, and of the spaces in between. Amidst it all, I privilege "story," and I privilege some stories over others, because we have favorites, and here, in this space, the elderly compete for space with their progeny, eventually taking a more central stage in the stories that get told. Even so, my effort here is to juxtapose moments of cross-generational storytelling in every portion of this book—showing how members tell, listen, agree, or sometimes contradict family stories. These moments, in their disparity and their resistance to being thematized, show the uneven ways in which Partition is remembered and resurrected. Ultimately what I have here are what James Clifford has called "partial truths" about homes, selves, and identity/s[88]—all of which, I emphasize, are truths that *I* chose to see and truths that shift with every angle I turn.

The stories performed and shown in this book enter a space outside/inside/alongside homes of modernity to show how home may be imagined against its antithesis; how people tell stories of home as a place made present by arrivals and departures; how un/homely homes, even as they destabilize, might be the only resource from which we claim our selves; how home is, perhaps, best approached as movement and motion rather than rootedness and stability; and how modernist homes may still be, ironically, the "rightful" homes that we want to achieve.

In particular—sometimes directly, other times not so directly—I work through Clifford's entwined concepts of "travel in dwelling" and "dwelling in travel" that have gained cultural currency in extant thinking about home and field.[89] We are now quite familiar with Clifford's admonitions that "diasporic conjunctures invite a reconception—both theoretical and political—of familiar notions of ethnicity and identity" and that "unresolved historical dialogues between continuity and disruption, essence and positionality, homogeneity and difference (cross-cutting "us" and "them") characterize diasporic articulations."[90] This approach deviates from nomadology, wherein locales and homes are projected as travel, persons as cosmopolitan, and spaces as deterritorialized.[91] The persons whose stories populate this book are refugees and their descendants who craft home/selves based on their consistently ambivalent relationship with space, location, and habitality. They might be defined as nomadic owing to the watershed moment that displaced them and the persistent discontinuities that shadowed some of their lives, yet they all inhabit and locate home in a multitude of ways—never fully settling into any singular articulation of home.

In "A Story Travels," I bring attention to how I heard a Partition story circulate amongst three generations of women in the Khanna family. I textually perform it in three reflexive movements—(how) a story travels; (how) a story struggles; (how) a story (is forced) to find home—to address how, in this particular family, the Partition account of the ailing patriarch (who romanticizes his house in Lahore) is held, and in fact domesticated, by female family members (and by this ethnographer) in (narrative) homemaking practices to discursively rescue a modernist idea of home. My goal is to show how home's modernist ideal is protected and "the conversation of struggle" deliberately sacrificed by the women in order to stabilize home and, I propose, a family identity. I also raise questions about how oral history fieldwork can evolve into a struggle between multiple interlocutors embattled in producing disparate versions of the emergent story.[92] Interspersed with the three movements are many reflexive moments where I show my own struggle as an interlocutor—Whose account to choose to tell? Why? And how?

The ambivalence with which women often view home is the subject of "Home Outside Home," which tells the story of Kiranji, an eighty-seven-year-old first-generation female refugee, who came to reside in home's loss because for her, Partition permitted a stepping out and away from the confines of feminine domesticity. When Kiranji asks me, and herself, "Would I be where I am or be what I am, had I not lost this home? I don't know the answer to that," I have no choice but to examine how departures and movements into un/home opened possibilities of selfhood that would have been impossible to either desire or actualize in a traditional home. Even while Kiranji longs for her old home and lovingly sketches it for me from memory, she dare not return. Her story shows "*the heaviness of home* for women who must consider many or all of these exclusionary structures" (italics in original).[93] The fragmented nation/home gave Kiranji the freedom to become something/someone more than the old country allowed. Does she reconcile the old and new? And how?

In "Adrift: Reluctant Nomads," I stretch further the dwelling-in-travel metaphor and the metaphor of drifting to address how subjects/participants, in this case three men, replace, respace, and reinscribe home and selves in passages and wanderings (of memories), and in building. The stories, and how I tell them, illustrate the ways in which home becomes synonymous with movement, even if that movement means miniscule shifts in neighborhoods and localities. While the stories presented here address drifting as a metaphor, taken together they explicate the experiences of Partition and its aftermath as movement, and home as a flexible and mobile notion deeply linked with subjectivity. The subjects in these stories live in a "perpetual present moment" and seem to be equally at home and not at home in different spaces.[94] I ruminate on how these homes/selves in movement remain, and indeed *are*, decentered subjectivities that help us to understand how home and self are an entwined spatial imaginary that moves from *here* to *here* to *here*.

In "Hearth Crossings," homes of the old country are agonizingly rejected and positioned as material and emotional spaces of terror and restrictions rather than of repose and equality. Swiftly dismissing the old country and home's traditional ideal, Veeranji pronounces, "Before Partition, there was nothing, we were nothing." In vignettes from five oral histories of women, I show how subjects craft home as what Julia Kristeva, in her book *Strangers to*

Ourselves, has referred to as a foreignness we experience within ourselves—as a place of no return, of unfamiliarity, of terror, and of absence. The stories here are un/homely in tenor and go against the grain of modernist understandings of home, habit, and subjectivity. They also run counter to émigré narratives that predominantly locate themselves in a nostalgic psychic space and place, where any sense of identity evokes longing for a glorious and stable past that can be renewed in the imagination. These accounts are an/other story of pre-Partition homes and communities—when home was always un/home.

Yet not all subjects align with the un/homely to tell an against-the-grain tale. "*Hum log sub hum hai*" (we people are all a "we"), recites eighty-year-old Roshanji on a humid August afternoon in his home in South Delhi. His unpublished poems, written in Hindi, Urdu, and English, are the rhymes through which he addresses the Partition (and this ethnographer). I sense the stories of some older male subjects as elegiac performances mourning lost selves, broken homes, and fragmented nations. "Remnants" is a collection of pieces and moments, some that fit together and some that don't, of how many first- and third-generation subjects, as described by Bachelard in *The Poetics of Space*, locate home in its modernist roots as a loving, stable, intimate space and imaginary. In particular, I show how these first-generation participants enter what I think of as a poetic realm—what Marianne Hirsch refers to in *Family Frames* as an "aesthetics of postmemory"—to memorialize the old country/home, pre-Partition India, and communal harmony, sedimenting the return of homes/selves to a secure modernist version. This aesthetic/poetic movement skips a generation and comes to be taken up by third-generation family members who re-encounter the old country on their own terms, returning us to Hirsch's idea that that our cultural homes are the spaces of "postmemory." I bypass analysis entirely, relying instead on puzzling ethnographic encounters to show how the old country survives in the aesthetic imagination.

"My Father, My Interlocutor," is a meditation—a lively one—both a beginning and a tapering off that concludes this ethnographic moment. I turn my attention to my father, whose presence—felt, seen, and heard all along—makes up both my home and my field. This part of the book can be viewed, broadly, as one encounter between a second- and third-generation participant, an encounter that emerged as a consequence of my decision to begin this project. Even though I endeavor to mingle storytelling with moments of emotional and methodological reflexivity as a loop that connects the stories, I consider these last moments crucial in addressing the generative nature of memory and fieldwork. I show, feel, sense, perform Papa's role in the doing of the oral history interviews, three-quarters of which would have been impossible without his presence in the homes of almost all of my elderly participants, who specifically (and repeatedly) requested that he accompany me. As my now seventy-two-year-old Papa, who was six when the family left Pakistan, partook in the interviews, he himself felt encouraged to remember, eventually taking us both into the crevices of some of our own family story, portions of which would have remained unremembered but for this project. Finding those stories as a generative response to those we heard is a sort of homecoming for this father/interlocutor–daughter/ethnographer duo. I conclude by considering where I arrive/where the ethnographer arrives in her thinking about home and who brings me/her there. More simply, I ponder the necessity to speak and story home.

The subjects of *Home, Uprooted* consistently straddle the dynamic tensions between homes of modernity and the actuality of their experiences, between stability and movement, between peace and terror, and between domesticity and freedom. These tensions notwithstanding, as displaced persons they attempt to "*continually imagine themselves at home*," to borrow words from anthropologist Bilinda Straight (italics in original).[95] Indeed, my participants' stories remind me, with remarkable consistency, that Partition was the loss of *many* homes, *many* selves, and *many* nations. The discursive terrain, here, is at best a constantly unfolding riddle. Each story could be many stories, each story linked, yet dispersed. Each story holds with another story (and does not hold). Each story forms and unforms thematics, which routinely fall apart. It is a terrain that I experience as so complex that I consider it imperative for the stories told here to be read together as oral history discourse, and to be read individually as personally situated history. It is even more imperative that these stories be read, re-read, and read again to engender newer interpretations of home and self. Both here and there.

THREE

A Story Travels

I would like to tell you a complete story, if there can be such a thing. I could begin dramatically, by asking you to imagine the moment when the Musalman's axe hits Labbi Devi's head and her husband's,[1] leaving them half dead on the rail tracks. They are on a goods train that is bringing them from Pakistan to India in September 1947, a month after the country has been partitioned. Before they are attacked, a Muslim mob has tried, repeatedly, to abduct Labbi Devi. She is a twenty-year-old beautiful young woman who describes herself, simply, as having had thick long black hair. She tells me, "They took me. I came back. They took me again. I came back. They were about to take me, and we were in the space between the train wagons, when the military arrived, so they left me right there. I was saved." Seventeen family members traveled together on that train; only four adults survived to reach Amritsar on the Indian side of the border.

Once I start, you may find your own beginning for Labbi Devi's story. Because, as Jeanette Winterson astutely tells us, there is surely "no story that's the start of itself, any more than a child comes into the world without parents."[2] Entering the space of oral histories can feel like circling labyrinths because the stories were already occurring when I joined them. They had been told before to many others in many forms; they have (perhaps) spiraled through various iterations, revisions, and receptions. Because, after all, an oral history is a "a repetition materialized in performance . . . history working itself out in narrative interaction, *on, through*, and *by* interview partners."[3] Stories are bits and pieces and wholes and fragments—experiences and remnants of experiences that we enter into at a pace determined by those who were already there. We may find a footing and stay in some versions, and we may depart from others. Only in such wanderings can hidden plots be unearthed. What is sure is that we are invariably escorted in these jaunts, helped along if you will, as I was on that summer day when I first met Labbi Devi.

(How) A Story Travels

It is a very hot Saturday afternoon in late June 2007. The first monsoon showers have brought with them a piercing clamminess that will last for a few months. During my field trips, I am staying with my parents in their South Delhi home, where I spent most of my teenage years and early twenties before leaving for the United States in 1997. My sixty-seven-year-old father has taken to accompanying me on interviews, and today we are heading over to Labbi Devi's home. We discover early on that when my father comes along, older members of the refugee families are friendlier, less reticent. Like them, he was born in Pakistan and lived through the Partition. I think they take comfort in that familiarity. And besides, his being closer in age to the first generation of my participants, who are in their eighties and nineties, reduces the awkwardness that is inevitable when talking to persons almost fifty years older than myself. When I request to meet older participants by introducing myself as a grandchild and child of Partition refugees, they ask if my father will be present. It becomes habit to have my now-retired father come along, and we travel into these stories together, a variant duo in different moments—father-daughter, researcher-informant, ethnographer-interlocutor.

We do not reach Labbi Devi's house. Getting there involves a stop in another neighborhood, a forty-minute drive from home, to pick up Asha, Labbi Devi's fifty-nine-year-old daughter. Asha has offered to take us to her mother's place because it is another hour away in West Delhi, an area that we are unfamiliar with. Of course we cannot leave immediately. These are Punjabi families from Pakistan. If a guest arrives, no matter who it may be—friend, stranger, acquaintance, or researcher—there is always tea to be had. In between tea and talk, we are given a tour of her newly renovated home. We are also shown the home of Asha's daughter Kavi, which is almost nested within the main house. I know I will be interviewing both Asha and Kavi in the coming months, so I am alert, noting the strong ties that bind this family. This married daughter has chosen to stay in a home enclosed by her mother's house, because as she says, "Why stay away from family, and why would I want my kid to grow up without grandparents around, I grew up with mine." And Kavi's mother wants to go with me to visit her mother. When I thank Asha, she laughs and says, "Now, you're talking like an American, I would go with you any day, and anyway it's been a few days since I've seen my parents." In that fleeting turn of phrase, I am reminded, not for the first time in home-fieldwork, that I am no longer from here; my movement to America has remade me.

Six months later when I return for more field research I record the first portion of Asha's oral history in this very house, with Papa, over a few more cups of tea. During this conversation Asha will lament the loss of socializing among extended families:

> When we were growing up, I lived between five or six houses, one day we were eating dinner at my cousin's, the other day they were at our home, if they had guests, we were always invited along, and vice versa. There is nothing like that now.

When I ask if it was Partition that changed these patterns, she replies, "Well, things have been dwindling since then. You know, they used to live in *mohallas* in Pakistan,[4] where everyone knew everyone and there were no strangers in your neighborhood, but who has time for anyone now?" A few weeks after this conversation, Kavi, a third-generation participant, close to my age, will visit me in my parents' home to "get interviewed." I've been trying to meet her for some time, and that day she will find herself in my neighborhood. Her mother, Asha, will be with her.

We are finally back inside the taxi that I hire at a daily rate to get to my field sites. I find myself in many ends of this city, with participants living over two hours away from each other. For 700 rupees a day (approximately $14.00), I get a sedan and a driver. The service is provided by the Bhoore Khan Taxi Company, owned by a Muslim family that stayed behind in Delhi after the Partition. Every day, a different male cousin from the extended family is assigned to drive me. It is ironic that as I travel around interviewing Hindu refugees who often wax nostalgic about their Muslim friends in the old country, I am accompanied by Indian Muslims, who are rarely befriended by Hindus and Sikhs in this new country. Of course, the wealthier Muslims and Hindus have always mingled, but working-class allegiances remain deeply communal. The drivers tell me about the various *bastis* where the family lives, parts of Delhi that, being a Hindu, I've never encountered. They even bring me recipes for *biryani*, a Mughal Hyderabadi rice and meat dish that is indigenous to their community, and then inform me that the best *qawwali*—Sufi devotional music popular in South Asia—is sung outside the tomb of the Sufi saint Nizammudin Auyila in South Delhi, where I live—something that is news to me. I wonder if they would talk to me, were we not in this client-service relationship. No, I would probably not have met them under any other circumstance. I've never spent this much time in the company of Muslims, having grown up in mostly Hindu areas and neighborhoods. I'm unsurprised when my reflection on this lack of intermingling is seconded by Asha's daughter Kavi, who says, "Well, I cannot say that I have any Muslim friends, I mean how could you when there were never any Muslims in my class in school, or in my neighborhood, or around any part of our daily life?" Yes, this is also my experience. In fact, I met and became friends with some Pakistani Muslims only as a graduate student in the United States, which I've come to view as a space that is a potential neutral zone for such encounters, even though rampant Islamophobia has overtaken the cultural surround, post–September 11. That I am meeting and spending this driving time with Muslims in Delhi, now, in this way, by paying for their services, is a simple reminder of the schism between the Hindu majority and the Muslim minority in most of the country. In story after story, I hear the statement "all our friends in Pakistan were Muslims," yet only a few of my participants will ever speak of befriending any Muslim families who stayed behind in India. In all my notes about this troubled relationship, the word *irony* is a leitmotif.

Asha sits in the back of the car with me and Papa takes the front passenger seat. We settle in for the hour-long drive. Her mother's home is only fifteen kilometers away, but in Delhi traffic it will take us a little over an hour. Asha starts telling us about her parents' departure and escape from Pakistan. She uses the word *Musalman* and speaks of *Mohammedans*—a term that Labbi Devi will eventually repeat—and I look worriedly at Ahmed, who is driving us today. I softy tell her, in English, that the cab service is owned by a Muslim family. She has not said anything derogatory, but there is always a possibility of unexpected utterances, of breaches that might be unknowingly committed. These drivers—Dilshad, Bhoore, Ahmed, Iqbal, among others—have become my comfortable companions. I spend as much time with them as I do with my participants, sometimes even more. Without them, I would not even be able to meet many of the families, as they live in parts of the city that are completely unknown to me. I must protect this curious conduit.

Asha begins again, this time telling us that her parents were injured by the mob; both were hit on the head with an axe, but they survived.

> You can see the axe mark on Mother's head even through her hair. She had long black hair down to her hips. My older sister was six months old and the mob was trying to abduct my mother—she was very beautiful, you see. When they saw her child they just threw the infant out of the train. Indian soldiers later found my sister in the woods; luckily she'd landed in bushes and was alive and crying. The train had not left, and they reunited her with my mother.

> My cousin, she was twenty at the time, was abducted by a mob that left her with a Muslim family. She was lucky, they were a sympathetic family and they understood that this was wrong. They gave her shelter for a few weeks. They waited for the worst of the rioting to subside, and then escorted her to a close-by refugee camp where the family was able to find her.

Asha concludes this with some satisfaction. We come to know that her mother's natal family were a family of gold jewelers whose train departure had been reported to a Muslim rioting mob, who were expecting to loot the gold.

Labbi Devi's natal and marital family traveled to India together. When the mob could not find anything, they massacred eight of the adult family members. I have been given one story in broad strokes—the details will come in numerous retellings. The jewelers escaped by train; most of the family members were injured or murdered; the survivors reached Amritsar, then Delhi; and the rest is a history of resettlement.

I am imagining another mob, this one made up of Hindus and equal in ferocity. No one is spared. No one but the very wealthy or the very lucky. An exodus is an exodus. New figures show that around twenty million people were displaced. One of the cab drivers had told me that some of his family escaped to Dera Gazi Khan, where they now live. My own family escaped the mobs in Quetta and witnessed Hindu mobs killing Muslims when they crossed over to the Indian side.

Asha moves me back to the present by saying, "Of course my mother is the only one who can tell you about any of this." "What about your father?" I ask. Asha informs us that he has Alzhiemer's and so his memories cannot be trusted. But he remembers his business—his shop in Pakistan and the clothing business he started here in Delhi after Partition—and he still goes to work at the shop every day. He also remembers his *kothi* (house) in Pakistan, and I will hear of both the home and shop when I am with Labbi Devi. The family has hired a companion who drives him to the shop and stays with him all day. In a tone of forlorn resignation Asha says, "Some days, he does not even remember us, but he always remembers his college days in Lahore and he never forgets his house and his shop in Pakistan."

The paternal moment is over and I am soon wandering Lahore with Asha. This recent trip, taken with her husband one year ago, is the highlight of all her conversations with me. "Why did you go? Was it to see your ancestral homes?" I ask. "Through our bridge club," she says, "to play a bridge tournament." Hers is not a wealthy family, but rather a middle-class one that has held on to some old British habits. Bridge is one of them. "I was not playing, my husband was, so I used to just visit different parts of the city with my friend whose husband was also playing in the tournament," she continues. They went looking for their respective homes and found the home of her friends' maternal grandparents in an old market. "Did you go in?" I ask. They went in; the house was in disrepair, as it had been taken over by a

Muslim family of small means. Asha admits surprise at the "shabbiness" of the home. The owners were worried that Asha's friend would want the home back, and when one of the men looked at them "strangely," Asha made a hurried exit.

"I took saris with me to Lahore, people had told me that if I wear saris, the Pakistanis will be friendly with me, and they were," she laughs. They would stop her on the street and tell her she looked very nice and ask her if she was from India. In fact, I have never seen Asha wrapped in a sari in the two years that I have visited the family. She always has on the Punjabi *salwar kameez* in all our meetings. Today she is wearing a floral-printed delicate cotton *kameez* (a long shirt), a white cotton *salwar* (trousers), and a pink *dupatta* (long scarf). "It's not like the movies, they like us, they want to talk to us," she confides. She has more good will stories:

> I went to a shoe shop looking to buy sandals; the shopkeeper asked me which Indian city I was from. He was curious about us and how we live. I chatted with him and then he tells me not to buy a shoe from his shop and asks his helper to take me to a better place. He could have made money from me, but he wanted me to get the best sandal available in the market. He kept saying, "You can buy it from me, but you would like those better and the quality is better too." See, these are good people.

Asha reports many more instances of kindness from strangers in Lahore. A nonvegetarian chef cooks a simple vegetarian dish for her at a midnight dinner in a street stall because vegetarian food is hard to come by in Lahore. In many of our meetings in the next few years, she constantly compares the streets of Lahore with those in Delhi, with Delhites always falling short on cleanliness, manners, and decorum. She insists that the Pakistanis have done for their major cities what we can never do in our Indian cities. With each anecdote, I experience a small reframing—the Other in her stories is being eroded. In Asha's talk the persons who walk the streets of Lahore are replacing the mob that killed most of her natal family. Yet the Other in them is also always emerging. This Other—consistently local and contingent.

Close to Asha's mother's place, we cross a very congested bazaar—a typical local market, found in every neighborhood in Delhi, old and new. They are especially typical in the neighborhoods settled by refugees. My mother,

Amma, calls these markets her lifelines, likening them to "little miracles" that are made up of square-shaped permanent or temporary shacks that sell plastic goods, medicines, cell phones, SIM cards, vegetables, and fruits. Nowadays they may contain trendy barbershops for men, hair salons for women, and even cyber cafes. Originally planned to house ration shops and milk stores for everyday supplies,[5] the markets have grown into miniature, albeit ramshackle, shopping plazas. They are a nuisance to street traffic and an eyesore but are indispensable for most homemakers like my mother, who can walk five minutes and find any item she might need for her home, even a tailor, a dyer, a drycleaner, or a shop that rents out news and social magazines on a weekly basis. "*Bara aaraam hai inki wajah se,*" they are such a source of comfort, my mother insists.

Asha is rapidly pointing to a yellow-and-red shop sign that reads *Kapur di Hatti* and telling Papa that this is where she gets the dough for *doli ki roti*. "Oh no," I think to myself when I hear the name of the dough being called. Papa, who has been napping in the front seat, is suddenly wide awake and almost out of the running car. *Doli ki roti* was the culinary bane of my childhood. A traditional leavened and fried bread eaten with mango pulp and other condiments, it is a summer special from the Punjab province in Pakistan. My grandmother prepared it every year and passed the recipe along to both her daughters-in-law, who are not too conscientious about cooking it on a yearly basis. My mother considers it too time-consuming to make and heavy to digest. My brother and my cousins are not particularly fond of it, but as kids, we were forced to eat it and pretend to like it for fear of hurting Biji's feelings. Insulting doli ki roti was like insulting the old country. It is the most significant, or at least the most remembered, edible symbol of my father's childhood in Pakistan. Since my grandmother's death in 1999, every summer he laments this lost delicacy, and some summers his complaints are strong enough for my mother to give in to the tedious process of preparing the dough, a process that can take days. "Really, you can just buy it here?" he asks Asha. "Yes, this is where I get it; who has the time to spend on the dough preparation?" she replies. We stop in the market and inspect the shop and talk to the owner, who is also a refugee from Pakistan's Punjab province. Papa beamingly purchases enough dough for about forty doli ki rotis. "Imagine, if we'd known about this before," he beams.

In ten minutes, we are parked outside Labbi Devi's home. Asha explains that the entire colony—neighborhoods are referred to as *colonies* in post-Partition Delhi—was settled by refugees from Pakistan. The house is a large imposing stone structure, and from that size it is quite clear that Asha's natal family has seen some affluence in the last six decades. We enter the home and are whisked up one flight of stairs to a small sunlit parlor. The atmosphere is airy, light, and calm. The stone floors have been immaculately swept and washed, and there are lovely Tanjore and Rajasthani paintings on the walls; it's clear someone has lovingly adorned this space.

(How) A Story Struggles

A woman, made small with age, sits sideways on a majestic divan ironing a cotton *dupatta* with a heavy iron. Her hair is cropped short, she has an olive-skinned, deeply-lined face, and she sits ensconced in a floral-printed cotton kaftan, the kind that women in my family also wear in the home in the 45 degrees Celsius Delhi temperatures. Asha gives her a light hug and asks in Punjabi, "*Ki haal hai, Mumma?*" (How are you, Mother?). So this is the woman I am here to meet. She tells Asha to take us to her bedroom. Later, I will come to know that ironing one flat garment a day is a type of exercise recommended by the doctor to strengthen Labbi Devi's arms and shoulders. "Otherwise, why would we allow her to iron her own clothes at her age?" asks Asha.

I have been expecting long hair down to the hips, and instead I am presented with a petite woman in a short pageboy haircut. I shake my head as if adjusting the new image to the old one in one portion of my brain. We are ushered into a large low-lit master bedroom, almost the size of a living room, and are led to a seating area that holds a largish loveseat, a few armchairs, and a coffee table in the center. A split air-conditioner unit is buzzing in the corner and the drapes are down; it is a very hot summer afternoon with the sun at its peak. Our eyes take a few minutes to get accustomed to the low light and we notice an old gentleman reclining on the large bed in the corner talking to a younger male who is sitting at the edge of the bed, pressing his feet. We presume this is Asha's father and his caretaker. Papa and I take the loveseat and have sat for less than two minutes when there is a flurry of activity at the door, and Labbi Devi, Asha, and another woman, Labbi Devi's daughter-in-law, walk in. My father and I spring up, place our hands together and bow our heads in the customary *namaste*. Labbi Devi takes the armchair next to me. The white *dupatta* that she was ironing is now wrapped around her shoulders.

Asha introduces us to her sister-in-law, Rani. A few moments later Rani's son and daughter saunter into the room. A helper brings a tray of cold water. As is the custom, we are asked if we would like to have tea. As is customary, we first refuse, then they insist, and we finally concede. If there can be an edible leitmotif in one's fieldwork, in mine it would be tea. Most of my field conversations begin and end with tea. Having spent most of my growing years sitting among family or friends doing *gup-shup* (gossip) over chai, I slide into the ritual with familiar ease. In fact, I expect tea wherever I go, and when over the years of fieldwork just one family—the Vermas—fails to offer it, I consider them an aberration, inhospitable, rude, almost un-Punjabi. I discuss them with Papa, who gets angry with them, advising me to not return to their house, saying, "Who does not offer tea/coffee to a guest?" It is petty, I tell my father, not to pursue a family just because of tea, and I was not really a guest. "Of course you are, you were in their home," he says. I understand him; for him tea is a sacred connector. As luck will have it, the Vermas are a busy family of small-business owners, difficult to connect with during subsequent trips. I don't meet them again.

We have established an informal circle within the seating area. Asha walks over to the bed to talk to her father, and from their conversation it looks as if today he has recognized her. She brings him with her to the seating area and we are all introduced to him. I am scrutinized by the extended family and asked various questions about my life in the United States, a predictable inquisition that I have become used to over the last decade of living abroad. The question I am most frequently asked is how I manage to live alone, and isn't it just so lonely to be on one's own? To them, just as it was with Biji, living alone is an aberration—a life outside home, unenclosed in filial ties. In the United States, living alone seems normal and reasonable, and I've learned (sometimes with reluctance) to savor the mental and emotional space that solitude can bring. The serenity of solitude would be unexplainable to this family so entwined with one another's lives.

After some minutes of chit-chat, I quietly turn to Labbi Devi and ask her if she would be amenable to my recording our conversations. I tell her that

I will do so only on some of my visits. In a mix of Punjabi and Hindi, she declares, *"Tusi is layee tho aaye ho, chalo shuru karo,"* of course, that's why you are here, just start right now. Our conversations are held in a mix of Punjabi and Hindi. I already know that I will have to talk to her alongside the extended family. I am never left completely alone with first-generation members of the family; it's a process I have become used to. I have various private meetings with members of subsequent generations, as with Asha and her daughter, but the first generation's stories are mostly told within the fold. Only when I talk to widows and widowers am I given more individual moments. Does a collective telling and listening strengthen the family's sense of self? Does it help to maintain the story of the Partition that the family wants to keep? Is it a way to anchor it?

I inch a little close to Labbi Devi. I start as I usually do with most of my participants, asking Labbi Devi if she will tell me her full name, and how old she was when the Partition occurred. She was twenty, and as for her name, she laughingly explains, "No one uses my real name. I'm just Labbi Devi." "Why?" I ask.

> *Labbi Devi:* When I was born there was so much trust between us Hindus and Muslims. My father and mother were not able to conceive, their kids would die in childbirth. I had six brothers and sisters who were born before me and they all died. A priest told them that you should get a cow and pray to it and serve it and you will have a daughter and she will stay alive. My father listened to him and domesticated a cow and I was born. Then my mother decided to not give me her own milk. She wanted me to stay alive and was afraid that her milk was what had killed her babies. I was breast-fed by a Musalmani [a Muslim woman]. My mother did not even raise me on her milk, I was raised on the milk of a Muslim woman. My mother did that to save me. That is why my name is Labbi. In Punjabi it means "we found her."

It seems to be a simple and seemingly routine explanation, for her. But I find myself thinking longingly about this lost world where Hindus and Muslims lived in peace, where Muslim women could be wet nurses for Hindu babies. It is common knowledge that economic inequities among Muslims and Hindus in small towns often meant that Muslims were employed by affluent Hindus, and Muslim wet nurses were not uncommon. So there is a logical explanation for the choice of a Muslim wet nurse. At the same time, a part of me wants to idealistically believe that the two communities were connected in this visceral way in that space and time.

This nostalgia for community is not a new feeling. My own grandfather, Pitaji, like many of his compatriots, believed that all the noise about Partition was merely a passing phase. His boss in the Indian railways, Mr. Abdul, convinced him to stay behind and wait it out. In fact, he invited Pitaji to move in with his family, which my grandfather did. As a precaution, Pitaji sent his wife, Biji, and his three children to Shimla, the British summer capital, in the North Indian Himalayan ranges. Meanwhile, Mr. Abdul began receiving death threats from his own community leaders, who were accusing him of harboring a Hindu in his home. Two months after Partition, believing the rift was final and complete, and fearing for his boss's life, my grandfather made his way to Shimla. He had packed up the house and placed the family's possessions on a goods train that was to cross Lahore. This train was looted by a mob and all their belongings were stolen. He arrived alone, empty-handed, but with a promise of a job in the railways in the new India. The family stayed afloat, barely. I grew up in an atmosphere heavy with such nostalgia about Hindu-Muslim friendship. I've wanted to hold on to this idea that we were one before we were forcibly separated.

There are echoes of such unity in many of the oral histories, yet something does not quite fit. The fact that Muslims are referred to as *them*, as *Musalman/Musalmani*, as *Mohammedans*, tells me that Hindus and Muslims were apart long before the separation. And "they" are always either employees, or helpers, or servants, or wet nurses—an underclass that no one acknowledges as an underclass. They are mentioned in the stories, but they are not important enough to be characters who stay in the stories. After 1947, it simply became easier to blame the rift on the physical and manufactured political divide. There is tremendous discussion about this rupture in other oral histories of the Partition. Historian Ian Talbot and migration studies scholar Darshan Tatla, for instance, emphasize these continuing themes narrated by refugees across many decades of oral history work: recollections of a fairly harmonious pre-Partition time; blaming the upheaval on politicians rather than on religion or culture; and a continued emphasis on personal roles rather than the state's role in rehabilitation efforts.[6] Now I am beginning to experience, both symbolically and semantically, the emotional chasm that was present long before the communities were politically partitioned. "Are you in touch with your friends in Pakistan?" is a question I continue to ask every participant who was old enough to have and remember friends. "No, there was no point in staying in touch," is the inevitable reply. Were the ties, I quietly (and now loudly) speculate, really so strong? Among the twelve members of the oldest generation (those who were at least ten years old in 1947) whom I meet, only one has ever returned to Pakistan or attempted to find friends left behind. Uneasy contradictions—friends and foes.

As if echoing my thoughts about these tensions, Labbi Devi's story shifts from kindness to killing. I've already heard some of this story from Asha in the car and will hear it again from Kavi, the granddaughter. I ask Labbi Devi to tell me about their journey across the border.

Labbi Devi: We took a goods train and that was attacked. Then we took a regular train and the military people who were escorting it were Musalmans, they harassed us.

Devika : What did they do?

Labbi Devi: My husband was sitting behind me, I was sitting in the front. My older daughter Prem was there, she was six months old. The Musalmans took my girl and threw her away on the platform. And the Musalmans took me away. They took me. I came back. Then they took me again, when they started to carry me I was hit by an axe. . . . see here. [Papa and I stand up and step behind her chair as she parts her hair and shows us the scar on her scalp, from what must have been a deep and painful wound.] They were about to take me and we were in the space between the train wagons when the military arrived, so they left me right there. So I was saved. There were three thousand, four thousand people on that train and only one thousand survived. My mother and father both died on that train. My husband's older brother's two children died on the train. My in-laws were also killed.

My husband was hit on the head with an axe, just like me, but his arms and legs were intact so he could walk. He fell down on his face and he had 400 rupees in his front pocket and that was saved. We used it to eat and buy food. The military trucks came from Amritsar to take us to India. They told us that the first trucks would carry the seriously wounded. His older brother was in serious condition, so they took him first. His wife said she wanted to go with him since he was her husband. My husband said, "I will not let my brother go alone." Then I was left alone over there. The Musalmans troubled me again, and I begged the Sardars [Sikh soldiers] to take me to Amritsar since they were troubling me. So they brought me to Amritsar.

The description is cut short by a *non sequitur* from Labbi Devi's husband.

Lalaji: There was a board in front of my shop in Lahore, which read, *"Rub bhalla kare sub ka"* ["May God be good to everyone"]. Do you know what *rub* means? It means God.

Rani (daughter-in-law): What else do you remember, Daddy?

I listen curiously to the exchange and smile, but I am quick to turn my attention back to Labbi Devi, since I do not want to lose the train of her thoughts. Given her husband's illness, I see her as the subject-repository where memory resides for this family. She continues:

All our possessions were taken by them. They took everything. In a milk box—where the baby's milk was kept—I had put a small gold brick of about 100 or 200 grams; I had got some gold melted and put the milk on top of it. After they threw my daughter away and after the military man brought my daughter back . . . I asked him what happened to our things, and he said, "the Musalmans have taken them." I told him that the child was hungry and that I needed to get some milk from the train and he said to go and get it. I went to the train and the box was lying there and I got it. There were the 400 rupees that my husband had in his front shirt pocket and there was the gold in the milk box. All other possessions were lost. We had anyway just left everything in our homes. . . .

The gold that I had hidden in the milk, you know? We sold it in Amritsar. After we sold that we got some money. We came to Delhi. There was some land on sale in Qutab Road, we bought it. We built the shop on it. His brother and wife stayed in a different house, we stayed in a different one. We did not want to live together. My husband's brother used to say, since we have lost everything, if we stay together there are bound to be fights and I really want our brotherly love to continue. They had two lavish houses in Pakistan, built side by side with a door between them. They wanted the same in India because they felt that we should live together but have separate kitchens, otherwise the wives will fight.

I quietly mention that if Labbi Devi had not thought quickly and saved the gold, they would not be where they are. I point out that they were able to survive and buy a shop because of that gold that only she was able to rescue. "*Ehh sub twadi kaarun haiga hai,*" all this is because of you, I tell her. Labbi Devi nods her head. Our discussion has been animated and has been heard by all members of the family, but this, her pivotal act of ingenuity and survival, is left unrecognized in this moment, and in many subsequent moments when this story is repeated. I glance around me looking for some support, but find none.

Why the silence, I wonder? The family and this story has traveled across the subcontinent, across three generations, but here in this space, this anecdote is muted into submission—the story disciplined, so to speak. My own grandmother Biji smuggled her gold, about 200 grams of it, across the border. It was this gold that enabled the schooling and subsequent higher education of a half dozen of her Chawla nieces and nephews. In my family, her gold story is told proudly, and my grandmother is hailed as its central protagonist. A similar story here, while neither silenced nor untold, is simply not placed at the center of the family's resettlement efforts. Even Kavi, Labbi Devi's granddaughter, fails to commend her grandmother's quick thinking. She refers to the entire history of escape and survival as the "conversation of struggle":

> *Kavi*: When we were children, during large family gatherings, when any mention of pre-Partition life came around, we were always told that we have had it so comfortable, that we have not seen suffering—there was always the conversation of struggle.

As if to clarify this further, Kavi announces, "The Partition is a storybook tale to me." "How is it a tale?" I ask. "Well, isn't it for you too?" she asks in turn. Yes, I nod saying, "I first heard it as a story from my grandmother and then there were all the films, the novels, and just the writing in the media." "Exactly," says Kavi. "When I think of Pakistan I think of it as a place—that was obviously home to my grandparents; at the same time if I visit it, I will visit it as a tourist to see just another country." "But your grandmother, her story, the axe that hit her head, how she—they—made a new life in India?" I question, trying to disguise my condescension. Unfazed, Kavi replies:

> Don't get me wrong. I am not at all saying that they did not suffer. I grew up feeling for them because we always heard the "conversation of struggle," and my mother has even visited Pakistan. But for me and my sister, Pakistan is a

place that was there, and now whenever we visit it—and we want to—it will be like another place that you see and enjoy. . . . See, we know more about their struggles in India than about their life in Pakistan. We were told more about the train journey and how harrowing it was and less about how they lived and what they did there. Yes, my *nana* [her grandfather, Lalaji] often talked about his college and how he was a bodybuilder and how he used to walk to school, but we do not know more than that about their life. I know that my mother's mother, my *nani* [her grandmother, Labbi Devi], was very beautiful and the Muslims tried to abduct her and they threw my aunt, her older daughter, out of the train—she was just a baby. But we know quite little about their life in Pakistan.

Kavi does refer to the gold story and how the gold was rescued by her grandmother, but like everyone else, she bypasses what I consider the importance of the role her grandmother played in the family's resettlement into a new business and new home(s).

I try to proceed with the story with Labbi Devi. I ask how they settled in Delhi.

Devika: So where did you stay?

Labbi Devi: In Karol Bagh.

When did they get their first homes? When did the business start taking off? What were the homes in Pakistan like? The answers come, not reluctantly, but in bits and pieces.

Devika: What happened after you came to Karol Bagh?

Labbi Devi: We stayed in Karol Bagh. My *jeth* and *jethani* [her husband's older brother and wife; her brother- and sister-in-law] were in another place. Then the shop started getting business and we were able to manage. First there was my older daughter, then three other kids were born, two girls and one boy. So we stayed like that for four, five years. Then we got claims from Pakistan and we got this house in the 1950s.

Devika: What did you get from that?

Labbi Devi: We got this house. We bought this house in exchange of that claim.

I try to ask her more about the claim, but she is reticent (or has simply forgotten), as is the case with many other first-generation refugees, and their stories align with others in the Partition literature at large. In *Since 1947*, Ravinda Kaur directly addresses this reticence in discussing her oral histories: "The arrival in Delhi and the resettlement remained a question that was frequently avoided when it came to the issue of state compensation."[7] Many affluent families had not relied on state compensation and had not been indebted to the postcolonial state for their post-Partition successes. Yet others were simply "reluctant to recognize the state efforts to afford them privileges in jobs and other such opportunities."[8] Interestingly, the less affluent, the untouchables and those of other lower castes, were more forthright about the state support they received. Labbi Devi's daughter-in-law interrupts us, saying:

> *Rani*: This whole colony is a refugee colony. All the people who were from there—refugees—they live here in the neighborhood.
>
> *Devika*: Do you remember your time in Pakistan?
>
> *Labbi Devi*: What?
>
> *Devika*: Your house and all that?
>
> *Labbi Devi*: I remember everything, *beta* [child]. His house was in the Keedon ki gali. The name of that mohalla was Keedon ki gali. That is where it was. His house was very good.[9]
>
> *Devika*: In what way?
>
> *Labbi Devi*: The house was very, very big and very lavish. There were two houses together and there was a door in between the two houses. Even there we had the same idea that we can live next to each other, but have separate households so that the mother and son do not fight over home territory or power in the house. The older brother and his wife lived in one house and the mother and my husband lived in the other house. They wanted to have a smooth relationship. Even in Lahore the shop was the same but the homes were different—the shop sold household goods, glasses, bottles, and all that. My *jeth* used to come to Lahore and get the clothes and . . . my husband was the younger one and he was the older one and his father had passed away, so his brother had raised him, so that is why he was close.
>
> *Lalaji* (her husband): There were only two, three people in that city who were B.A. pass, all the others were matric pass.[10]
>
> *Devika*: Only two or three?

Such anecdotes are common. My own maternal great-grandfather was the only graduate in his district in Dera Ghazi Khan.

> *Labbi Devi*: Yes, there were two. He had gone to study and get his B.A. People in the neighborhood used to tell his brother, what has happened to you, why have you sent him away to study? [Going away was atypical.]

> *Papa*: So, he did his B.A.?

> *Labbi Devi*: Yes, he did his B.A. before we were married from the Lahore Dyal Singh Mahavidhalaya.

> *Lalaji*: These are all old stories now. Everything had some value in those times. This is nothing now.

> *Devika* (questioning Lalaji): Do you remember the college?

> *Lalaji*: I remember everything. The board on my shop said, "*Rub bhalla kare di Hatti*." ["May God be good to everyone."]

Papa asks some more questions: "What subjects did you study in college?"

> *Lalaji*: I studied Urdu. I studied English. I used to also study Farsi. Farsi is almost like Urdu.

> *Rani*: He tells *shairi* [Urdu sonnets]. Can you recite some for us?

> *Lalaji*: Our shop in Lahore was four stories high and you could see the train station from the terrace, so people used to come there to see whether or not the train they were about to take had arrived. There was no shop like this in town.

> *Rani*: Why don't you recite a *shair*, Daddy? "*Unke . . .*"

> *Lalaji*: "*Unke aane se jo aa jaati hai muh pe raunak . . . unke aane se jo aa jaati hai muh pe raunak . . . wo samajte hai ke beemar ka haal accha hai.*" [When I get a sighting of my beloved, I get such a smile on my face, then everyone thinks my illness is over.] . . . "*Ooncha apna naam karta hain wo sab salaam karta hai . . . chal chal chameli bagh mei hum phool layenge.*" [A boy said, get a garland of flowers for my house . . . his friend said, your wife is so beautiful that you do not need a garland of flowers.]

We all laugh.

> *Rani* (prompting): "*Jaate ho khuda . . .*"

> *Lalaji*: "*Jaate ho khuda haafil, par itni gujarish hai, jub yaad hamari aa jaaye milne ki dua karo.*" [You are taking my leave, so goodbye for now, but when you miss me, grace me with your presence.]

Papa: *Wah wah!* [Hear hear!]

Rani: Make them listen to the other one . . .

Lalaji tells the station, shop, and home story again and recites another sonnet:

"*Neend kub aati hai yaaron ishk ke beemar ko, dekhta hi rahte hai wo chaand ki rafter ko.*" [The man who is lovesick cannot sleep at night and spends his time tracing the movement of the moon across the sky.]

"*Chal chameli bagh mein hum phool layenge, arre phool kya laoge, phool to tum khud ho.*" [Let us go to the garden and get the flowers, says the girl. Her man replies, why would we need a flower, you are a flower yourself.]

I inch closer to Labbi Devi, attempting to resume our conversation:

Devika: How did the shop start doing well?

Labbi Devi: First, we got one agency,[11] then we got another one. We knew people, we used to call them. Then we got another agency. So we kept getting agencies and our work kept going. God was kind to us.

Devika: Where were you from in Pakistan, even before your marriage?

Labbi Devi: Khan.

Devika: Even before your marriage?

Labbi Devi: Yes, even before that. You can say that . . . our houses were the same distance apart as my daughter's house and mine. About one hour away.

Devika: So what year were you married?

Labbi Devi: 1945.

Lalaji and Rani both interrupt with the house story, the shop story, and recite some more poetry.

Devika: What did you sell?

Labbi Devi: We used to sell socks and all that, handkerchiefs and things like that.[12]

A maid enters the room with some snacks and Labbi Devi invites us to eat. Lalaji continues with the story about the home and shop.

Devika: What year were you married?

Labbi Devi: 1945.

Papa: You were married a long time.

Labbi Devi: Yes, yes, it has been over sixty years since I was married.

Papa: It was during the war.

Devika: Yes, World War Two was going on.

Labbi Devi: When Prem, my older daughter, was born in 1946, the war had stopped.

Snacks and tea are offered to everyone and Lalaji refuses to eat, and instead continues with his home and shop story.

Devika: Did you have many friends who came here with you?

Labbi Devi: From Pakistan no one really came with us in terms of neighbors and friends. My sister-in-law was there, she came with us. Her husband came with us, he died in the train. Their kids, they also came with us.

Lalaji recites the home and shop story again. At this point, I decide to fully turn my attention to his story, and I ask Rani:

Devika: It's interesting what he remembers. Isn't it?

Rani: I try to make him remember every morning. I tell him one word and he reconstructs the rest of the sentence.

Rani tells her father-in-law to recite some more of the story and some sonnets. He repeats a small sonnet. Papa jumps in and provides some prompts. Lalaji still mixes up a few sonnets. Meanwhile Labbi Devi invites her husband to drink tea. He then tells the home and shop story again. I turn to Labbi Devi again and prompt, "Tell me a little bit more about the resettlement in Delhi."

(How) A Story Finds (Is Forced to Find) Home

When I first returned from meeting Labbi Devi, I was inattentive to the circuitous nature of our conversations. Even though much of my time was spent asking her about the process of relocation and rehabilitation in India, I unconsciously refused to acknowledge that we were both forced to submit to the memories of her husband, Lalaji, who was prompted to remember poetry and envision the old home by *all* of us. At first I explained these constant interruptions as part of this family's lively remembering of its history—a process that was both homey and homely. My notes reflect such thoughts:

> An oral history with multiple interlocutors. The family members seem generally interested in the family history. They all help their grandfather to remember and recite the poetry that he used to enjoy. Really delightful. There is a lot of affection in this home. I was taken into all these stories by women, there seems to be a matriarchal structure at work. Of course, I cannot be sure.

Yet, as I lived with the oral history, my thinking about it shifted. I found myself viewing the multiple interlocutions by the women, which privileged the voice of the patriarch, as the story that was performed by us all. In my notes, I pondered:

> Yes, a methodologically important oral history vis-à-vis the multiple interlocutions. Why is Labbi Devi not allowed to own this story? But then, I should also ask, can oral histories be contained in one person? In this case, Lalaji, who has Alzhiemer's, is constantly deferred to. His medical condition makes it imperative for Labbi Devi to tell/take over the telling of the story, yet the family intervenes to make sure his loosely remembered stories stay center stage. His age and illness ought to diminish his patriarchal authority, but even though he is the only grown man present during all my visits (not including Papa), patriarchy is maintained and produced by the women themselves. What am I to make of this? On the one hand, this is not news, since they are probably socialized to uphold patriarchy, yet on the other hand, these are strong women who have been working inside and outside of the home, running households as well as businesses. And what about me? Why am I unable to intervene and speak with her alone and elicit her story? What makes me defer to this storyline? Can I take this story any further? How can I insert Labbi Devi into her own family story when her family won't allow it?
>
> I thought this was one of my more detailed interviews, but now I am unsure. I just notice myself struggling to get the story out. I know stories are not stored in bodies and really come into being in the telling. I suppose what comes into being in this account is unsatisfying for me. And why is it important that the story "satisfy" me? Am I failing as an ethnographer and oral historian?

It is now quite obvious from these notes that I was forcing myself to address patriarchy, gender, and power structures—pressing a feminist analysis, so to speak. I felt it was crucial to show how Labbi Devi was being silenced, left unvoiced, and disallowed from owning her version of the family story. I admit I felt a twinge of guilt because I was unsuccessful in enabling voice, in itself a problematic idea. I wondered if I was failing as an ethnographer, feminist, and oral historian, because after all, "to facilitate access to the muted channels of women's subjectivity, we must inquire whose story the interview is asked to tell, who interprets the story, and with what theoretical frameworks."[13] And Kaur astutely notes, "Even though many consider story-telling a female pastime, it is not publicly performed by women. . . . [T]hough the gendered differences in the narrations are not surprising, it is important to remember who within a family is telling the story."[14] To confront these matters is to begin, in a sense, to interrogate both ethnography and oral history. Indeed, oral histories belong to no single constituent and are often considered "repetitions." There is no singular/insular oral history, just as there is no single history of an event. Remarking on this quality in "Moving Histories: Performance and Oral History," Della Pollock explains:

> With the frame of a performative culture, the oral history is itself a repetition without stable origins. It is a form of cultural currency that flows among participants. As such it does not "belong" to any one teller. Its vitality lies in exchange, at the dialogical intersection of teller and listener. . . . In a horizontal economy, a performance of oral history is a tale told *alongside* another. It enacts the inter-subjection of interview partners, and their mutual becoming in the fraught negotiation of subjectivity, temporality, memory, imagination, and history. It does not disown the "original" teller, though it does elaborate the displacement of what is ostensibly his or her story into the co-relation of multiple others.[15]

The teller, notes Pollock, is doubly burdened—not only by her own, but by other histories. If the teller, here Labbi Devi, was performing as expected, the question then is: Was the failure mine? Was it I, the ethnographer, who was not doing enough to accomplish a satisfying narrative or at least one that satisfied me? Moreover, had I become complicit in resubjugating Labbi Devi by passively entering an ongoing family dynamic? Had I become complicit in the process of silencing this woman who was already subjugated by historical forces, and then resubjugated by family discourse because the patriarch's story—fleetingly remembered—needed to stand in and stand for family remembering? Or was I experiencing what Geertz had long ago predicted in describing anthropological analysis "as a task at which no one ever does more than not utterly fail"—confronting "the un-get-roundable fact that all ethnographic descriptions are homemade, that they are the describer's descriptions, not those of the described"?[16] But I took pause from these thoughts and noted that there *was* a story (among stories) that had been performed—the interrupting story of the "home and shop"—a story that Asha had been preparing me for on our way to meet her mother. I could either turn my attention to this story or relegate it to the archive.

In worrying about the failure of feminist ethnography, Kamala Visweswaran describes a common strategy of reinterpreting failure as success by viewing it as a valuable lesson for refining one's methods, but she warns that better methodology does not necessarily mean better results.[17] Here I want to focus on ethnographic work in general. In order to generate a more satisfactory account, should I have insisted on meeting Labbi Devi alone, should I have insisted on getting her story of the Partition? Visweswaran asks that ethnographers, instead of reinterpreting failure as a lesson in methodology, track failure at the epistemic level addressed by Gayatri Spivak's notion of "cognitive failure,"[18] which occurs when projects are faced with their own impossibility. Visweswaran notes that feminist ethnographers fail because they continue to see women as "simply" women and not as historical subjects often primarily constituted by race, class, and sexuality. She urges us to look at failure as both an epistemological crisis and as an epistemological construct, because "failure might signal a project that may no longer be attempted, or at least not on the same terms," and she argues that the ethnography must hold in tension the "desire to know and the desire to represent."[19] Ultimately, Visweswaran observes that a failed account can engender new kinds of positionings that might alter the contours of the fieldwork. With the Khanna family, I arrived at what I consider a failed account; instead of a movement from failure to success, my analysis moved from success to admitting failure.

Domesticating the Idea of Home/Self

What choices do I have and what must I do? It is entirely possible to conduct a deconstructive transnational feminist analysis of the family story and indeed show how female subjects are subjugated in historical discourse. One can also suggest that women may, and often do, become the instruments of their own oppression. In undertaking such an analysis, I can reinforce and reify the disciplinary mechanisms of the gendered nation-state,[20] and thereby position Labbi Devi as an unwelcome and marginalized subject of historical discourse.[21] But I am forced to wonder how far such an analysis will take me. What might it reveal about these interlocutors and their experiences? I decide, instead, to take another route—to attempt to hold steady with how the story "is," why it "stays" where it does, and ultimately what that might tell us about our *narrative quest* for homing amidst the chaos of forced migrations.

I choose to remain with the home and shop story and consider the following questions: Why does this family entrap its story in a circuitous repetition that is encouraged by everyone, including this ethnographer? I revisit segments of Labbi Devi's account and find (again) that she is unafraid and in fact eager to tell the story of the family's post-Partition struggle, since she was an active participant in the family's economic mobility over the last five decades. But she is persuaded to stay passively outside the intricacies of narrating that struggle, because remembering the home and shop appear to be crucial to the family's selfhood. I want to propose that this seemingly unconscious maneuver allows the family to hold the story and thereby preserve a stable sense of the idea of home. And when a home is preserved, then subjectivity, in this case the family's identity, can be salvaged from becoming an identity that finds itself destabilized in the "conversation of struggle." In that conversation, the family must acknowledge the trauma of displacement, an acknowledgement that means an inevitable loss of footing, a loss that they would prefer to not remember. Stability is achieved and a self is preserved by subjugating the subject and muting her story.

Consequently, the only way that the story can enable home, indeed *find* a home, is for the interlocutors to perform the rules of domesticity by controlling both the story and the subject (and even as I veer away from reducing this to a feminist analysis, it's inevitable that the scope of patriarchy in shaping these stories be addressed). The story has traveled and is forced to find roots in "the home and shop" image of the patriarch through the encouraging machinations of the female family members (and myself, and my father). I want to consider this strategy as a *narrative homemaking practice* that relies on cross-generational repetition—the image of the home and shop must be repeatedly evoked to bring home into relief, to maintain home, and so to replenish a family identity. This narrative homemaking practice is a performance of domesticity that coincides with the modernist visions of home and dwelling that we want to preserve in this story. If we understand domesticity as, in Karen Hansen's words, "a set of ideas that over the course of nineteenth century . . . have associated women with family, domestic value, and home, and took for granted a hierarchical distribution of power favoring men," then these narrative practices stand parallel to how homes of traditional modernity were conceptualized as feminine spaces.[22]

In studies that trace the modern history of home, the evolution of home into a private and intimate sphere is seen to coincide with domestic arrangements being taken over by women, making it not only a feminine space but also a place under feminine control. Such control gave rise to the idea of domesticity as what Witold Rybczynski has described as "a set of felt emotions . . . [having] to do with family, intimacy, and a devotion to the home, as well as with a sense of the house as embodying—not only harboring—these sentiments."[23] Homely domesticity was ultimately the result of women's role in the home, a role created by patriarchal arrangements. John Lukacs considers domesticity one of the most crucial achievements of modernity, observing that "domesticity, privacy, comfort, the concept of home and family . . . are . . . principle achievement of the Bourgeois age."[24] Rybcznski refers to it above all else as a "feminine achievement."[25] In the second half of the twentieth century the idea of domesticity has been critiqued, deconstructed, and reinvented, leading to rearticulations of domestic roles. Of course disagreements abound over the private/public split in domestic/work life brought forth in a modernist era.

My goal in invoking domesticity here is simply to emphasize how traditional domesticity—if we understand it as a process whereby women stay home to keep the home intact—circulates in this family story, and why I believe the "home and shop" remain central to how they view themselves. Our discursive home-work is a performance of conventional domesticity that ensures the narrative dominance of the patriarch's "home and shop" story over Labbi Devi's "conversation of struggle." Curtailing her account keeps Labbi Devi confined to the home space—the feminized space in traditional narratives of home. This privileging of her husband's story safeguards the patriarch's version of home despite the fact that new homes came to be because of Labbi Devi's labor in the post-Partition world—labor that involved being physically active in the means of economic production. I am forced here to recall and remind us that Lalaji (Labbi Devi's husband) continues to go to work by being taken to the shop by his companion every day, securing the separation between home and work. Finally, we all become co-conspirators (wardens, if you will) who sediment this illusion by disallowing Labbi Devi's account, preventing it from becoming an achievement. Our actions result in domesticating her to/in the home/house—a sort of colonial maneuver that keeps the hierarchical power lines intact. Domestication is generally understood as a "reintegration or re-assimilation into the dominant culture," comparable to the colonial endeavor as an assimilating and civilizing mission.[26] In fact, the etymological closeness of *domesticity* with *domesticate* is not coincidental; "domesticity is often considered as being part of a civilizing mission and as such the import of domesticity was a crucial factor in the colonial encounter."[27]

Having noted the above, I stop short of emphasizing that our homemaking strategies are colonial (and civilizing), but they are certainly meant to assimilate (and subsume) Labbi Devi's story into the story that the family members want to remember and repeat. I am also disinclined to argue that this narrative homemaking is a conscious or deliberate tactic. Rather, I want to emphasize how pervasive and persistent traditional meanings of homes and identities are, and how easily a patriarchal and modernist adaptation of home can come to be. For this family, the repetition of the patriarch's construction of home is so crucial that women in the family take upon themselves the task of keeping alive and favoring the rendition of their Alzhiemer's-ridden patriarch.

But I want to end by offering an even simpler explanation. Perhaps this family story, told forcefully and collectively with its patriarchal, modernist, ideological reproductions of home notwithstanding, is really about *homewell*[28]—the desire to belong in and with something—to recover the fragmented self, lost in national fragmentations and Partitions. *Homewell*, according to Lisa Knopp, can mean a few things:

> When you are *homewell*, you feel rooted, aligned, nurtured, synchronized, whole, plugged in and flowing. When you have *homewell*, what is essential— hearth, home, love, community, belonging, memory, creativity—is with you.[29]

Perhaps being and keeping *homewell* is at the heart of the storytelling process for this family. For as Tonya Davidson has noted, "when a place is lost, through exile or voluntary movement, the loss is reconciled through a type of traumatic storytelling—revisiting the place over and over again by narrating it for others."[30] Among scholars such as geographers Porteous and Smith, who position home as a psychosocial space, "being at home is defined as being close to self," and home is seen as a

> [s]econd body . . . as a symbol of self and self-identity. Home shapes you and, in turn, is shaped in your image. . . . Ironically, the strong sense of self created by a strong sense of home may also be the factor that preserves you when home is lost.[31]

Indeed, I approach the domestication of Labbi Devi's story as a critical narrative act that recovers and sustains the self-identity of this family. If the home is the second body, it must be saved because its death could foretell the end of the self. After all, as Richard Daniels asserts in his gracefully poetic essay "Scattered Remarks on the Ideology of Home," home is

> among other things, the desire to go on living without transforming changes; the wish for the ongoing reduplication, the endless repetitive loop, of one's everyday life, idealized, even sacralized; the desire for things to stay as they are, and to consider them right and just; the wish for the end of history. Home is also the desire to be at home with oneself, as well as the deep wish to have a unified originary "self" to begin with.[32]

Home for this family perhaps lies somewhere along routes that their story travels as they perform it, for themselves, for each other, and for me.

FOUR

Home Outside Home

An image secures itself in my mind. A young refugee woman, no more than twenty-one years of age, rides an old black bicycle around the streets of Darya Ganj in what is now called Old Delhi. She's in search of an old man said to be hoarding books.

An image is often the place where a story anchors itself. An image might even become a story. This image is not Kiranji's story, but these scenes are how I first came to know her. So here, I travel into a story before the story—a necessary wandering that led me to the account I eventually tell.

Something Real, Something Imagined

It is a few months after Partition and many *galis*, narrow side streets, in this otherwise bustling neighborhood are deserted. As a young Sikh woman on her bicycle, Kiran seems oblivious to the danger she might be in;[1] the communal riots have not entirely dissipated, and Hindu and Sikh mobs are still hunting down any Muslims who have not yet fled to Pakistan. She is looking for an old *maulvi*, a Muslim religious man, known to be sheltered in various homes in these streets. Since fleeing Rawalpindi in September of '47, Kiran has spent her days volunteering at the refugee camp, writing and reading letters for other refugees. She has enrolled in the camp college to complete her final exams for a master's degree in literature. Such colleges have mushroomed in refugee camps soon after the Partition, allowing students to complete their degrees.

Imagine: A young boy at the camp whose immediate family was murdered at the hands of a rioting mob, for whom Kiran writes letters to extended family members, has alerted her to the Muslim holy man said to own copies of Chekov, Tolstoy, and Dostoyevsky—books Kiran needs for her M.A. exams. How does this young boy (let us call him Suraj) know this man?

Imagine: Suraj has survived a mob that was chasing him down these very streets because the maulvi grabbed him into his room as the boy frantically turned into an alley. The maulvi hid Suraj until the worst of the mob violence had abated, and some while later, in the middle of the night, delivered him to the refugee camp. The boy tells Kiran that the old man was hiding in a ten-by-ten-foot room that was mostly full of novels by foreign writers. What writers? Kiran asks. Suraj recites, in halting English, the names he can remember—Chekov, Gogol, Tolstoy. There were piles and piles of them on the floor of the room, resting against the walls. The maulvi-bibliophile read novels most of the days that he and Suraj stayed together.

Why did the maulvi save the boy? And what was he doing with the Russian novels? And what does it mean to read, just read, in the midst of all this bloodshed and chaos? Perhaps explanations are unnecessary. This was a time when Hindus, Sikhs, and Muslims were risking their lives to save one another. This was also a time when Hindus, Sikhs, and Muslims were risking their lives to kill one another. Perhaps there could be no better time to read Dostoyevsky or Chekov, who explored the motivations that impel human beings to commit sin, to suffer, and yet to live with grace. The Partition is no different from any other time and place of tyranny. That the Russians are a part of the equation and that the maulvi—a man of faith—is reading them seems both natural and magical. Besides, there is something Chekovian in the figure of the maulvi, a man married to faith, a healer of sorts, desiring literature. Chekov, the doctor-writer, was famously known to insist that medicine, healing, was his lawful wife and literature his mistress.

And Kiran—the real and the imagined—risks her own life in search of both the maulvi and the Russians. She needs these books for an exam, yet the desire to find them exceeds the purpose; it becomes an obsession. The search returns a semblance of control to a world ripped apart by Partition. Finding the books—a tangible link to the place she can no longer call home.

This is *real*, because she tells me, "I would cycle out to that neighborhood on those really warm days wearing a really thin cotton *salwar kameez* with full sleeves to protect my arms from the sun, to look for this old man who had the books I needed for my exams, but I never found him. Just one day before I had left Pakistan, I had sent all my books to the nuns in the convent where I had studied." She would knock on doors describing him, but people were either unaware or too afraid to tell. "What happened to your exams?" I ask. "I had to manage from notes, I did not do well but I passed with a low pass and completed my degree." Undeterred, Kiran would go on to complete another graduate degree in education with high distinction and would become a life-long educator.

Kiran on a bicycle in search of an old man with books is a peripheral moment in her experientially and durationally rich oral history. I am so enchanted by what I hear that I begin thinking of her life as a story, "The Maulvi, the Refugee, and the Russians." The fusion of the real and imagined is both exhilarating and discomforting. From the moment of its inception, I question myself: "This is not her story, it's mine. Can I tell it this way?" I even consider removing her story from my field record.

The image spurs my creation of two strong characters brought together by historical circumstance. One, a man of God, hiding from Hindu mobs, the other, a young woman cycling unchaperoned in 1940s India in the midst of communal violence—both on a quest for Russian novelists. What could be more romantic and more improbable than a twenty-one-year-old woman cycling in search of the Russians who were in the hands of a Muslim man of faith?

An Imaginative Digression

Kiran returns to those galis every day for a few weeks, until someone in the neighborhood, an old woman perhaps, takes pity on her and leads her to the old man. The mullah, flattered by Kiran's interest in the Russians (and in him), offers to tutor Kiran for her exams. He has been reading these novels for years now and considers himself something of an expert. Imagine that the story's center is the evolution of this relationship. A god-fearing Sikh woman, Kiran has married into a fairly traditional Sikh family. She wants the tutoring and is in a quandary, since it is unsafe for her to travel to these streets every day. She's been using attendance at the camp college as a cover for cycling here, but she knows it won't be long before she is discovered by her teachers and family, who would be unhappy about her choice to befriend this man. She must convince her husband, an Air Force officer, to allow the maulvi to move into the *chummery* with them. *Chummeries*, originally meant for bachelors, were like boarding houses where refugee couples shared quarters, bathrooms, and kitchens. Her husband, a quiet and unassuming man, agrees. The maulvi moves in and continues to stay even when he could return to resume his religious work in Pakistan. Over the years, he is often mistaken for Kiran's father, who has died of heart trouble owing to the stress of the Partition, barely a year after the event. The maulvi is like a grandfather to Kiran's two sons, born a decade later. They assume he is a grand-uncle from Pakistan. He dies in 1970 at the age of 100. Since he is Muslim he must be buried. Kiran must reveal his religious identity to friends and family, who are expecting a cremation. Only her husband ever knew the truth, and he is dead. The story ends with Kiran's decision to gather her family around her and deliver the news.

A Relinquishing

The story is imagined in broad strokes. It has contours, but something continues to stop me from adding to it—from giving it nerves and bones—a body. I hold it as a summary scribbled in my notebook, a scratch note that I fondly cohabit with for three years. Unwilling to fully put it to paper, and yet unready to let it go. So, why tell it here? Why not leave it unmentioned? Why not just start with the story that I eventually choose to tell? Why fuss and fiddle with the narrative, you might ask? Why must I confuse you, the reader, with such layering? But bother (you) I must.

Listening to oral histories is neither straightforward nor unitary. Stories undergo numerous iterations between teller and listener. They travel, and we travel with them. The listener grapples with many versions of a narrative before settling upon an interpretation that seems suitable. And all oral histories are "generative" ethnographic encounters, which illustrate that all our narratives sit on the interstices of our memories, our notes, our observations, and our imaginations.[2] I find that my first story about Kiranji resembles what Michael Taussig calls "the first phase of inquiry—that of the imaginative logic of discovery—which in the case of anthropologists and many writers . . . lies in notebooks that mix raw material of observation with reverie."[3] What emerges—in fiction or ethnography—is often (or always) a coupling of the seen, the heard, the felt, and the imagined. Under these conditions, how the ethnographer veers *away from* or *comes to* a story seems critical.

What had troubled me about formalizing the fictional account? As a contemporary ethnographer, I believe strongly in the slippage between genres—the flexible and friendly gray areas between fact and fiction. I am untroubled by fictional or poetic or imagined ethnographic accounts; they compete for attention on many of the pages here.[4] So why then was I disconcerted by what was being left unsaid about Kiranji? I was notably conscious of and cautious about how Kiranji's story had become *my* story—an offspring of my imagination.

While some amount of authorial control is inevitable, to detour a participant/character into a plot entirely controlled by me, created by me, is difficult to reconcile. I recall Bakhtin's warning that the author has the tendency to select "excerpts that lay claim to some sort of meaning, while completely ignoring the whole of the hero and the whole of the author."[5] I would have to let go in order for Kiranji's story to emerge.[6] Even while I reprimand myself for the diversion, I acknowledge that any encounter with a historical subject is necessarily an "insertion" as well as an "intrusion" into his or her history. Oral historian Della Pollock writes:

> History cannot be held privately. No one person "owns" a story. Any one story is embedded in layers of remembering and storying. Remembering is necessarily a public act whose politics are bound up with the refusal to be isolated, insulated,

inoculated against both complicity with and contest over claims to ownership. That's her story, we might say, ostensibly valorizing the teller by remaining at arm's length and failing to recognize, much less reckon with, our places in the network of social relations her story invokes. In this way, we may neutralize by privatizing a given history.[7]

Dare I suggest that we may also neutralize by *de*privatizing an account? Surely the relationship can work in either direction? I had done the inverse of what is noted by Pollock; I deprivatized the oral history to such an extent that it distanced me from Kiranji's experiences. How could I salvage this account from myself? How could I reprivatize Kiranji's history? How could I let go?

Having lived so long with the imagined account, I realize that relinquishing the image requires systematic attention. It needs a (re)tracing of my steps by (re)listening and (re)hearing the recordings, in order to (re)imprint Kiranji's voice in my ear, to (re)mind myself that she had a story before it became mine The "listener as storyteller" is also a responsible witness, and oral history performance, says Pollock, is concerned "with the 'response-ability' of the person who hears oral histories and the corresponding strength of that person's agency as someone who acts on hearing, if only by telling again."[8] At the same time, I note Jacques Derrida's words, "There is no testimony that does not at least structurally imply in itself the possibility of fiction, simulacra, dissimulation, lie, and perjury—that is to say the possibility of literature."[9] This, according to Peter C. van Wyck, places testimony in the "zone of undecidability" as something that is "strangely complex."[10]

So, I begin by re-embedding myself in Kiranji's story. I spend months with the transcriptions, notes, headnotes, dreams, daydreams, and impressions. An iPod attached to my ears, I wander the winding streets of my hilly college town in the Appalachian part of Ohio. This peripatetic habit—the rhythm of my feet with the ground—allows me to listen more carefully to the patterns, themes (or lack thereof), and dreams in the stories I bring back.[11] Essayist Rebecca Solnit explores this relationship: "The rhythm of walking generates a kind of rhythm of thinking . . . suggests that the mind is also a landscape of sorts and the walking is one way to traverse it."[12] Walking is a bridge between my fieldwork and homework. These peregrinations, which I trace back to those walks with Biji, are my way of initiating, inviting, hosting my participants in my world.

This activity is yet another encounter with my notebook, which is both a guardian of my memories and a "continuous revision as well."[13] Taussig playfully describes the field notebook as a "slumbering repository awaiting the lighting glance of a re-reading."[14] My first jaunts with Kiranji lead to my domestication of her story. Of course, any account is still my account, because the ethnographer as interlocutor is always making individual, and some might say arbitrary, interpretive choices.[15] I remind myself of a mantra I like, a popular phrase from writer Joan Didion's now famous 1976 *New York Times* essay, "Why I Write": "It tells you. You don't tell it."[16] I want to listen to how the story is telling (me).

Months later I can recite large portions of the long interviews verbatim, as if Kiranji's words have settled inside and sunk into my body. I keep mulling over a pivotal moment in her narration—a moment that I now know from memory, but it has been in my fieldnotes all along. I must have hastily transcribed while Kiranji spoke:

> Home is the mother, the real mother is where you are born. . . . It is like losing a limb . . . like you've lost a life that you would love to live over again. . . . But, would I be where I am or be what I am, had I not lost this home? I don't know the answer to that.

I have written a small note on the margin: "absence/presence; it's there, but not there." Ordinarily, I avoid note-taking during interviews, but something prompted me to transcribe these lines, quite diligently. Where was I going before the image and fiction took over? I cannot un-imagine my fictional account, nor dismiss it. It exists. So, like Taussig, I want to ask, "But then what is fiction? Or what is not fiction? might be the better question, since the first way of posing the question assumes a nice safe world of the real upon which and after which we create fictions."[17] Perhaps this is the reason I have begun this story in this manner—to show how stories take us inside and outside of themselves. And that our diaries are like scrapbooks that we "read and reread in different ways, finding unexpected meanings and pairings as well as blind alleys and dead ends."[18] Or how histories lead to fictions, and how fictions can return us to histories. Eventually, the stories we tell are the stories that may have been there all along.

Another Beginning

Gurgaon, a New Delhi suburb, is a forty-minute drive from my parents' home. Kiranji lives here and has asked to meet me at 10:00 on a Sunday morning. She makes it clear that Sundays are the only days that she will be available. I am surprised because Meher, her grandniece, told me that Kiranji is a retired eighty-seven-year-old widow who lives alone. Kiranji is the fifth member of the Suri family that I am meeting. I reach her through her relatives—a cousin, a nephew, a grandniece—who insist that she is a family member I should most definitely meet. Meher is adamant that I meet the rock star of her family. Meher is an important conduit for me in the Suri family; she takes charge of making all of my first appointments with her family members. Her father, sixty-nine-year-old Amritji, whose stories are also a part of this book, says of his aunt, "We all made a life for ourselves here, I mean we have done well for ourselves here, but Kiran, she *became* something. You *must* talk to her." Yes, I must.

Meher requests her mother, Roniji, to introduce my oral history work to women in her "kitty," of which Kiranji is a member. Every month Kiranji, other older women of the Suri family, and some female friends meet for lunch in different restaurants around the city for what are known as kitty parties. A digression is necessary here so I may explain what kitties are.

Kitty party is a familiar phrase for most Indian women in small and large Indian cities. I don't know the history of the kitty; I suspect it has something to do with how wives of colonial administrators socialized with one another in the afternoons during the Raj, but I know that this is a space for women to mingle outside the confines of family homes. In urban areas, kitties are often held in restaurants, but they are also hosted in various members' homes. Men, however, are almost never invited. I think even daughters and daughters-in-law are only reluctantly included. But I've seen that rule broken. Over the years, I've noticed that kitties tend to be generationally divided. But I've also seen that rule broken. Some women hold memberships in various kitties, thus expanding their circle of friends. I have been invited by Amma to her kitty only one time and that too because some of the members were new and had never met me, since I no longer reside in India. Amma gently coached me to leave after a drink and an appetizer.

As a child and teenager, I was disdainful of my mother's commitment to these women and these parties. We—friends and cousins—thought they were just a space for housewives (as we referred to them at that time) to gossip about their in-laws and their husbands, because most of these women did not work outside the home. As an adult woman, now, I see them differently—as necessary avenues for women of my mother's generation who either never worked or were briefly in the workforce before marriage. This once-a-month gathering was their only respite from domestic life, providing a social network mostly unfettered by natal or marital ties.

Just why are they called kitties? Once again I have to speculate. Each woman in a kitty of ten to twelve women puts in $5 or even less, or $1,000 or more into a pot (kitty). Every month a drawing is held and one woman wins the entire pot. It cannot be called a lottery win, because she simply recovers the money she has put into the pot in the last ten months. Most women, like Amma, tend to save this money and recycle it into the same kitty every year. In a way it is the paid membership of a group, yet it is not quite as materialistic as it sounds. Amma's closest adult friendships with women have emerged from her kitty. While the members gather "formally" just once a month, they have forged close friendships. They meet for dinners, coffee, lunches, and even take short weekend trips together. They are a strong presence in one another's homes during weddings and other familial celebrations. In fact, when my father underwent heart bypass surgery some years ago, it was Amma's kitty friends who waited with her outside the operating room.

A few days go by and Meher's mother telephones, saying, "*Bache* [child], I talked about your study to the ladies in my kitty, and Kiranji volunteered to be interviewed. I didn't even have to ask her." Kiranji has requested that I call her in a few hours to set up our meeting. I'm happy that she has volunteered and surprised when she tells me that she would prefer to see me alone. I had expected that she, as is routine for her generation, would ask Meher (if not Papa) to accompany me. Meher calls soon after and jokingly says, "You must tell me a little about the interview, she's a legend in my family, we all know her, but we are so curious about her life." Surprised, I ask, "You can see and talk to her anytime, can't you?"

Meher: Yes, but she doesn't really talk about the Partition and post-Partition days and she only joined my mom's kitty after she retired from work, she worked all her life—she was the principal of Shastri School,[19] so there are a lot of gaps in what we know of her; and really, she does not talk much about it.

This is an interesting characteristic of the persons I am encountering, a point that has been noted by Partition scholars[20]—many (but not all) men and women of this generation are reluctant to talk about their struggles in India to younger generations in their own families. But I cannot call it a pattern, a theme, or a redundancy, because that would be a tidy simplification of why stories remain untold, are held on to, or just let go. For instance, Labbi Devi has made known and storied her struggles to her children and her grandchildren, but when *I* enter the family dynamic, her "conversation of struggle" is muted. Kiranji has held the struggle very close to her heart and from her family, and once in a while she offers an explanation.

> *Kiranji*: Because if you haven't seen it, if you haven't struggled, then you don't know how hard it was. The youngsters see the movies—about Partition—then they come back and they say, "All this happened and you've never mentioned it." . . . The loss was too much and you can't talk about it that often, because it makes you very very sad. . . . Both my sons do not know this story.
>
> I had a friend, this friend, a Hindu from Rawalpindi who died just last month. It's amazing that we never asked questions of each other . . . just to avoid the hardship that the other had gone through. I met her so many times after Partition and she came and stayed with me for a month, but I've never asked her what happened. She's dead and now of course I can't even do it . . .
>
> *Devika*: It was avoidance?
>
> *Kiranjii*: Yes, I think so. To avoid the misery. To avoid the misery of the other person. You've gone through some misery yourself and you don't even want to think of what the other person has been through. . . . That is why when Roni asked in the kitty about meeting you, I offered myself. I said I would talk to her. . . . When you came here I asked, "Why are you doing this?" Because if it has got to do with a government agency or something, I would hesitate to talk. You hesitate for this reason that you don't want to get into any problems with anyone. But you opened yourself to me and I want to tell my story and I don't want to sugarcoat anything, I want to tell the truth, to you. You see, you don't want people who know you *now* to know what happened. While some of them would think highly of me, there are others who might think differently. So we never talk about these things to ones who we have known very well . . . those who are close to you.

That she will tell this account here, to me, away from any government agency, is also a/her resistance to its being considered an official account or witness— the account that is presented to us in official Partition historiography.

Devika: In my family, using the word *refugee* was considered bad.

Kiranji: Yes, I told you, I did not even want to register with the rehabilitation projects, in the beginning, because for us, *refugee* just meant charity.

Devika: One of my grandmother's friends, a very close friend who used to spend summers with her in Quetta, invited my grandmother to stay with her and her family during the first week after the Chawlas came to Delhi (my family came to Delhi through Shimla). This friend was a part of a social service group, and in a meeting with this group in her living room, she referred to my family as *sharnarthis* [refugees]—she was trying to use the Chawlas as an example of how everyone must work to help families. My grandmother, who was in the room, was very offended, and that very evening after my grandfather returned home she had packed all the bags and they moved out, never to meet this family again. My father told me this story just recently; my grandmother never did.

Kiranjii: Yes, I understand completely.

Papa had indeed told me this story a few weeks previously when we were talking to Anilji, who kept referring to refugees as *them*; and I wonder what motivates the need to separate oneself from what one is and what one was, or as Papa says, "what one was forced to become."

Why not, I wonder, share with those close to you? Biji did share some of the post-Partition hardship with us, but excluded many episodes, such as the above story. I cannot generalize, but in my own experience of North Indian Punjabis (and I am one), there is a sense that you avoid sharing weak moments with loved ones lest that weakness be held against you at a later time. Amma constantly cautions me not to share too many "personal matters" with close or extended family, and advises, "Share them with your friends; you choose your friends, but not your family." Perhaps we cultivate a culture of distrust; at the same time I think such rules are a legacy of joint families that would often include cross-generational units under one roof. But here, the lack of sharing is linked with feelings of shame and helplessness at the loss and subsequent struggle, even when shame over Partition—a political decision over which ordinary citizens had no control—seems irrational. There is always a self-imposed logic to familial secrecy.

Meher wants to know more about those hard times, and while I feel an obligation to share my materials, I am wary of carrying stories from person to person within the family, lest my participants lose trust in me. I tell her that I will let her know how our meetings are going. Curiosity about other family members' stories is natural. In fact, another cousin of Kiranji's, Mrs. Chopra, inquires, "What did Kiran tell you about those days, did she tell you about Lahore?" Well, Kiranji does not really mention Lahore, and I wonder why not. But I learn to give ambiguous (not untruthful) answers. I have no interest in verifying one story against another. That is not my task. Oral histories like these are linked up in watershed events, but they are also individual and unique. What stays in the stories and what is left out is as much a pronouncement about the life as the told story itself. After all, absences are their own plots.

Papa is disappointed that he will be absent in my meetings with Kiranji. He insists that I might need him: "What if she speaks pure Punjabi? Some of the refugees have difficult dialects, you know? How will you understand her?" "That's not possible, Papa, she was the founder of the famous Shastri School in Delhi, she will speak both English and Hindi, and I know enough Punjabi to understand most people," I tell him. And anyway, I remind him, I've already spoken with her on the phone, so I know that I will not need a translator. I feel as if I am betraying our partnership, but I cannot insist upon his presence nor request it. Undeterred, Papa decides instead to accompany me to Gurgaon in the car and visit some of our relatives while I interview Kiranji. He is curious about her as he has not been with other participants. I've mentioned her pivotal role in setting up Shastri School. He says he knew that this school had a female founder and headmistress, but he is astonished to learn that she is still alive and that she will be one of my participants.

Kiranji's success is anomalous for women of her generation, and hence I understand Papa's interest. She and I are almost five decades apart in age, but in some ways, my own choice to live alone in the United States to pursue an education and an academic life (with neither extended family nor ties here) is considered divergent from the norm, and I am viewed as an aberration. My own parents, even while they support it, have never understood the decision to leave home. Just knowing that Kiranji was a successful educator from the

1950s to 1980s is enough for me to feel connected to her. And in all my years of fieldwork, with Partition refugees now and with urban Hindu women in arranged marriages a decade ago, Kiranji is the only participant who asks, "Are you happy there in America?" I am touched by the question, since I expect to be reminded of my un/belonging and critically interrogated about why I choose to live alone in America. I hurriedly reply, "Yes, I am happy. I left when I was quite young. . . . I left at the age of twenty-three. I wanted to study." She smiles knowingly and says, "Good, I'm glad." It is curious how a mundane question can forge a bond. I don't want to pretend that my entry into the lives of my participants is as momentous for them as it is for me. But what is perhaps, for her, an unremarkable moment brings me closer to her.

Mr. Haq is driving us today, and he parks outside a white-colored old-style but newish-looking *kothi*, a bungalow, with midsized iron gates that are locked (which is typical for bungalows in many parts of Delhi). Papa accompanies me inside to make sure that Kiranji is home. I ring the bell, and a female house helper unlocks the gates and leads us into the house. We are taken into a living room that looks more like an office workspace, with a seating area in one corner and at least four or five computer workstations in the rest of the room. There are a few people at work on the consoles and a split air-conditioning unit is quietly buzzing on the corner wall. I assume that we are being temporarily seated in the more public area of the house where Kiranji is getting some work done.

A few minutes later a diminutive woman who looks no more than sixty years old enters the room and introduces herself as Kiranji. She is wearing a soft pink mint-patterned *salwar kameez* with a long scarf, a dupatta, in light pink, in a way that I think only Sikh women are able to. I mean this as a compliment, because the outfit, now a staple in most of India, is traditionally the garb of the Punjabi-Sikh community and of Pakistani women, who wear it with the utmost grace. Many of my Sikh friends have these outfits stitched by tailors who have worked with their families for years. Even though Kiranji's hair is almost fully grey and she wears it in a small chignon at the nape of her neck, I am surprised at how young she looks, at least twenty years younger than her eighty-two years. I glance at Papa and he too looks surprised. I introduce him and tell her that he is just dropping me off and cannot stay. She softly offers, in very, almost British-accented English, "Oh, please have some tea before you leave." Papa refuses, saying, "I just wanted to drop her and get going, I am meeting our relatives who live close by." She does not insist, but as soon as he leaves, she turns to me and asks, "At least you will have some tea, no?" I tell her that I will have some water and tea a little later, maybe in the middle of our conversations. "Of course, but have something, a little *nimbu pani* [sweetened lime water]?" I nod, yes. Kiranji points to the rest of the room and says:

> Sorry about this workplace, my son markets online tutorials for some public schools. He is in between offices, so for now the work is happening out of my home and I am supervising; I can use my experience in education [laughs].

I nod again, expecting her to move us to another room, because, after all, she is going to talk about family history, Pakistan, and her early life, but she settles into the sofa. I cannot help make this observation, because I am surprised that I am not invited into the rest of the house. Kiranji and I will have the longest conversations among all my participants, yet I do not see the inside of her home beyond this workspace. While I am too polite to ask to be invited inside, the pattern is not lost on me. It becomes crucial to how I read the way that Kiranji sketches the sense of home and self, in between the old and the new country.

Leaving Home: Plotting Absences

My older participants inevitably start our conversations with intricate details of the days before they left Pakistan, and of their journey to India. It is like a ritual that they must perform—both for me and for themselves. It is a punctuated marker implying that a story can begin. And for some, such as Sarlaji, a female participant, this journey-narrative is *the* story of her move from Pakistan to India. She tells it like a mystery, revealing key information with dramatic flourish, with insertions of various phrases, such as, "*Accha phir Batoun Kya hua?*" (Then you want to know what happened?). Arjunji, an elderly male participant, stories the journey like an escape adventure, showing how he got away.

Kiranji's rendition is low key in comparison, but the departure narrative is a similarly detailed exposition. It is also where she begins. As always, I am struck by the vividness of the memories. I do speculate whether such moments in the stories are ways of saying goodbye to the old home, as if the final rupture must be clearly remembered to make a separation from the past. In some families where these departure stories are repeatedly told, each repetition is perhaps a reinforcement of loss, and a salute to home. Or is it a relocation? Sara Ahmed proposes that stories of dislocation might "help to relocate: they give a shape, a contour, a skin to the past itself."[21]

Biji would repeat stories and often end them by saying, "*Sub chut gaya*," everything was left behind.

A repetition.

A reminder.

Of loss.

Of home.

Papa, on the other hand, guards many stories, telling them infrequently and fleetingly. His home in Pakistan is one that he barely remembers. I think he would prefer to forget.[22] Just as Aniliji's fifty-five-year-old son, Ravi, too, would prefer to forget it: "We just grew up under this cloud, it was difficult for us psychologically, there was a lot of sadness." Papa, who was only six when it happened, insists that it is just a story.

A repetition.

A guarding.

Of inherited loss.

Of home.

What is significantly different in Kiranji's story is that even though she was married, she departed for India alone, with no family with her. A lot of her family had left while she stayed behind to finish her final exams for the M.A. degree. She never did take those exams, since her father wanted her to leave for India. So, Kiranji traveled from Rawalpindi (Pindi) to Lahore, a journey of about 230 miles, and then took a flight to Delhi. Some members of her family who were left behind in Pakistan were flying to India by procuring seats through some connections in the Indian Air Force (her husband would eventually make a career in civil aviation). Her father, a doctor in the army, chose to stay on, but conditions were difficult for Hindus and Sikhs who stayed behind—more often than not, their Muslim employers or friends were threatened with death by rioting mobs. The situation was no different on the Indian side of the border. About her arrival in India, Kiranji tells me:

We came one by one, there were very few seats available. I was traveling with the brother of a Muslim friend (she is dead now). My sister came to Delhi first and was already there, she was to take the train to Dehradun to join her in-laws. The plan was to meet my husband who was already in Delhi. But I could not contact him, the phone lines worked intermittently, and it was dangerous to just go looking for him, so where was I to go? So I went to Dehradun with my sister.

Now that journey was so harrowing. We were at the Old Delhi station at 6:00 in the evening to go to Dehradun.[23] We got stuck there because there was word that in Ghaziabad there was a mob of Muslims waiting for this train to pass to take revenge for some carnage that had taken place a day or two ago against Muslims on another train. There were supposed to be twelve people in the train compartment, but it swelled to thirty-five, then there were forty and there was hardly any breathing space. And you know, ever since then I am claustrophobic, that has not worn out, the feeling of suffocation actually . . . just last month I had to get an MRI done for an eye surgery and I could not sleep for three nights because the thought of being placed in that enclosed space was scaring me. . . .

While we were waiting in the compartment, a train, they said it was from Peshawar in Pakistan, came to a halt at the station. There was a tall Muslim, I think from Afghanistan, he looked like he was from the frontier. He was an army person. When he got out, twelve or so people surrounded him with grass-cutting scythes. He defended himself . . . but they ultimately slit his throat.

Now to have seen that? I saw nothing in Pakistan, no killing. It was so shocking, you couldn't take your eyes away from this . . . and every few minutes you would hear someone scream and then baggage being thrown out from that other train . . . there was a policeman who was passing and I said, "Why don't you stop this?" He said, "You can say that because you don't know what has happened." I said, "I can say that because I have come from a place where all has happened." After all, I had been in Pakistan for the entire riots. The police just turned their faces when everything was taking place.

I marvel at her bravery in admonishing a police offer. And such instances of courage shape much of her life story post-Partition, confirmed also by her cycling alone to find those books. The move to India split her family to such an extent that for many years they lived in different cities in India—her father in Meerut, her mother in Chennai, one sister in Pune, another in Mumbai, and Kiranji in Delhi. Fragmented families within India were an inevitability, a consequence, a mirror of the fragmented nation.[24]

Kiranji's husband's family had moved to India in March, but, as we already know, she'd stayed behind in the hope of taking her exams, since she was in her second, penultimate year of a master's program in English literature. We also know that she eventually took the exams in the camp college and passed with a very low pass. Explaining this, she says, "There was nothing to write about, but we had done some social service in the community and in the camps and that was considered a part of the exam." This desire for an education amid communal chaos is an important element of the life that Kiranji eventually made for herself. This desire is also the generative impulse that had captured my fictional imagination.

I am accustomed to participants talking at length about their homes in Pakistan, romanticizing how life was lived in the old country, and how the loss still shadows the present. The home of the old country is steeped in tradition, stability, and warmth. Such characteristics do emerge in Kiranji's narrations. Yet they seep into her voice as mere traces, forcing me to mark them as both absence and presence. That rushed scribbling in my notebook—"absence/presence; it's there, but not there"—comes to be slowly deciphered by me, for me. Later on in my notes, I scribble:

> She longs for Pindi, it is there in the tone of her voice, but why won't she talk about it in any depth, with any directness? Pindi is *in* her, but she won't reveal much of it. She barely even describes her home, something that many older generation members know and tell and show from memory. The childhood home is placed on a pedestal, tragically ever present, yet, semantically, absent.

When Kiranji does mention the old country, it's almost as if she wills herself to mention it in intangibles, in all the ways that she can bear the weight of her loss:

> You see it's been very heartrending. You've left your birth-place. We are Indian citizens, no doubt about it, but it is the birthplace that you always think about. So that is something that has happened and you feel very, very unhappy and emotional and sentimental that you can no longer freely visit it. You know anytime you see it as a flash in the news, Pindi, it's nostalgia.

She reminisces about summers spent in the hill station, Murray. Her school, Chelsea Convent, had branches in both Pindi and Murray. If one left Pindi on Friday, one could join the Murray branch on Monday and not miss a day of school. She yearns for both that time and the education:

Now our summers, we had never spent them anywhere, except in the hills. Pindi was just thirty-eight miles from Murray. The weather was hot, but the breeze was so nice in the evenings and the mornings; and you could see the mountains when you stepped out of the house. I can still visualize the streets, the roads, where I lived and how we lived. It can't come back, so it is a tragedy for us. . . . It's a limb that has been torn apart.

The education system in Pindi was something that one can never even think about. And then it was not difficult to get admission in any school. Those who wished to admit their child anywhere, they could do it. And the activities we had . . . Whatever I had as a child I tried to do in the schools here.

She alludes to the streets, hints at them, seems to remember them, and insists that they are "etched in her memory," yet ultimately she leaves them undescribed. Similarly, she talks about her school, the nuns, the education, but omits details. In puzzlement, I turn to Bachelard to understand this hide-and-seek and am reassured by a few contemplations:

> Over-picturesqueness in a house can conceal its intimacy. . . . For the real houses of memory, the houses to which we return in our dreams . . . do not readily lend themselves to description. To describe them would be like showing them to visitors. . . . All I ought to say about my childhood home is just barely enough to place me. . . . All we communicate to others is an *orientation* towards what is secret without ever being able to tell the secret objectively.[25]

And I have to tell myself that *I* am a visitor—just a brief interlude in Kiranji's life. And even though Bachelard's meditations about how homes of our childhood reside in our memories might not have resonance in all transnational views of home, here in Kiranji's absent-present ruminations his thoughts hold sway. To make these particular memories too easily accessible can mean losing the secrets/presence that she holds dear. Mia Couto, the Portuguese writer, aptly notes that "forgetting is an activity—it's a choice that demands the same effort as remembering."[26] Perhaps Kiranji has not even made these memories available to herself; or perhaps, as Ahmed proposes, "It is this home, which, in the end, becomes Home through the very *failure* of memory."[27] The dislocation is both spatial and temporal, so much so that " 'the past' becomes associated with a home that it is impossible to inhabit, and be inhabited by, in the present. The question then of being at home or leaving home is always a question of memory, of the discontinuities between past and present."[28] At another moment in our conversations Kiranji longingly confides:

> Home is the mother, the real mother is where you are born. . . . It is like losing a limb . . . like you've lost a life that you would love to live over again. . . . But, would I be where I am or be what I am, had I not lost this home? I don't know the answer to that.

This last "stanza," one that I transcribe verbatim amid our conversations, is momentous and intrinsic to *my* understanding of Kiranji's life. I repeat it here, for it is the emblem by which I begin to (re)read her life. To explain it simply, it displays Kiranji's ambivalence toward home and loss. In a more complex reading, one that I endeavor here, it becomes the way that she comes into being in a post-Partition world. It is rightfully noted that away from home or exiled from it, "horizons expand, and an individual may discover new aspects of the self that result in an inevitable reordering of the intimate world and reevaluation of past, present, and future situations."[29]

There is no ambivalence, however, in the way Kiranji, and so many of my older participants, emplace home as a "place one starts from."[30] Pindi/Pakistan/home is positioned as the originary (the real mother), as a being who is coterminous with the body, so much so that its loss is like losing an integral part of one's body. Kiranji again echoes Bachelard's idea that "the house we were born into is physically inscribed in us. . . . The house we were born into is more than an embodiment of home, it is an embodiment of dreams."[31] Bachelard, quite directly, aligns home and mother, when he notes, "Life begins well, it begins enclosed, protected, all warm in the bosom of the house."[32] Freud's notions of home-dwelling compliment this thinking of home as mother, as origin, and is elucidated well in his statement, "the dwelling-house was a substitute for the mother's womb, the first lodging, for which . . . man still longs, and in which he was safe and felt at ease."[33] And losing this organic entity—home or mother—is a sort of death, but one that allows a different being to emerge—the person that Kiranji is able to become post-Partition. In loss, a birth.

I cannot help but compare myself to her. It is an indulgent and even self-serving urge, since our political circumstances could not be more disparate, yet I feel an immediate kinship with her. In fact, I have compared Kiranji's stories to the stories of other refugee women from her generation and wondered why they made different choices—most of them contributed, in large measures, to the resettlement of their families, but primarily within the confines of domestic life. For instance, when I ask Poonamji, a seventy-five-year-old woman from the Vohra family who was seventeen when they were displaced, if she considered finishing college, she despondently states, "What would have been the point? And my parents wanted us to be settled."

Compared to Kiranji, my own displacements feel lighter, mellower, and certainly more peaceful—I left home because I feared a conventional life of marital domesticity. I use the word *displacement* out of habit, knowing full well that displacements are always the product of political unequality.[34] I was not being forced to marry nor being discouraged from working outside home. I came of age in the '80s and '90s in Delhi, so having a career was already an option, but a career, in my family, was also considered secondary to marriage. I was advised, "You must do something before you get married"—as if the chances of doing anything afterwards were minute. And when I look around my family, no woman in my generation or my Amma's holds a full-time job outside the home. One maternal grand-aunt pursued a successful full-time career, and the traditionalists in the family still grumble about her overt independence. Another aunt, an artist, is considered selfish because she cajoled her husband into stepping back in his career so she could continue with her art.

Ultimately my own leaving was most unlike Kiranji's—unforced and uncoerced. All I knew—much before I understood the conceptual frames of displacement, diaspora, identity—was that leaving was about becoming. But I moved by choice—the privilege of the expatriate. The expatriate (I, the ethnographer) is a "subject who has chosen to be homeless, rather than is homeless due to the contingency of 'external' circumstance," and for such a person "having or not having a home does not affect their ability to occupy a given space."[35] I do not consider myself an exile and do not consider my loss of home "a political condition of singular and irrevocable absence."[36] When I left home, I was not escaping any watershed historical circumstance. Tradition, maybe. All the same, this is where Kiranji and I share a bond. For me, it is in tradition (or a resistance to it) that our stories find a link, the loss of home (leaving in my case), the unforced shedding of familial bonds—an impetus to another life.

The choices Kiranji made were an involuntary response to a circumstance that had historically presented itself, one that she found herself in.

Admittedly, the meaning I am attributing to this moment is a rhetorical and interpretive overreach, but it allows me bring coherence to the story she and I experience. If I begin to consider that home's loss can be understood as the gain of a self-identity, my understanding of our conversations takes on another life. Settling into this explanation is transformative, insofar as, instead of trying to understand why the old world is absent-present in her oral history, I step into exploring how absences announce themselves in remarkably loud ways in the story that Kiranji tells about her post-Partition struggles and ultimately, successes. I attend to how the loss of home allows her to gather a self that would have otherwise remained unborn. This self is her response to history.

Replacing Homes—Gathering Presence

I've come to understand Kiranji's life after Partition as a story with two dominant yet parallel threads. One is an instrumental pursuit to build and procure living spaces—houses. The other, what I consider central to her life story, is her quest to provide good quality education to children in Delhi—the kind of education that she was given. Albeit, "given" might be too generous a word to use here, because her desire for an education, consistently encouraged by her father, is never supported by her in-laws, nor by the women in her family.

> *Kiranji*: You see I got married at the age of eighteen. We had been betrothed as children—seven years old. Common at that time. Our parents were family friends and our fathers were both in the army. One year our fathers were on leave and we were spending holidays with each other. The families decided that since we were all together [they should] . . . *shaadi kara do* [get them married]. The wedding was arranged in about fifteen, twenty-odd days. I was okay with it, but I told my father, "You better tell them that I am still studying." I was in my third year of a B.A. when I got married. I finished, and then wanted to do an M.A., but my in-laws would not let me enroll in the same college as my husband. I approached the nuns in Chelsea Convent, where I had studied since nursery until my B.A. So the nuns told me to get some other girls and they started master's classes. So there were twelve of us who started and only three remained. But they carried on. They didn't say that they would end it.

Amidst these ambitions arrives . . . the Partition. Kiranji is determined to complete her degree. So she stays on in Pakistan when everyone leaves. She simply explains, "I wanted to take my M.A. exams." After a traumatic arrival in Delhi, unable to reach her husband, she leaves for Dehradun, but she returns in a week, after he manages to contact her. Unsurprisingly, the first task is to find a place to stay:

> *Kiranji*: My husband was sharing a room with someone and when then he realized that I'd come he asked the man to move out. So I moved in. But things were not simple. My mother-in-law was in Mumbai and other relatives were in Pune, but I did not want to move there since I wanted to stay in Delhi and finish my post-graduate work. My husband took a job, he got a job with the help of my brother-in-law who was in civil aviation. So a little help from here and there and you carried on. My in-laws helped a little and his salary was there, so, we managed. But it was difficult. . . .
>
> It was not a refugee colony; we were sharing rooms. There was a whole row of *chummeries* [bachelor quarters], in Gol Market. But if a wife/sister/mother moved in, then the other man who was sharing would move to a different room. There was a common kitchen and bath. So one would get up early in the morning to make sure that you took a bath before anyone else had. To share a bathroom with twelve people? Life was not easy. Fortunately, we moved out and began sharing a government flat with another family. Two wives.
>
> *Devika*: Two wives? He was Muslim?
>
> *Kiranjii*: No, a Sikh gentleman.
>
> *Devika*: Two wives?
>
> *Kiranji*: I mean he did not have a child with the first one and she forced him to marry a woman of her choice. They lived very well together. The women used to beat the hell out of the husband. [She pauses because I look surprised.] I mean it was amazing, but they were very nice people.

Her memories about home-building are distinct. She is exact in the ways that she manages to secure houses that they live in. She successfully builds a house in Delhi, but I sense no attachment to it—it is a place that houses her, rather than an abode. That she does not consider these homes in Delhi as anything more than structures, roofs over her head, is increasingly clear to me. It is she, not her husband, who brings these houses/buildings to fruition.

Kiranji: Then we moved to Nizammudin. This is where I built my own house in 1952. Now this was a refugee plot. We were allotted it by the rehabilitation ministry. Now at that time when they started the ministry my father was alive, and he asked me to register myself. He had registered in Meerut as a refugee. I never bothered, you understand?

Devika: Why?

Kiranji: I think it was because you have a silly notion sometimes that you don't want to take anything from charity. But I had done other things, like get a ration card. I did what was required of a good citizen, but the registration, I had that feeling, to hell with it, you know? Because you feel at that time of your life that you can do anything, so why ask for charity. Now little did I understand that there could be a lot of benefit from this process. Then in 1950 we came to know that they were allotting land in place of the land that you left behind, and we felt that we had made a mistake (my husband's family had a lot of land in Pindi and in another place called Kahouta). Even though we had missed the deadline for registering, I decided to meet the rehabilitation minister. He said they would give me land on a condition, "If anyone can verify that you left Pindi after the Partition, and give us proof of your birth, then we may consider your application."

The pursuit of these papers—the verification that she was born in Pakistan and that she left after the August 15, 1947 Partition date—returns us to Chelsea Convent and the nuns who taught her. It seems poetic, yet obvious, that Kiranji's love of learning makes possible the procurement of land in India.

Kiranji: I wrote to the Mother Superior, because I was in the convent from nursery to my M.A. degree, and said that I could get land here if she could send a certificate saying that I was a student there and I left Pindi on the second of September. Just the day before I left I had sent a cartload of books to the convent with a letter saying that since I was leaving Pindi I wanted Chelsea to have these books. I had a huge collection of books—school books, novels—a huge collection. I mentioned in my letter that I'd sent books on the day I wrote the letter and that should prove that I was there and that I left afterwards. She sent me a certificate mentioning all this within four days!

A Mother Superior in a convent would not lie about this. I went back to the minister and gave him a piece of my mind telling him that my old ration card was destroyed and if this letter had not arrived I would have been going on a fool's chase. He was upset over my tone but said, "All right, we'll give you land." They gave me some land in Nizammudin. My husband thought I was being stupid and wasting my time because that place was, the whole area was a jungle, barren. But you know, it paid. I built a house there in 1952 and it was because we sold it that we were able to buy this house, here.

Kiranji's last contact with the outside world before she leaves Pakistan is her generous book deposit to the convent, a deed that eventually helps her to secure land.

Her voice has the ring of achievement, but she speaks of the home-building in Delhi in detached tones. She remains proud of her home in Pindi because nothing can compare with it, or perhaps it's that nothing must be allowed to compare with it—an act of guarding memories, of keeping them alive. Getting a home in Delhi is about receiving what is rightfully hers/theirs from the government, but the feeling of home seems to have been left behind. She treats the homes in India as objects, and her oral history is told from the standpoint of the "self" she became "outside" and "beyond" home. I wonder if this is the reason I never see the inside of her home, just the outer living room and work area. Is it that home, once left behind, can never be re-experienced in the same manner? So that anything after home is irrelevant? Thomas Wolfe's famous phrase comes to mind, "You can't go home again." And someone else once said, once you leave home, you could be anywhere. Can that be the reason for the absences that shadow how home took shape in Delhi?

And yet I am tracing presence in very tangible ways. The feeling of home seems to have been displaced to another area of Kiranji's life—in the self she comes to be. The interiority of home is replaced by the exteriority of the identity that she forges as a working-woman. Even though she does not mention it, I believe that like all nomadic and displaced persons, Kiranji acquires a "spatially dispersed" notion of home because her strongest sense of "home coincides spatially with the site of the domicile," in her case, Rawalpindi.[37] Julia Kristeva observes about the diasporic subject, "His origin certainly haunts him, for better or for worse, but it is indeed elsewhere that he has set his hopes, that his struggles take place, that his life holds together today."[38] In the process of the search and struggle for living spaces, Kiranji completes her master's degree and enrolls for another graduate degree in teaching from the most elite teaching institution in India, located in Delhi University.

What follows here is the story of her beginnings as an educator in Delhi, a career that spanned over three-and-a-half decades.

Kiranji: After my M.A. in Pindi the idea of taking up a job would never have happened. As a girl, medicine was the only thing you were allowed to do. I had said that I would marry on the condition that I would be allowed to continue my education. My in-laws agreed, but they said, "*Humne naukri thodi karwani hai* [we are not going to have her work]." I was fond of studies. . . . When we came things were different and my husband told me, "If you want to take a job then you go in for teaching."

So I went to get my B.Ed. in teaching, after my master's, from the Central Institute here. . . . This was in 1952 and I got a distinction. I was also very involved in activities like sports, singing, dancing and such with the students. Then, I got a job in a school in Gol Market, I took it and then went to visit my mother for the summer break. When I returned, they were making the job permanent, but asking me to sign a document that said I would make X amount, but in reality the salary was much less. I walked out saying I would not do it.

Devika: Wow. How did they react to your walking out?

Kiranji: I don't know. I never went back. Then the first job I found advertised in the paper was a job in the Air Force School at Palam. They wanted a headmistress. It was a question of going from Gol Market to Palam every day. It was a long bus ride, but I found a company—Burma Shell—that used to run a van there, so they would pick me up at my doorstep in the morning. But when we moved to Nizamuddin it became difficult . . . it was far away and I used to have to take an auto-rickshaw along the way and change buses. Then I read that a school was being opened in Lodhi Road and I applied, but the station commander who oversaw the school in Palam would not let me go, he said, "You can't go, I've already spoken to the station commander in New Delhi saying that your application is not to be accepted." I said, "This is not on, I have worked here for three years, and it takes me three hours to commute here every day." He said they would give me a house here, but then my husband would have to make that trip. So I said, "Please ring up the gentleman and tell him to consider my application."

I left there and moved to Lodhi Road. By the time I left I had expanded the school [in Palam] and when I moved to the new one I was expecting my first baby. Not my first one, I lost the first one, so you know, the second child. I didn't want to take the new job without telling the chairman that I was expecting. I told him that I would need to take maternity leave for a month in the winter. He asked me how many children I had. I said, none. He asked, "When did you get married?" I said, "Ten years ago." When he heard this, he said, "It will be my pleasure to give you maternity leave." [She laughs a little tearfully.] . . . You see the stress of the Partition was difficult to bear . . . my father died of a heart attack just a year after the Partition . . . he could not get over it.

It is a somber moment and we are silent for some time. This is one of few instances in our conversations when Kiranji sounds melancholic, almost tearful—always referring to the lost baby as her *first one*. This late-term pregnancy loss was brought about by a combination of medical factors and extreme hospital negligence. I am so used to Kiranji's stoicism that I am tentative about probing her, afraid of causing distress, because I sense fragility beneath the strong exterior. But Kiranji interrupts her education account and explains:

You see my kids were born practically eleven years after my marriage. But it was a deliberate attempt not to have children because I wanted to study and then I did my B.Ed. I couldn't have had a child at that time. Then it was a struggle, how to bring up a child in a single room? No. When my younger son was born, my first son, I had him at home. He was born in 1956, the other son was born in 1962.

These lines signal an end to the fleeting familial moment. We return to talk about school. Once Kiranji moves to the school closer to her home, and the stress of the daily three-hour-long commute is behind her, her career flourishes. The school is connected with the Air Force, so it is located on Air Force land, and she is given two barracks to house the classroom and administrative units. She begins the process of school expansion, and tells me, "If you have experienced something as a student yourself you want to make sure others have the same facilities." There is pleasure in her voice as she talks about how she replicated, even resurrected, the school of her childhood. The home is lost, but here in the outside world of school, its sense and presence are gathered. A re-homing begins to take place.

Kiranji's goal is to offer an experience of schooling that equals her own in Pakistan. Shastri School eventually becomes something of an elite institution in Delhi. She is meticulous in the details of its rise from a small school

housed in barracks to one with a full-fledged building. Unlike her instrumental descriptions of homes for her family in Delhi, this quest is a labor
of love:

> *Kiranji*: I asked for more barracks. One of the units moved out so fortunately
> we got another barrack and then another one. I went to the station commander
> and told him that his children must go to school here (they were in other
> private schools). I told him if people see that his children are studying here,
> they will also admit their children here. His wife was not happy, but he said
> that his younger kids (he had four, five daughters) who had not started school
> yet would be admitted here.
>
> There was a lot of land around Lodhi Road. I wanted to get ahold of that. It
> was difficult because that land was earmarked for other things, but I approached
> the sports minister, Buta Singh, that I wanted this. My proposal was that I would
> offer sports facilities to all the schools in the neighborhood, but we would own
> that land and maintain it. The offer came with just 3.5 more acres, but we grabbed
> it. I was a little disappointed considering how well my school had been doing in
> sports and other things. We were national badminton champions, in music we
> were national award winners, we won the Cadbury Quiz. . . . The school was at
> the top. But I wanted money for a school building, we were still in barracks. I was
> told I would have to wait. So I started a scheme for a double shift for the school
> for three years—people were unhappy—but we got a five hundred enrollment.
> I was scared, but I knew it was the only way I would bring in money. We did.

The school continues to be recognized in both extracurricular activities
and academics. At one point, Kiranji hears that parents are paying for their
children to get private tutoring at home. The cost of these sessions was
bloated and home tutors were making a lot of money. She is, of course, disturbed by this trend:

> I sent circulars to parents offering tutoring in the school for a mere 20 rupees
> added to the fee. Teachers were unhappy since they would have to stay back to
> coach students. I told them that I could get outside teachers to do it, but I was
> not going to have parents spending 500 to 1,000 rupees [about $20 in today's
> currency] for tutoring when they were supposed to be getting this knowledge
> in their classes.
>
> We also started school lunches [something that is unusual in Indian
> schools]. Because of sports we had a lot of kids in school after schools hours, so
> we started providing food at a very subsidized rate (5 rupees for both students
> and teachers). Things were cheap at that time. The lunch was so good that

parents would come to us and say, you give them this stuff in school and they won't eat at home on Saturday and Sunday [laughs]. Of course there was a fixed menu, but we had a kitchen garden in school.

The school graduated from being a primary school to being a higher secondary school. In many ways, Kiranji was a pioneering educator. One of her most controversial decisions was to do away with testing. She says:

I abolished exams. There were no exams until class 8 [grade 8]. I was doing this for the students. You see, because teachers have to work harder when they don't have exams. When there are exams, the teacher just marks the paper and it's over. But without them you have to assess the child from scratch. They have to pay more attention to what is happening in the class. They were not happy with this. I retired in 1985 and they brought them back the day after I left.

I grew up in an Indian educational system where rote learning and test-taking were central to our school and college experience, and even now, only a few innovative schools use the kind of teaching she is describing. So I am curious about how this shift was received by parents.

Kiranji: The parents were very unhappy; they thought that their children would have difficulties later. But the kids did much better. We had started child counseling—the first school to start it in Delhi—and we kept each child's profile from nursery onwards. So we were able to track their progress before and after I abolished exams and the reports were that they were doing much better.

I abolished them because there was a child who had epilepsy, and exams and the stress brought on his attacks. I had spoken with his doctors, and he was promoted from one class to the other wherever I could do it, without a test. He was unhappy; he was a good student—he's dead now. But when I saw him going through those phases before his exams—with him we could see the stress, but imagine with the others when you cannot see physically what they are going through? So I did away with them. Things got back to the way they were, so I feel unhappy.

Devika: You were committed.

Kiranji: Each brick, I can lay my signature on it, this is what I built. I feel very happy about that.

I am once more reminded with some force how Kiranji defines herself through school, education, and her professional life. Many of my participants describe every corner of their home in Pakistan or having built new homes in India "brick-by-brick." Papa oversaw the building of my family's first independent home in Rajouri Garden in Delhi, and he often says, "I knew every brick of that house as if I built it with my own hands." Even as I compile this monograph, Papa often mentions that when he remembers his dreams, they are always about him in his home in the Rajouri Garden house—H-14 is what we called it (house number 14 in H block). Even though he has lived in at least three subsequent houses, H-14 shadows him like a benevolent ghost—like the childhood home of memory.

But here in Kiranji's story, it is the space outside home—the school—that shapes her, almost as if she has given a physical structure to the old world. She is reconciled to the idea that her home of the past cannot be resurrected, and in fact she makes no attempt to rebuild that sort of a home. But that sense of home—the stability, the goodness, and the warmth—is gathered elsewhere, showing us that "home is not so much a place as a complex set of emotions linked to our earliest memories."[39] In this elsewhere-outside a new person emerges.[40] Or, as her relatives continuously remind me, "We all made a life for ourselves . . . but she *became* something."

Before she retires, Kiranji wins numerous regional and national awards for her contributions. In 1980, she is chosen by the then Indian prime minister, Indira Gandhi, to travel to Moscow as one of five government delegates for the summer Olympics. I am almost bursting with pride, with her, when she speaks of being chosen:

> *Kiranji*: It came as a big surprise because that experience was like a big paid holiday [laughs]. I was there as an observer and I had to report back what I did, but still. . . . There was a Physical Education person whose name had been proposed and Mrs. Gandhi—when the file was put on her table—said no, and said she would like to send an educationist, and I was chosen. When I came back I met her, Indira Gandhi, and the schoolchildren all lined up, and the ones who had done well in cricket were there too. . . . She was very happy to meet me at that time. It was an experience one does not forget.

This honor seems like a culmination of the person she became, the life she made for herself. So, I smilingly ask, "Had the Partition not occurred, would you have been able to do all this?"

Kiranji (laughs): Never. You see I would never even have been allowed to take up a job. I might have studied further, done a Ph.D. in English or something. I am not sure what I would have done, but I would not have worked. In some ways, as an individual the Partition was good for me. The going was tough, but very job satisfying. I've lived to the hilt in that sense.

Devika: Do you think of visiting? Now that people are going back and seeing their homes?

Kiranji: I would love to go, I was too busy before, I couldn't get away, but now . . . but I don't want to go with Jattha.

Devika: A Jattha is?

Kiranji: A Sikh pilgrimage, they go to the *gurudwaras* [Sikh temples]. I just want to go see Pindi.

Yet she does not visit, even when her nephews and cousins invite her to accompany them on their nonpilgrimage trips. Is it because the old country might look different, might not fuse with the home of memory? Is the refusal to visit an act of self-preservation, a desire to keep safe the stable sense of home? Does she dare not return because the old home is a reminder of a self she no longer recognizes? A self that is difficult to coalesce with the one that she became? Is a return home impossible? For Sara Ahmed the answer to the last question is a positive:

> It is impossible to return to a place that was lived as home, precisely because the home is not exterior to the self, but implicated in it. The movements of selves between places that come to be inhabited as home involve the discontinuities of personal biographies and wrinkles in the skin. . . . The process of returning home is likewise about the failures of memory, of not being inhabited in the same way by that which appears familiar.[41]

This impossibility is not just emblematic of Kiranji's re-homings, but spreads across this oral history record and those collected by other Partition scholars. Anilji, an elderly participant who revisits his home in Karachi, confirms some of these/my wonderings about safeguarding and failures of memory, and the symbolic impossibility of being at home in the old country, when he announces:

> The house we lived in, it looked so small and almost like a ruin. And my school classroom looked the same, as if nothing had been renovated in fifty years.

When you are younger, I was seventeen when we left DI Khan [Dera Ismail Khan], everything seems grander. It was not what I had imagined or what I remembered.

And again and again in our talks, Kiranji insists that the Partition should never have happened, even though the event was a sort of rebirth for her. It sanctioned another life, yet she would prefer the old equations:

It would be much better if there was still one India. Things change. East and West Germany could meet again. So, why not us? Pakistan has not benefited in any way from this division. India has done well, but of course, would be much better with them. We have independence, but if we were together we would not worry about our neighbors. What we could have achieved. Let's hope some day all this tension goes away.

The infamous Mumbai terrorist attacks occur in 2008 in the midst of my three-year-long fieldwork. I watch the attacks on television during Thanksgiving weekend at the home of a friend in Brooklyn—another expatriate like myself. That experience, in itself surreal, is made more real because my spouse, Anirudh, is acquainted with one of the fallen Mumbai police officers. India and Pakistan, while not at the brink of war, stand then at the most conflicted crossroads in their entwined histories. The tension now is overpowering, and any hopes of its disappearance are unlikely, near impossible. For my generation, any reconciliation seems like an idealistic yearning, so I can only view Kiranji's hopes as a sort of unrequited longing—much like her nostalgic desire to see her old home—a wish that, as I write, seems to have remained unrealized. My own desire to see the old country in the course of this fieldwork is curtailed. Since the 2008 attacks, and Osama Bin Laden's assassination in 2011, my family will not hear of my going to Pakistan, because it is too dangerous there both for Indians and for me, the Indian-born naturalized American citizen. I don't resist; maybe I am just not so brave.

I want to tell Kiranji that she would not be who she became if the countries had remained together. I also want to tell her that her old patriarchal home, the home presented to us in Bachelard's poetic and romanticized theory of space, the home that she so longs for and imagines in memory, would have shackled her to the hearth and domesticity. Because such homes, Edward Said argues, are more fanciful than lived, like history and geography, they are more or less imaginative spaces.[42] Pointing all this out to Kiranji would mean forcing her to be disloyal to the old home whose memories have sustained her and whose loss has motivated another personhood.

Yes, the contradictions between her longings for the past and the present/ future are glaring, but I feel it impertinent to intrude. Why cause unnecessary discomfort when she is able to *live* and *live well* in between the two worlds? Why unravel this condition to which she seems reconciled? Is it my place or my role to displace (yet again) her sense of home and self? I think not. I am not here to disrupt her reconciliation. As an interlocutor, I want only to show what I understand, knowing full well that any understanding is always incomplete.

And so, the old home, the limb that has been torn apart, hovers as a ghost that insists on appearing, ephemerally as a presence, always there. It remains, in Avtar Brah's words,

> a mythic place of desire in the diasporic imagination. In this sense, it is a place of no return, even if it is possible to visit the geographical territory that is seen as a place of 'origin.' On the other hand, home is also the lived experience of locality, its sounds and smells.[43]

Flitting between presence and absence even in ordinary unrecorded moments, Kiranji continues to salute the old country:

> Anytime Pindi is talked about, whether it is a restaurant, whether it's a person who is visiting, you don't know the person, but you want to talk to them.
>
> I was on a layover in Frankfurt once and on my way to Munich with a cousin. We were considering what to do with our luggage, you know, whether to leave it at the airport or not since we were only staying a few days. I was in a *salwar kameez* and so was she. A group of boys heard us talk in Punjabi, so they came over and asked if we had a problem. So we told them that we were trying to figure out where to store our luggage. They told us don't worry, we'll help you drop it in safe custody at the railway station. They were from Pakistan, but just because we were in *salwar kameezes*, they wanted to help us. They thought we were Pakistani. We took their help and then I was embarrassed so I told them to please carry on with their day. But they said, "No, nothing doing." So we had tea at the railway station, and I asked, "Where are you from," and they said "Rawalpindi." I told them we were from Delhi. He said, "It's amazing, I was drawn to you because of your language. . . . We've been refugees from our own country [Pakistan] for seven years." I think they were supporters of the Bhutto clan.

. . . See, they just wanted to help because of the language and the fact that we were wearing those clothes. Even though we were not Pakistanis they did not leave us in a lurch. They stuck around [laughs].

They stuck around, just as the old home sticks and clings to her psyche. The home and its dialect appear and are recognized even in moments of traveling through *elsewhere* places, where something—an accent, a tone, a garb—conjures home. My task as I see it is to reconcile with the idea, as I have done with Labbi Devi and her family, that there is a version of home that persons in these families want to maintain, solidify, and repeat for specific purposes. In *my* reading of Labbi Devi's life, remembering home outside of the Partition struggle keeps *in order* and *in place* a stable sense of family identity. In Kiranji's case, romanticized memories of home keep alive an old self that she might not recognize, but a self she is nonetheless unable to let go. Because, as Ahmed and others tell us, after all:

Being at home and the work of home-building is intimately bound up with the *idea* of home: the idea of a place (or places) in the past, and of *this* place in the future. Making home is about *creating* both pasts and futures through inhabiting the grounds of the present . . . and for those who have left their homes, a nostalgic relation to both the past and home become part of the lived reality of the present. . . . Thus the work of making home, affective and physical, is an ongoing process.[44]

For Kiranji, remaking herself has been the process of homing in the new country. What I consider a contradictory struggle seems to be but a balancing act for her. The past must live in her psyche, so she can live in the present.

I avoid taking phone calls from Kiranji's relatives who are curious about her. I am able to temporarily appease them by providing them with transcribed copies of their own interviews, and I often present them with digitized recordings. But I do not stall when her niece Meher, over a cup of tea with me in her home, asks, "She's a dude, isn't she?" I grin and retort, "I hope you mean that figuratively?" We both giggle. Yet I think about her being called a dude—equal to a man in those days when women did not work? Someone who bent gender roles when the lines were strictly drawn? How could I explain my experience of this woman in a small conversation? What could I tell? How could I tell Meher what Pakistan, Partition, and home meant for Kiranji? How home (and self) came to be lost and found? How the work of keeping home was done outside the home? How she "*became* something" while the rest of the family made lives for themselves in the new India? It is a long story, one that I almost did not tell.

Adrift: Reluctant Nomads

New Delhi, Summer 2007

The first months of fieldwork are the most strenuous of the seven transatlantic trips for this project. I am trying to locate the families that I will work with—a task that might seem easy in a city where there are millions of Partition refugees, yet is a little more complex than one would think. The blistering 45 degrees Celsius (about 110 degrees Fahrenheit) temperatures of the North Indian summer drive families to the hill stations along the Himalayan foothills, and so much of my time is spent trying to coordinate meetings in between their travel schedules. And then there is, of course, the other matter of many participants asking my father to accompany me. Within the first few weeks, Papa has taken on the role of my unofficial informant. The Bhoore Khan Taxi Service drivers have been driving us to different corners of the city—Patel Nagar, Rajouri Garden, Lajput Nagar, Transjamuna, Vasant Kunj, Pusa Road, Karol Bagh, Gurgaon, among other neighborhoods. At summer's end, Papa and I have met about twenty of my participants. I return to the United States in the autumn and start the process of sorting through my field recordings and notes.

Bangkok, January 2008

Winter finds me in Bangkok for the semester to teach in a doctoral program linked with my university. My fieldwork and oral histories go with me. My goal is to stay familiar with the persons and the stories that I will meet again in a few months. I am listening to the stories, transcribing, and taking notes—all the usual work at this stage in the project. Amid these mundane interpretive routines, the act of listening begins to make me nervous, almost adrift. I am jumpy, unable to sit still for too long, and have taken to drifting into long walks around the apartment complex where I am staying for the semester.

Blaming it on the heat and humidity of the Thai summer, I press on. For a week, I am too busy with doctoral teaching, and cannot make time to read or listen to the oral histories. My nervousness, I notice, has stopped. I return to the oral histories, and just like that, the nervousness too returns. I can only conclude that the stories themselves or the act of reading or listening to them is making me fidgety. Bemused by what I begin to refer to as *narrative lightheadedness*, I tune my attention to them even further. I might be experiencing what Kathleen Stewart calls atmospheric attunements, which she identifies as "an attention to the matterings, the complex emergent worlds, happening in everyday life."[1] People can develop attunements to the atmosphere around them, and "what affects us—the sentience of the situation—is also a dwelling, a worlding born from an atmospheric attunement."[2] She explains:

> An atmosphere is not an inert context but a force field in which people find themselves. . . . It is an attunement to the senses, of labors, and imaginaries to potential ways of living in or living through things. . . . Things can remain ungathered into meanings. . . . Or they can throw themselves into a full-blown ideology. . . . Attending to atmospheric attunements means . . . chronicling how incommensurate elements hang together in a scene.[3]

Something in these stories is ushering in more than just a discursive and narrative experience. Of course, I was there when the stories were gathered, but here and now in the listening and the reading of these lives, a different experience—an extralingusitic one—is occurring. Was this nervousness present when I first experienced the storytelling? I have lapses in memory about those ethnographic moments. So, I look over my notes, I scratch my mind for my headnotes, and I cannot recollect any kind of dizziness. I cannot ignore these symptoms. I must not. To sideline the sensory emerging here is to treat the present context as inert, and to privilege the discursive over the felt and heard.

In general, we ethnographers are repeatedly scolded for our scriptocentrism, for repressing bodily experiences (our own and those of our participants) in "favor of abstract theory and analysis."[4] That cultures are performed and that bodies matter in the way that we represent lives are matters now commonly addressed in contemporary sociocultural anthropology.[5] We are consistently pressed to think of ethnography as an *"embodied practice,"* to recall that "the embodied researcher is the instrument."[6] There is no longer a disregard for "sensory" and "embodied" knowledge, the kind of knowledge that is only made available because ethnographers (as beings and bodies) are physically immersed in their fields—containers, connectors, collectors of knowledge. Undoubtedly, the ethnographic encounter, like all human encounters, is an embodied and atmospheric encounter, at least in sociocultural work where field or home are physical locales and participants are material bodies with whom we intersect. It seems pertinent to invoke Clifford Geertz, often critiqued for his own textocentrism, who writes, "You don't exactly penetrate a culture, as the masculinist image would have it. You put yourself in its way and it bodies forth and enmeshes you."[7] Trinh T. Minh-ha calls attention to these matters, emphasizing that interpersonal experiences are sensual encounters; "[S]peaking and listening refer to realities that do not involve just the imagination. The speech is seen, heard, smelled, tasted, and touched."[8] All sense-based activities, notes Mieke Bal, are profoundly "impure," and these can include looking, listening, reading, tasting, smelling. This impurity "makes such activities mutually permeable, so that listening and reading can also have visuality to them."[9] Listening, in fieldwork, is often stripped of its affective and sensory qualities and reduced to interpreting, even when we know, as Bal emphasizes, that all sense-directed activities are "inherently framed, framing, interpreting, affect-laden, cognitive and intellectual."[10] In the words of W. J. T. Mitchell, "all representations are heterogeneous."[11]

Michael Taussig critiques our failure to literally "draw" out (in pictures) our field experiences, blaming the prevalence of a "writing and reading" middle-class culture that infantilizes drawing and pictures—the very things that our senses are most attuned to.[12] One must and can draw for many reasons, because the more the ethnographer writes down in her note-book, "the more you get the sinking feeling that the reality depicted re-cedes, that the writing is actually pushing the reality off the page."[13] Even though many of these criticisms are directed at bourgeois (often white) in-tellectuals and scholars hampered by their inability to express and repre-sent ideas in any medium other than writing, the argument obviously extends to embracing the untextual means through which we also arrive at understanding.[14]

My nervousness and sense of being adrift is an ethnographic encounter— it is *my* body putting itself in the way of and into the stories—an embodied acknowledgment that I am enmeshed, even more completely than I was in the field and the home and here in this space, this other city that lies in between the already-muddied locales of home and away. Is it my body's performative response to listening to home-field stories here in an elsewhere place? This drifting is *my body* alerting *my mind* to focus on something I must observe. I tune in to the sensations to find the cause.

Refugees are persons who have lost either homes, or homelands, or both. So a literal and figurative feeling of homelessness lingers in this oral his-tory record, making nostalgia and homesickness inevitable emotional threads that weave together the plots—stories of humans forced to stray out of their comfort zones. Yet in many participants' lives, in time these feelings become muted. As their lives are reconfigured, some of the pain of loss either recedes or is willingly relinquished. Some, like Kiranji, build a home-self outside home. Others—such as Labbi Devi, even as she struggles to re-home in the new India—bow to the memories of husband and family. A few poeti-cize the loss. Still others, such as the subjects of this chapter, stay unmoored, stories and selves and bodies adrift in movement.[15]

I have expected this loss of moorings to be performed in all the oral histo-ries. But in some stories—including the three that I am telling here—the narratives, along with the persons crafting them, seem unable to settle into an explanation. As if mirroring them, I too am unable to find a footing. I struggle to both contain and control how to tell (of course, ironically in writing this I accomplish a containment). I attempt to sidestep the storied dizziness by telling myself that carrying the stories across countries might be the cause for this drifting—a psychosomatic narrative dizziness; because the notion of a field as a monolithic space/place is as fictional as any other interpretation.[16] When have ethnographers not carried their fields and homes with them?

Of course, this nervousness also stems from an evergreen ethnographic representational quandary—how to tell these stories? How to enliven the heard and the felt experience of being adrift—both their experience of it and mine?[17] I cannot negate any *crises* of representation. All representational dilemmas are real; novelist Yanik Hamel has written, "To write in the twentieth century is to become witness to the unrepresentable,"[18] and that has not changed in the twenty-first. My drifting is both a representational dilemma and something more than a representational dilemma. Something in the form and content of some of these oral histories is generating a sensory response. I take heed of what Tom Jacobs writes about representation: "[W]hen pushed far enough, the apparent distinction between faculties and senses breaks down, and the terms through which we produce or understand a given form of representation reveal themselves to be thoroughly hybrid. . . . [W]e are left with images and words, and in some profound way, never the twain shall meet."[19]

The three stories that I tell here are a compromise between my participants' stories, my words, and the senses. Three movements.

Movement I: Passages

ORIGINS

Anilji and I have spent two hours combing every corner of his retirement flat. The birth certificate must be found, because Anilji says, "We must begin at the beginning." We eventually find it, well preserved between two old photographs from Karachi. It establishes Anil Vohra as a "British Subject" born in Karachi in 1930. It was registered in his name by the Karachi Municipal Committee. "Why is it important?" I naively ask this seventy-seven-year-old-man (he has turned eighty-two as I write this chapter). He says it's not important, but it establishes where he's from. He wasn't born in Pakistan;

there was no Pakistan, he was Indian, and a British subject. Once I have inspected the birth certificate, Anilji proudly tells me, "You can photocopy it and keep it." "Thank you," I smilingly reply.

To claim origin/s is as human as speech or symbol-making, is it not? When people ask where I am from, I have difficulty just saying that I am from India. I feel a need to provide a preface: "My family is from Pakistan, my father was born in Quetta, they all moved to India in 1947." The tone of pride in Anilji's voice as he evokes his British legal status, and alongside it, British subjugation, is a reminder of how colonial legacies trail postcolonial subjects. My fondness for my Biji's Taj Mahal box, our pride in knowing how to speak "good" English, our tea-drinking and toast-eating habits are all symptoms of colonial nostalgia. Moreover, for the postcolonized, origin can only be a plural idea—a plurality that cannot be ignored in the way that three national identities are evoked here: there was no Pakistan when Anilji was born in what is now Pakistan; Anilji was Indian; Anilji was a British subject. Origins are important, just difficult to define, contain. The birth certificate is a material reminder that identity and home are movable, mobile, and moving notions, much like borders and selves.

The search for this piece of paper has delayed our conversations, and I am feeling anxious, not knowing whether Anilji will have the energy to continue talking to me today—he is in his late seventies. We have set aside most of the morning for this first meeting. Just as I am beginning to settle down to my questions, Anilji jumps up and calls out to his wife, "Where are all the photographs?" We spend another half an hour searching for pictures of his father from Karachi. In the process of doing this, we are in and out of most of the rooms in Anilji's modest flat, which is home to him, his wife, and his adult son, who is recently divorced. My father comes to my rescue, eventually convincing Anilji that maybe we can see these pictures later. Of course, in retrospect, I scold myself for ending the search, because I wonder whether his story would have taken a different structure and form with the pictures. Of course, I know it would have. In subsequent visits, even when we have a chance to go through the photographs, it is not the same. Firstness comes only once.[20] Later, when we finally view them, I see pictures of home both pre- and post-Partition—the old and the new. Anilji is among the very few of my participants who have visited their old homes in Pakistan.

We finally settle down in a corner of Anilji's sitting room. And as I do with all of my participants—old, middle-aged, or young—I ask him to recall the days preceding the official Partition, how his family left, how they made it out safely. For the older generation, this is a fitting way to begin, and even without my prompting, it is where we often start. For subsequent generations, this is a way I am able to gently force a recollection of family memories—what do they remember being told about the journey? The departure story remains the most circulated of the Partition stories. Anilji repeats the tale numerous times and wants his grandchildren to "know everything." He also says, "It is like an adventure story, I enjoy telling them about this."

A lot of time has passed between that meeting with Anilji and the writing of his story. And, in the years that follow, I visit his home a few more times. I also interview the older of his two sons, his sister, and his aunt, in their homes. I hear many iterations of Anilji's story. I spend time with it and take it with me to Delhi, to Bangkok, and back here, to Athens, Ohio. Everywhere it puzzles me with its resistance to any sort of plot. I find it (and him) made up of fragments, incomplete parts, interrupted plots—unsettled and unsettling. Nervousness is almost inevitable. I frame it here in two passages, with many pieces in between.

PASSAGES (DEPARTURE)

On August 8, 1947, Anilji's father asks him to leave for India. It is a week before the country is officially divided. Anilji tells me, "We had come to know that something was going to happen; my father—we used to call him Lalaji—told me to leave." Lalaji cannot be released from the electric company in Dera Ismael Khan where he works as a foreman, so Anilji is entrusted with taking his five-year-old brother and his mother to Delhi. An eventful journey, he describes it vividly:

> *Anilji*: We lived in Dera Ismail Khan—DI Khan—it is a frontier province.[21]
> We are from Karachi and our house was in Karachi, but my father worked in
> DI Khan. We used to have to walk fourteen miles to get to the Sindh River,
> then we had to cross the river using a steamer. There was only one steamer at
> that time. On that day, August 8, I don't know how, but we got a spot on the
> steamer. We were even checked on the way.

Devika: Checked, in what way?

Anilji: The Muslims entered the steamer. Luckily, we were saved. I don't know how. I think they did not check our cabin. Whatever else they checked they looted and took away. We were saved.

By now, I am used to the conflation of rioting mobs with simply the word *Muslims*, or *Mohammedans*. I make a mental note to ask/remind Anilji who he thought the mobs consisted of—on both sides of the border. While I don't get to that question in any direct manner, it does get answered in a fashion, in the story of his return passage to Pakistan fifty-nine years after Partition, reinforcing how the categories of Muslim as enemy and Muslim as friend can coexist in Partition memories. Meanwhile, Anilji continues:

This is an adventure story. The river was flooded. So the steamer used to go up to a certain point up to some place and then you had to take a *tonga* [a horse-drawn cart or carriage]. So the entire river was full of water, the river was flooded. We had to take a tonga to go halfway up and the tonga had to go through the river. The tonga man said that he would not be able to take that much of a load, so he asked me to get off. My mother stayed on, but I had to swim in the river. I was also lifting my younger brother. I put him on my shoulder. We could have drowned, but . . .

Devika: So you knew how to swim?

Anilji: Yes, I was a very good swimmer. There was a swimming pool in the cantonment DI Khan. There was also a tube well there.[22] My father worked in the electric plant, so the key to the tube well used to be with me. I used to go in and take a bath there on my own. It was at least seven foot deep, and as big as a room. I used to fill it up and this is how I learned to swim. I used to also go to the Sindh River and take a bath there [laughs].

So, you had to cross the river and get to the next station. The next station, after crossing the river, was fourteen miles away. It used to take a full day of travel. If we started in the morning at eight, then you would get there at night and take the train in the morning. From here we went to Lahore and then from there we went to Delhi on another train. I thought I would try and get a ticket for the second class on the train. This train was leaving for Delhi in the morning and there were no seats. So I just bought a first-class ticket, but forget about first, second, or third class, everything was the same—jam-packed. Then later I got a spot in the third-class compartment near the toilet. I think there were thousands of people on that train, they were also on the roof of the train.

We got in with great difficulty, we also had some luggage. We had one, two trunks. We were carrying bedding. At that time we used to carry bedding with us for the train.

So we arrived in Delhi. My uncle used to live in Delhi. My *mammaji* [his mother's brother]. They came to receive us at the railway station. We stayed with him for some time.

PIECES

I cannot say that there is a break in Anilji's story here, at this very moment, but it feels as if, after describing this departure, his memories, his experiences, and *my* listening take on a fragmentary tone. The rest of his story of post-Partition life seems bereft of a discernable trajectory. In some ways it seems logical: a break from home leaves him adrift, and thereafter there is no continuity in his life, just movement and motion. There are no plots, just incidents; the character (Anilji) wanders, and the settings are a series of localities that he attempts to call home. Consider these pieces a trajectory of rupture.

Anilji: I think we stayed with my mammaji for six months. We stayed for quite a long time. There was nothing to do. We just wasted time. We did not know what our future was going to be like. Then my mammaji started getting more guests, and we had to leave. We had been intending to leave anyway and had been searching for places.

There was a college in front of their house—Tibia College—many people told us that people were getting rooms there and we should also try and get a room there. So we went and took over a room. And, for the rest of my family, the story starts here. My mother, my younger brother, and I moved in here. It was a big room, I even remember the number, it was room number 4. Then after six months my father arrived. We did not know whether he was fine or not. He flew from Dera Ismail Khan. He was sent by someone. And the aeroplane had managed to land there—you could not land aeroplanes—there was no strip there. At that time there used to be the Dakotas [a widely used transport plane]. So he came in that. One day he just entered Tibia College. He knew we were there.

It is a small detail, but I am often left stunned when my participants tell me they did not know where many immediate family members, even parents, had scattered. I always ask my participants how they dealt with the anxiety of not knowing. Anilji does not reveal his emotions, but his younger sister, Poonamji, who managed to come to Delhi with a young aunt on a train that was delayed for many days in various North Indian villages, resignedly asks, "What could we do? That is how it was. We worried about each other, we were all just trying to get here." Anilji's son Ravi, a second-generation participant, addresses this unknowing in a different way. Born in India in the 1950s, he tells me, "We always grew up insecure, a little unsettled; I think that came from the way my father and his brothers and sisters grew up in those years after Partition, and between their memories of their old home in DI Khan, the places here in India." Ravi's feelings echo Marianne Hirsch's ideas about family, what she calls *postmemory*, and how family is "structured by desire and disappointment, love and loss."[23] What is set aside by his father and aunt is psychologically present in the way Ravi grows up.

Most middle-class homes at that time did not have telephones, the telegraph was not regularly used, and there was no other way of knowing what was happening to another family member who had not made the passage.[24] My father, Papa, tells a similar story:

> Pitaji [Papa's father] stayed behind because his boss wanted him to stay on, wait for the chaos to be over. Everyone thought it would be temporary. We had all moved to Solan in June.[25] Then the Partition happened and Pitaji was still there. In August, we got a telegram from Pitaji telling us that he would be leaving Pakistan and would come to Solan. His boss had started receiving death threats from the mob—they were accusing him of harboring a Hindu. Biji used to send me to the railway station every day at three in the afternoon. This was the time the train from Delhi used to arrive. We knew that Pitaji would have to get take a train to Solan from Delhi. I would be there every single day. One day, I think it was some time in the middle of September, he got off the train, and we saw him walking to us.

Just as Anilji's father walks through the gates of Tibia College. Slowly Anilji's extended and immediate family members are reunited. They stay together in the one room, about seventeen of them. Then the group starts scattering. Pieces.

> *Anilji*: We just kept living there. My brothers arrived. They used to go to college in Karachi and Lahore. One went to Bombay to study and the other one got admission in Pune.

I was left alone. I joined the camp college. Over there we only wasted time, there was hardly any studying. It was an evening college.

I left that summer and went to Kanpur. I had a cousin there who told me there was some work in some company. I had another relative who was working there. I went to visit him and he said there was a job opening. At that time, I was also learning stenography. I used to practice in Delhi, I used to type. He got me a job. I did not know anything, but I got the job. Then I started learning English. There were British people there and they gave me some dictation and I could not understand a thing. I had a bad time. My relative told them, "He is new to the job, he will learn." I stayed there and kept practicing. I also joined evening college there.

The moment ends; Anilji does not tell me what happened afterwards, just that his career started with that job and that he got married. I ask him what he thought about the Partition as a sixteen-year-old. "What could we think about it, we were too busy thinking about ourselves, and how we would move ahead," he replies honestly. And then, we are back in Tibia College:

> *Anilji*: We moved out of the college. We got an allotment for a refugee house in Jung Pura [a South Delhi neighborhood]. We had to get the house emptied, people were living there illegally. We settled there.

When I question Anilji on who the illegal occupants were, he brushes off the question. Historical literature on Partition rehabilitation makes note of "evacuee property." During the peak of the riots in 1947, many Delhi Muslims had been asked to move—and often were forcibly moved—from their homes to refugee camps in Delhi for their own safety. Some of them later returned to claim their homes; others went to Pakistan. Their property was referred to as "evacuee property" and was meant to be in the safekeeping of the Indian state, which used these houses to provide temporary shelter to Hindus and Sikhs arriving from Pakistan. However, Vazira Zamindar argues that "one could say that most Muslims of Delhi were forced out or evacuated from their homes. But in discussions that ensued these homes came to be described first as 'abandoned' and then as 'vacant' and 'empty houses,' which could then be used for rehabilitation."[26] Many Muslims, as is the case of Rafi Bhai, whose story is told in Zamindar's book, were unable to return to their homes, which were parceled out among Hindus and Sikhs, who were seen as "central to the task of rehabilitation."[27] It is entirely possible that Anilji is referring to the home of a Muslim evacuee that was claimed by a Hindu/Sikh refugee family illegally and outside of government intervention. It is also possible that the people who were "living there illegally" were a Muslim family that had returned to claim their home, only to find it had been allotted. Still evasive, Anilji continues his story:

Anilji: I used to come and go between Kanpur and Delhi. I asked for a transfer to Delhi and came there in 1953. Then I changed that house. I did not like it.

Devika: Why not?

Anilji:: All these refugees lived there.

Devika: But you were a refugee too?

Even as I ask the question, I know that many older participants felt so ashamed of the refugee identity that had been thrust upon them that they made every effort to distance themselves from it. Kiranji almost did not apply for rehabilitation funds. My grandparents were allotted land in Faridabad, a little outside Delhi, but sold it and built their home in Rajouri Garden, a neighborhood that was mixed—populated by Dilliiwallahs (those native to Delhi) and refugees.

In *Since 1947: Partition Narratives among Punjabi Migrants of Delhi*, Ravinder Kaur tells a similar account about this evasion of the refugee label. One of her participants from DI Khan tells her, "Earlier we had to write 'refugee' in every official document but in the 1960s we refused to be so described."[28] Kaur notes that "[t]he important feature of this approximate date is that it was around this time that the Indian state decided to formally stop the resettlement schemes . . . in 1965, when the Ministry of Relief and Rehabilitation closed down and all residual resettlement work was transferred to the Ministry of Home Affairs."[29] The use of the label was, however, always a bit conflicted, and Kaur further notes that "the legal documents used terms like 'displaced persons' or 'evacuees,' while the official writings use the term 'refugees' to describe the plight of the migrants."[30] Even though Anilji unmarks himself earlier than these dates, there is agreement across the oral history record that the label of *refugee* was being consistently unclaimed. Once refugees began owning property, argues Kaur, they began to "contest the notion" of being refugees; "a claim to an immovable resource seemed to link them to a new place."[31] The movement from refugee to local was therefore both a symbolic and spatial process.[32]

To be rooted is often what drives our search for home places and spaces. Even here in the United States, "Where are you from?"—a question loaded with cultural identity politics—reveals our need to find comfort in location and a located identity, even though we know that any answer to this question is neither straightforward nor simple—*anywhere*. I resist such emplacements and often roguishly respond by saying that I am from "here," and that I lived in Indiana and Michigan before I moved to Ohio. And sometimes, if I am feeling generous, I invoke the subcontinent: "I am from Delhi, but my family is from Pakistan." When one is so variously located, resistance to place is inevitable. Symbolically, Anilji's need to remove himself spatially from other refugees seems to me a sort of movement to hold secure an emplaced self amid the chaos of displacement.

> *Anilji*: There were so many refugees. My job was permanent and I was getting a transfer to Delhi, so I told my parents I would not live there [in Jung Pura]. I never used to like that atmosphere—dirty ramshackle homes. So I moved us to Patel Nagar. We took a house on rent. Then, the landlords—an old couple—started harassing us. Don't do this, don't do that. I was disturbed by this.
>
> My mother and I went to see Rajouri Garden. We saw that some builders had opened offices there and they showed us houses that they were making. The houses were open, there were flush toilets. I liked the model house. I told them that I liked it but I did not have money. They asked me how much money I had and I must have had 40, 50 rupees in my pocket. In those days 50 rupees was a large sum. My mother had about 10 rupees in her pocket. He said, "Give us 50 rupees and we will book a house for you." They said we could pay off the house in installments. I bought the house for 7,500 rupees. This was 1955.

These post-departure moments—pieces—show a self that is trying to find a footing in the new country, a self who resists the refugee label, and ultimately a self who seeks a piece of home in place after place in Delhi. Anilji now lives in a ground-level flat in a housing development partially funded by the state, close to the international airport—flats built by the Delhi Development Authority. We are standing in a modest verandah with its outdoor potted plants and bougainvillea vine, and I remark that it is restful. Anilji looks around despondently, unconsciously dismissing my mention of the landscaping and the greenery, and answers, "It's okay. . . . We are nothing compared to how people live in Lahore." "When were you there?" I ask.

Anilji: Just last year in April [2006]. Should I tell you the story?

Devika: Yes.

Anilji: It's a long drawn-out story.

Devika: Please.

And in this way I enter the second-most important passage in Anilji's life. His is a life, as I see it, lived not between, not beside, not in spite of, but *in*—passages. The long drawn-out story is the tale of the second passage. After fifty-nine years.

PASSAGES (RETURN)

In 2005, Anilji, his older brother, and his sister-in-law decide to travel to Pakistan. "Why did you want to go?" I ask curiously. My participants have shown ambivalence about seeing home again—many long for it but don't do it, others don't think about it, yet others are adamant about their refusal to ever see it. "I lived in Pakistan for sixteen years. I wanted to go and see the places where I grew up," Anilji replies. He adds:

> We had been planning to go for a long time. My brother and I. We really wanted to go badly. We had such a strong feeling that we wanted to go. We wanted to go to Karachi, DI Khan, Islamabad, and Lahore.

The journey back begins with Anilji's brother making contact with an old army colleague and close friend from Pakistan.

> *Anilji*: A Musalman. He was a Mohammedan. A brigadier. He used to study with my older brother in veterinary college. After Partition, he tried to work in India, but he was unable to. Musalman. He was a Mohammedan. They shared the same room in their hostel in college. They had lost contact, but my brother knew that he was somewhere in the army. He used to live in Hyderabad, that is where he migrated from. My brother called the Hyderabad cantonment. Somehow we made contact, it took some time. We started communicating. He recognized us very well. We told him we wanted to come to Karachi, and he said, "You are most welcome, come right now and stay with us, I have a huge

house and just don't worry, just come here." We told him that we also wanted to go to Dera Ismail Khan. He said he would organize wherever we wanted to go. He said, just come. So we started planning.

The enemy (Mohammedan) who checked and looted the cabins in the first passage is replaced by the friend (Mohammedan) who is host and companion in the second passage. It is the refrain, the redundancy, and the repetition that I cannot help but note. Oblivious to it, Anilji, with very little prodding from me, announces:

> The Partition was bound to happen. It was inevitable. Because I don't think we ever got along. Never. Hindus were moneylenders. They were people who did not work too hard, but sat and enjoyed the interest from their money. They used to lend at high interests and the Mohammedans were prejudiced against them. Where we lived in the frontier province, it was close to Afghanistan, the Musalmans used to come once a year and burn the villages and loot them. They took what they needed for the year and then they would return.

And another framing of the Other takes shape here. Muslims and Hindus have coalesced into one. They are both *they*. So, I tentatively ask, "But you are Hindus too?" And he says, "Yes, but we were not rich moneylenders, we never had that kind of money." Here, he distinguishes his family from both sets of people—Hindu moneylenders and Muslim mobs.

Such contradictions follow the story of every generation. They reveal themselves in my own family moments, such as when Biji, my own grandmother, was quite upset in 1974, when my father wanted to give me the name *Shireen*. "It is a very Muslim-sounding name, she must have a Hindu name," she said. I am eventually named *Devika*, the name of a not-very-significant goddess in Hindu mythology. More notably, it is the name of the first Indian female film legend from the early twentieth century, Devika Rani, who is also famous (or infamous) for being the first woman to have lip-kissed on the Indian screen—not a vamp, but a "forward" star. When I heard the naming story as a teenager, I was upset only because I liked the name *Shireen*, it was different, and like all teenagers I wanted to feel less ordinary—everyone around me, mostly Hindus, had names derived from Sanskrit. I asked Biji why it was a problem; she loved Pakistan, she missed her Muslim neighbors, and she longed for Quetta, so giving me that name would have been appropriate. She laughed (sheepishly, or so I want to remember) and said, "We are Hindus, we have Hindu names, we are not Muslims." Unresolved, uncertain, uneasy contradictions. Yes, irony continues to be a leitmotif.

And here, fifty-nine years later, despite the contradictions, the Other is met as friend. The brigadier, Saif, receives Anilji's entourage at the Karachi airport. He brings along his entire family to welcome them. He recognizes them very easily, also because Anilji's sister-in-law always wears a sari—an easy way to mark Hindu women of her generation. They are unable to go to the cantonment because the visa disallows it, so they stay in a hotel for two days. But they do break a visa rule and visit Saif's home for dinner in the evenings. "He smuggled us in," laughs Anilji.

> Our excursion began right there. All the arrangements were made by Saif. He took us around all day. He stayed with us all the time. His daughter's son, his grandson, a young teenage boy, was also with us all the time. He did not leave us alone for even a minute.

This passage is about matching memory of home to the remnants of houses that still exist. The past shadows their every trip within Pakistan—a return to and of memory. In these travels, a feeling of home does return, fleetingly, despite the inevitable transformations:

> Karachi has really changed. It's like Bombay; it's full of multistoried buildings. It's become really commercialized. But I found it very peaceful. I never felt as if I was a stranger there.

The feeling of being home is so heightened that the disappointment of not locating his *own* home in Karachi does not leave Anilji anguished. They look for it all day, but conclude that it was either demolished or the street names were changed. From Karachi they go to Rawalpindi, because that is his sister-in-law's birthplace. This trip is organized by Saif's son, who lives in Sargoda. This house is not lost, and they are eagerly welcomed by its current inhabitants. Anilji happily notes:

> They received us very warmly. The house was not a house anymore; it had been converted into a shop. They showed us everything. The nameplate outside the gate was the same as it used to be (that is what my sister-in-law told us), they had not removed it. Many of the buildings around were also the same. It is a beautiful city, you can see a hill station from there—Murray. We were in

Pindi for one night and from there we took a taxi to DI Khan. We reached there at 4:00 P.M. We checked into the hotel—it was even air-conditioned. In those days [pre-Partition], there used to be nothing there—no flush system, only dry toilets . . . I mean there is a lot of change now.

The return to DI Khan seems sacred for both the brothers. For it is this home that connects them to their childhood. It is where Anilji spent most of his first sixteen years, where he started school, where he learned to swim in the tube well, and the port from which he departed for India.

Anilji: The school was exactly the same. No change. Absolutely no change. And the person who has put the foundation there, his name was Bagri. He had put the foundation stone for the school. That was still there, intact. They showed it to us. The furniture that we used to use when we were in school, it was the same. I felt that they had not even whitewashed the place. There was another school that I used to go to, the Islamia School, we went there too. That too was the same. There was an old *chawkidar* [guard] there who was so surprised to see us. The poor man, on his own, went and bought a cake. We did not want to eat it.

Devika: Why?

Anilji: Since it was dusty there. He was a guard, you know they are not clean. To show respect, we each took a piece. And you know the electric company where my father worked? We went there too. Even there, after sixty years, there was no change. There was one person I wanted to meet there, that person used to work under my father. His name was Jumman. I remembered him and I asked where he was. They told me he had recently died.

Even in DI Khan, we could not see our house. It had been demolished. But the area was lying as it was. It is a jungle, there was no change there. There are refugees there from Afghanistan and they have taken over some of the places. There were a lot of Afghanis there.

From here we went to Lahore. My brother's college was there—Dyal Singh College. The name of the college is the same, the foundation stone of the college is the same. The principal came to see us. We went to see my brother's room, it was the same. After a lifetime, you got the same atmosphere.

In Lahore we stayed with a friend of my nephew. My nephew lives in America and has a very close Pakistani friend there. His Pakistani friend's family took care of us in Lahore.

Papa and I look at each other in surprise and ask Anilji if they were worried about staying with strangers. Anilji asks, "What strangers? My nephew and his friend practically live in each other's homes in America." The irony is palpable; the nephew would have very few chances to befriend or even meet a Pakistani if he lived in India. Anilji continues:

> We stayed in their huge bungalow. It was centrally air-conditioned. We had a car and driver at our disposal. They were lacking for nothing in that place. Very rich people. We have no standards compared to them. Their house was worth seeing. Even all the food we ate in the house seemed like it was imported. It was like this in Islamabad. We went there too.

> *Papa*: Their rich class is very, very wealthy.

> *Devika*: I have heard this too, but mostly because these are landowning families.

> *Anilji*: Yes. But our home, where we lived and where my father worked, it was all the same.

The frontier remains the frontier. Timeless. A quality that we gladly associate (or want to) with the homes of our childhood. The frontier is where Anilji calls home. He is happy to see that things have remained the same— the home-place of Karachi and DI Khan (while not the abode) coincides with the home of memory. I discern in him a feeling of satisfaction that it resembles the old home of memory, echoing Bachelard's thoughts on how childhood homes conjure a "land of Motionless childhood."[33] It is our "first place," and for most people it is remembered for the security it invokes. The timeless and motionless quality is reconciliatory for Anilji. And yet, it gives him pause:

> One thing we cannot say is that had we stayed there we could have been better off. We would have had to go to work in the frontier. There was nothing there at that time, but at least my father had a job with the electric company. Now even that is torn down. There is nothing there now. What would we have done?

Even when the home is the reason for the return, to find that it is the same and yet somehow empty, seems disloyal to the memory of home. Yet to find that it is "nothing" is crucial for Aniliji, because the displacement then becomes justified, it becomes worth *something*. It finds an explanation. But then we return to his stories about Lahore and Islamabad, the high status of people there, the quality of life and the wealth, and I hear him say, again, "We are nothing compared to them." I argue with him, telling him that for the very wealthy, such as these persons (here or in India), the Partition was just a moment in history—their life was not disrupted. But Anilji shakes his head negatively and vehemently insists, "We are nothing."

This statement and Anilji's general despondence about home here/there forces me to ask whether the journey back has been for naught. He wanted to see the old home, but seeing it has not generated a feeling of stability nor any resolutions—"there is nothing there." And here in India, too, there is "nothing." Does the passage of return *erode* rather than *reconcile* Anilji's sense of home and self, similar to the passage of departure? Wandering and wondering what home was, what it is, what it might have been. Wandering and wondering who Anilji was and would have *become*, had he stayed home. But here he is, a person who has spent his life living inside these passages and pieces. And as if this dissatisfaction were contagious, my nervousness persists.

Movement II: Wandering

This is another story of drifting. Of a life lived wandering willingly in the past. A story and a self that do not make a reach into the present, so much so that home becomes a flexible, moving, movable idea that is lived uncomfortably backward—in memories and (their) dreams. And as if to reinforce motion, people on the move, we meet its subject at a crossing. On a road.

Arjunji lives in a part of East Delhi that neither Papa, nor I, nor even our cab driver, Iqbal, are familiar with. So Arjunji generously offers to stand at a Metro station stop, also a four-way crossing, waiting for the car. It is almost 44 degrees Celsius outside in mid-June; the North Indian summer is at its peak. "No, no, just give us the directions," Papa insists on the phone. After he hangs up, Papa declares, "He won't listen, he is almost eighty years old, he could get heat stroke."

Such generosity will announce itself in almost every member of Arjunji's family. His son, Veer, will offer to come to see me at my parents' home. Veer does not live in Delhi, and my visits fall during months that he cannot visit. We are unable to meet, but I am touched by his gesture. Arjunji will offer to accompany me to see his daughter, Rekha, in Gurgaon, a Delhi suburb. When we do meet Rekha she will take hours off from the Montessori school she runs to talk about her memories of her father and his life in Pakistan. She will talk of her father's Pakistan with a longing that will surprise me. From a console in the drawing room, she picks up an ornamental box placed on the center table:

> This box is from Pakistan, it used to be there in my grandfather's home, my father gave it to me. It's very precious to me. I love it. I keep it close where I can see it.

As I watch her caress the wood of this foot-long rectangular wooden box, I can almost hear Arjunji's words in my ears:

> I must tell you that daughters feel much more than sons. My son knows about all this, my home and my struggles in India, and I think he feels for me. But I think daughters are somehow more caring than boys. They are more sympathetic.

Rekha's reminiscences take me to Biji's tin Taj Mahal box. I am reminded of the longing it evokes for a place I have neither seen nor visited. These exchanges reinforce the simple idea that "memory . . . involves things and care,"[34] even if or when things-objects-materials bypass a generation. Having been born in India, Rekha and I are second- and third-generation refugees, and ours might even be considered the category of privilege rather than displacement, because the Hindu and Sikh community in Delhi has always been a prosperous community.[35] The nostalgia for the old country that both she and I feel would seem to be a function of what Hirsch calls *postmemory*—an imaginative investment in an unremembered past that we have only experienced in stories.[36]

Arjunji is waiting for us at the Metro crossing, right under a flyover (or overpass, as it is called in America). As soon as the car stops, he jumps into the front passenger seat and declares in relief, "Ah good, you did not overshoot this point. Our flat is just ten minutes away from here." A man of average height, Arjunji is dressed in dark cream trousers with a brown belt and a cream-colored shirt—a kind of summer uniform for retired men of his generation. He talks nonstop on our way to the ground-level flat, telling us how good it is to have company: "It is lonely you know when you get old, not too many people come by to meet you, earlier our kids used to live close by, now they live in two different directions." Papa points to me and exclaims, "Yes, but at least yours are a driving distance away, see she lives a twenty-hour flight away." We all laugh, but underlying the jest, I also feel a bit chastised for having left home. Even sixteen years have not softened the blow of separation for my parents (and, to some extent, for myself); they continue to encourage me to search for a faculty position in Delhi. Is that why, I ask myself repeatedly, I stay suspended between field and home—caught between fieldwork and homework?

Arjunji's wife, Meenaji, greets us both with hugs. They live in a very modest two-bedroom flat in a semi-government housing development. Arjunji immediately takes us on a small tour of his home. It takes no longer than five minutes to see everything. He keeps insisting, "It is a humble abode, but we like it here." He asks where I might like to sit and when I mention the dining table that is placed in a corner in the drawing room, he is pleased; "My wife can also listen to some of it from the kitchen, she likes to hear these stories." The kitchen is diagonal to the living room, about fifteen feet away. Since it is midafternoon, I ask what she is making. Arjunji replies, "Some snacks for all of us." "Oh, she shouldn't, we ate lunch and besides I rarely eat between meals, nor does Papa," I implore. Arjunji laughs and says, "It's a good excuse, and anyway it's for tea and I will also get to eat some *pakoras* [vegetables deep fried in chickpea flour] and *mithai* [sweetmeats]. So think of it as a treat for me." We all laugh. Papa, also fond of these snacks— North Indian junk food—nods smilingly.

DREAMS/MEMORIES: UNBREAKABLE HOMES

Even before we have settled Arjunji announces, "I went to Sibbi last night." I'm confused. Sibbi was his village in Pakistan. He laughs, his wife's laugh tinkles in from the kitchen, and they explain that every few days he "goes away" to his *ghar* (home) in Sibbi in his *sapne* (dreams). "I wake up and my wife and I discuss all the details of my dream, where I was playing, which room in the house I was in, and what we were doing—it's almost real," he smiles. We are all quiet for a while and then I ask, "Did your wife see the house? You were not married at that time." "No, but over the years she has come to know it from my descriptions," he explains. It has been sixty years since the Partition, and for this man to still dream every few days about his old home is poignant, almost heartbreaking. Yet he is delivering this information laughingly.

This passing moment sets the tone for the kind of self-in-movement that Arjunji symbolizes for me. Someone who wanders in the past, who is not absent, but who is not fully present—in the now. Bound by my own fieldwork habits, yet wanting to break away from some of them, instead of asking him to tell me how he arrived in India, I ask instead, "Tell me about your life in Pakistan:"

> *Arjunji*: My father was a very influential person. He used to write legal documents petitioned by people to be written in Urdu. He used to get paid almost 60, 70 rupees a day for this, in today's world he would be a millionaire. He never knew English, but these legal documents used to go right up to London. There was one case, he drafted a case and it went to the Privy Council and the judge there asked, "Who has drafted this case, I want him to be brought before me." The judge was told that my father was in Baluchistan and he knows only Urdu, he does not know English, and this is a translation by us. The judge said that there was no error in the document and the judgment was passed. My father got a lot of congratulations for that. It was passed by the Privy Council and was written by a man who only knew Urdu.

And so here it is again, this homage to the British, who were co-conspirators in causing the fragmentation that displaced him and us. Like the original birth certificate that Anilji is compelled to display, Arjunji must prove his father's status by showing me how he was honored in the metropole, in London—the power center of the Raj. Of course, I mean no sarcasm in noting his devotion to the British; I mention it here to reinforce my point about the consistent deference to Empire. That he and Anilji, among other participants, even the now ninety-seven-year-old Dadaji, always begin by speaking to me in English, sometimes broken English, despite my readiness to converse in Hindi and Punjabi, is a salute to the British. Of course, many merely begin by speaking in English, and gradually shift into Hindi or Punjabi. Anilji continues:

> We had a villa there in Sibbi. My father was earning about 100, 150 rupees a day. In those days, in the 1930s, it was a lot of money. He was a rich man. He was always traveling. We had a big house with big grounds. There were about seven rooms. We were eleven brothers and sisters [five brothers, six sisters] a huge family. And there were always a few guests staying in the home at one time. We also had two houses in Quetta and in the summer we used to shift there because it used to be too hot in Sibbi. Then there was an earthquake in

Quetta in 1935 and the entire Quetta was razed to the ground. Only our house was still standing.

The story of the deadly Quetta earthquake, or the *Quette ka bhuchal*, as Biji referred to it, is one that no one in my family is allowed to forget. My grandfather and great-grandfather's homes were razed to the ground. Biji inevitably mentioned the *bhuchal* alongside the *Batwara*, the Partition. We lost our homes two times in twelve years, she used to say. For Arjunji, whose home was not lost to the *bhuchal*, the unshakeable and indestructible quality that defines the material house also permeates the way that home and its habits are remembered—as if they are still there, ready to be accessed or escaped to, when the present home/country/life encroach with their inescapable and everyday burdens, because Arjunji constantly refrains, "We were very happy there, we came here temporarily, we thought there would be peace and we would go back." Sibbi holds strong in his memories:

> Our family life was very, very good. We siblings used to quarrel, but we used to love each other. We were very afraid of our father, when he came home, we used to be quiet. We used to get up at five in the morning. We had two cows. I was active in the family. I used to do all the domestic chores. I used to carry buckets, bring the milk, give it to my mother, go shopping—buy sugar or this and that—this was all my duty. After this I used to go to school. After school, I used to play with kites. We used to pester my sisters. They would cry and tell on us and we would hide.
>
> Then there was a time when I hurt this good friend of mine. I was too big and he got a cut. I ran away from his house and came and hid in a dark room in my home. This boy and his mother came to complain to my mother saying that I had beaten up her son. The boy had a cut that would need stitches. Another neighbor came and saw the cut and said it would need stitches, but she filled it with *soorma* and bandaged it.[37] He was fine in two days. If you put in stitches, you often get infection. Then this boy became my friend and he gave me a picture of Mahatma Gandhi as a gift because he must have thought I am a quarrelsome person and this would give me peace. [We all laugh.]

From here Arjunji's stories flit from topic to topic, detailing life in the old country, the habits, the adventures, his schooling—as if it all happened yesterday. Sibbi is so much part of his subconscious that it returns in his dreams. As it is for so many of his compatriots, Arjunji's memories of home sketch a picture of communal harmony entwined with the ever-present vestiges of communal tension and material inequities.

Arjunji: In Sibbi, we were staying with 98 percent Mohammedans and just 2 percent were Hindus. I say that 80 percent of the Mohammedans must have taken meals in our houses. I used to live in the company of Muslims. We used to go to the chai shops in the evenings. I had money at the time because my father was rich. I used to take them out, I used to pay the bill, so they used to be my supporters [laughs]. If there was a quarrel or a fight, they used to come to my rescue.

Also, no Hindu ever went to an Islamic school there—a Mohammedan school. I was the only single person who studied in the Islamia School in that town.

Devika: How did that happen?

Anilji: In Sibbi there were annual examinations in December. In Punjab there were annual examinations in March. In 1942, I was in class eight [grade eight] and I could not pass. I failed. I was very upset and I told my father that I would not study further. So my father asked me, "What will you do? Graze goats?" [Laughs.] My brother had a friend in Lahore [which is in Punjab], he wrote to him and said that he was sending me there so I could take the exams there in March. I went there and they gave me admission. There was a man called Mia Abdul Hakim who I explained my situation to. He told me I could join the class the next day, to repeat the eighth. I stayed there for three months and cleared my exams. The children would ask me what I was doing there since my name was Hindu, Arjun. They would ask me why I was there since I was not a Musalman. I passed my exams and returned to my school. But I was the only Hindu person who studied in the Islamia School.

Arjunji seems thrilled as he ushers me into this anomalous situation, not realizing that he is simultaneously providing me with the same contradiction and ambivalence that I encounter in story after story. It is the story of two communities more "apart" than "one," (arguably both effect and cause of the Partition, as noted by Khan and Zamindar[38]), and each accesses the other when convenient. If it were not for its flexible exam schedule, there would have been no other reason for him to join the Islamia School in Lahore. And so irony resurfaces in my notes.

Arjunji shifts the conversation, not deliberately, and tells me about Jawahar Lal Nehru, who became the first prime minister of independent India:

Pandit Nehru[39] came to Sakkar in 1942. At that time I was in class seven [grade seven]. I told my father I want to go and see Pandit Nehru. My cousin offered to take me. My older brother, my cousin, and I, we went to Sakkar. Pandit Nehru was standing there and there was a great rush, he was giving a lecture for the Quit India Movement[40]—the movement had begun. I still remember when he took the mike in his hand. This was the time I came to know that there is something called a demand for independence; otherwise we were in a remote corner of the country and we did not know about these things. I remembered the speech and I thought if I go there (to India) I will meet Pandit Nehru. After Partition, I came here and I met Pandit Nehru in his office.

Devika: What did you do in his office?

Arjunj: I was a parliamentary assistant, doing parliamentary work.

I want to know more about Arjunji's life in India after he arrived. I ask him to tell me how that took shape. His memories of relocation are not only brief, but also checkered, as if he does not want to revisit them, showing me how we make choices about the memories we want to keep and inhabit. He has chosen to live in memories of the original home, one that he witnessed as a child, and one that witnessed his childhood. He wants home to *stay* there. Making *here* is the homework of memory.

NEW HOMES/EMPTY VESSELS

Arjunji: I moved on May 24, 1947. I left Quetta and I reached Lahore the next day. I left my luggage in the cloakroom and went to meet my uncle in his home. I hired a *tongawallah* [a driver of a horse-drawn carriage] to get to his place. I said, "*Bhaiya* [brother], take me to Prem Nagar." He said yes and took me till a crossing, one side was Prem Nagar and the other side was a road. He told me to get off because the Hindus were there across the road. He said, "They will kill my horse and they will kill me. I know you are a Hindu and I could have killed you, but I did not, so you can walk from here." So I walked to my uncle's house and told my cousin to get my luggage from the station. My cousin wanted to find the tongawallah and hand him over to the Hindus. But I said, "No, no, don't do that, he saved my life." I was in Lahore for seven days. In the meantime my two younger sisters, my younger brother, and my mother had already reached Dehradun. Then I went to Dehradun and I stayed there. There was an outhouse with three rooms. We stayed there. There was no work, no money, nothing.

India is experienced in moments of trial and error—fits and starts—mirroring the departure. Unlike many others who speak to me about their ambitions for a post-Partition life, of wanting to rebuild, to resecure their wealth, Arjunji leaves his dreams and ambitions behind. He had hoped to be in the legal profession like his father. His post-Partition narrative is that of a nineteen-year-old who just gets by in the present, and with some deliberateness, stays firmly ensconced in the memories of the old country. As he gets older he builds a narrative (a life, a self) that is the opposite of the one he lived, one that rejects wealth and affluence. A life that is littered with innumerable failures and disappointments. Drifting, but stagnant. Mobile, but not:

Arjunji: I had an account in the New Bank of India. I had transferred some money from Quetta to Dehradun. One night there was an announcement that the bank was liquidated. I did not lose the money, but they gave it much later.

Then what happened? There was an announcement that there would be a train to Allahabad and there were jobs at a refugee camp there. So I took that train and worked there for some time—just a week. They paid us 70 rupees plus ration for the week.

Then a recruiting officer came and asked if we wanted to join the army. And I thought, why not? You get free boarding, lodging, training, and a good salary. So they took me. They took my weight and height and said I was too thin and underweight. Our recruiting officer used to get 5 rupees per recruitment of a *jawan* [junior soldier] so he told me to wait and gave me some *chana* [roasted garbanzo beans]. He said to eat that and [drink] a lot of water. I did. I went on the scale and my weight was okay for the army. *Chana khaa liya paani pee liya* [I ate garbanzo beans and drank water over them], and I was recruited. [We all laugh.] They told me I would get 57 rupees a week plus boarding and lodging and clothing, et cetera. I was to get up at 5:00 A.M., go for drill, PT [physical training], all these things. For three months I was in Lucknow and then I was sent to Ferozpur.

The stint in the army does not last long. Arjunji's father and older brothers move to India and his father is distressed by his decision to join the army. Arjunji feigns (and orchestrates) a medical condition that forces him to be discharged from the army. A mirthful look in his eyes, he relates the discharge:

One day we were doing PT and I kept rubbing my leg where I had a mark. My friend asked what it was and I told him it was from a cycle accident and I cannot do certain exercises. The officer asked us to turn right, I would turn left, when he said turn left, I would turn right. He called me out and asked me what was happening. I told him my leg hurt from the old injury. He made me get an x-ray, of course nothing showed up, but I kept insisting that I could not walk. My officer got fed up and said, "You are not fit for my company, this is your discharge certificate, go" [laughs]. So I left and came to Delhi.

Arjunji's experiences of relocating to Delhi are haphazard, and even after trying to understand the movement chronologically, I am unable to map how he moves from one job to another or from one place to another. I think of his time in India as a montage of movement—from *here* to *there* to *elsewhere*.

There is a home in Delhi's Patel Nagar neighborhood (bought jointly by the family), where Arjunji lives for many years; he is forced by family to sell this, and he distributes the money among siblings. This is a bitter moment: "I was very upset, but there was no way out." He moves to where he lives now, a humble abode, in modest state-built flats in East Delhi.

He opens a bicycle shop in Chandni Chowk (in Old Delhi) with a partner. The Korean War starts, leading to a shortage of bicycle parts from Korea and forcing the closure of this business. He starts a clothing shop with a friend, but owing to some internal conflict is forced to sell his share to his partner. He leaves Delhi and takes a job in a refugee claims office in Gujarat. This lasts a few months. He returns to Delhi and works for some years in a government agency that resettles Partition widows. He gets a modest job in the prime minister's office in 1954. He stays in this job for almost thirty-two years, until 1986. He is offered an extension to work longer, but refuses it.

Arjunji: I retired and I am continuing with whatever pension I get. I am not a greedy person and my wife, she is cooperative, and seems comfortable with what we have. I have suffered a lot in my life financially. Moneywise I am not at all rich, but I am happy. I am the poorest person in my family, but I think I am happier than those who have money.

Devika: Would things have been different without Partition?

Arjungi: Of course, but . . . I have no worry that I do not have money. So what? My health is good. I wake up at five in the morning. I do all the work, I bring vegetables, milk, my wife and I sit together, we play cards. In the evening we go for a walk and in the night we watch television and sleep.

Home cannot be resurrected, but Arjunji renews some of the habits of his childhood world. Habits trail us into new places, or as Edward Said observes in his famous essay "Reflections on Exile," "For an exile, habits of life, expression, or activity in the new environment inevitably occur against the memory of these things in another environment."[41] And while he resurrects his habits, Arjunji resists restoring his economic status. Contrary to many refugees of his generation who wanted to restart by replenishing their resources, Arjunji wants to travel into his memories, "These are my memories. When I sit alone, I remember all these things, I remember Sibbi, I dream of her, and I feel comfortable." Would you return, I inquire?

> *Arjunji:* Yes, I still feel that if I get a chance I will go back. We never thought we would settle here, we thought there will be peace again and we will go back to Pakistan. If we go back, if you take me, I can show you the entire Baluchistan. I feel as if, if things were normal, I would go back and settle there and then I will be finally happy.

Arjunji's daughter Rekha, on the other hand, tells me that she and her children would be too fearful to go to Pakistan: "If you ask any person if they want to go there, they would say yes, but they would hesitate, they might not want to visit." But your father would like to visit, I tell her. "Yes, but you see, he was born there, we don't feel for it like him," she replies. Many other second-generation refugees (not all) echo this emotion. Rohit, a fifty-nine-year-old second-generation participant whose family was from Lahore, tells me, "When I was growing up we would meet people who had formed associations, refugee associations, but for me Pakistan is a dot on the map, I would visit it, but only as a curiosity." This sentiment is echoed also in Ravinder Kaur's book *Since 1947*, in which second-generation refugees exhibit a similar curiosity about their parents' birthplaces, and yet for them Pakistan denotes a national region associated with violence, loss, anti-Indian sentiment, and forced movement. Rohit elaborates on this delinking of home from Pakistan, "By and large there are negative feelings about Pakistan. There is a huge element of negativity. The new scars of terrorism will take a long time to heal." We are speaking in 2009, less than six months after

the infamous Mumbai attacks. And yet none of my first-generation participants has mentioned these attacks in the three years of fieldwork.

I ask Arjunji, "You have never been happy here in India?"

Arjunji: There is nothing here. There is no brotherhood. There is nothing.
There is no love between people. Everybody is selfish here.

Devika: Why is that?

Arjunji: Money. Materialism. Everybody is after money. There is greed.

In his mind, the desire among refugees to replenish their past lives and
livelihood has reduced the new country to nothing. He finds no fit here. All
the same, his longing for the past, too, comes with its summary contradictions, as it does for many refugees. I come to a similar conclusion with regard
to other participants' dreams of return that also do not come to fruition.
Arjunji too wants to return, but has not traveled back. When his son, Veer,
a horticulturalist, has an opportunity to visit Pakistan to be a judge at a
rose species contest between the two countries, Arjunji asks him not to go.
Eyes widened in disbelief, I ask, "Why did you tell him not to go?"

Arjunji: That is not a reason to go back. What is the point in going there to
choose one rose over the other? If he chooses the rose made by the Pakistanis,
the Indians will hate him, if he chooses one made by Indians, the Pakistanis
will hate him. [We all laugh.] So, I told him not to go. That is not why one
must return to Pakistan.

A trivial reason, in his eyes, is no reason to travel to Pakistan. Arjunji does
not want home to be belittled in this manner. His words describe well the
separation that many first-generation refugees make between home and
Pakistan, whereby *home* brings forth warm nostalgic memories of ancestral
towns and villages, whereas *Pakistan* evokes the violence of Partition and
the "unbridgeable gaps that led to a Muslim Pakistan and a Hindu India."[42]
Dissuading Veer from making the journey is an attempt to protect the
home of memory—an act of preservation; an act that the architect Juhani
Pallasma contemplates:

We have just as great a need to keep secrets as to know them. Our imagination
fills out the compartments of the places, rooms and buildings with memories,
and turns them into our own personal territories.[43]

The home of the old country claims Arjunji's imagination and he, in turn, marks it as a sacred sphere, showing us that places are not fixed entities and that the "places travelled to depend in part upon what is practiced within them . . . And at the same time as places are dynamic, they are also about proximities, about the bodily co-presence of people who happen to be in that place at that time, doing activities together."[44] This home-place must remain untarnished so he can travel into it—in his dreams and his imaginings—with his memories intact. Pure spaces. Inviolable territories.

Arjunji: I miss it. I miss my bed. I miss my house. I miss my friends. My friends may not be alive now, but I still feel for them . . . and there was and there is this place, *my* place, *my* home, where I used to roam around.

And so he dwells deliberately in this childhood home of memory, dream, and imagination. Speaking about the relationship between the self and the house that has witnessed childhood, Davidson proposes that "the childhood home remembers and is remembered as a virtual space, constantly called upon for idealistic understandings of security and imaginative possibilities."[45] Will Arjunji not return because home's reality would interfere with the memories that have sustained him, because we leave childhood homes without ever leaving them? Or is it because, as Michel De Certeau notes "they live in turn, invisible and present, in our memories and our dreams. They journey with us"?[46]

A return, even if it is a return by Arjunji's son, could mean a disappearance or a shift or a dislodging of memory. A return is a potential for disappointment. It could mean the death of a past self of memory that has allowed Arjunji to navigate the new country. To continue wandering is an act of preservation. *There* must be kept there, so that it can be remembered. To keep there *there* is to protect the self of history, the wandering self of memory. This protection is the homework of memory.

Movement III: Constructing

Hotel Noor is a fixture,[47] an almost necessary landmark in central Delhi. It takes up an entire block of Connaught Place, which is the financial hub of the city. Named after the Duke of Connaught and an almost exact reproduction of the Royal Crescent in Bath, England, Connaught Place and its surrounding areas were the center of British Delhi in 1931. It is an area of the downtown with concentric inner, outer, and middle circles that house some of the oldest and newest city businesses. Its inner circle runs many blocks, and one can literally walk the entire circle (more than a few miles) under high-ceilinged colonial-style verandahs. Seven radial roads connect Connaught Place to the rest of the city, including India Gate, the Parliament, the presidential residence, and other important state buildings.

Spaces claim corners of our memories about home, and when I think of Delhi, I don't so much think of a house or my home, but of days spent gallivanting in Connaught Place with my mother, to shop for her saris in the government-run Cottage Emporium,[48] to her tailor in Shankar Market who stitched her sari blouses, to search for "junk jewelry" on Janpath, and to drink cold coffee at DePaul's, a small cosmetic store famous for its homemade cold coffee. We used to bully Papa to take us on after-dinner drives to India Gate so we could eat *chuski*—a kind of locally made spicy popsicle—and popcorn, and run around the lawns that circle the gate. When we were older, we were taken to the India Coffee House to drink their famous Irish coffee, and to Kwality's to eat the "best *chole bhature*" in Delhi (a common North Indian street food—fried leavened white-flour flatbread with curried and spicy garbanzo beans). In our late teens, summer nights would find us driving to the India Gate lawns, and in the winters we spent many after-dinner leisurely hours sipping coffee in cafés around Connaught Place. Hotel Noor was always a presence in these visits. I have never stayed at the Noor (mostly because I have never had to stay in a hotel in Delhi), but I have eaten in its famous Delhi cuisine restaurant.

Amrit Suri owns Hotel Noor. He did not build it. It was built by someone else in the 1930s. Amritji has owned it since the mid-1970s. Meher, his daughter,[49] tells me the story of how Noor came to be family-owned. "It's quite dramatic and romantic how it came to us," she says as she begins.

> My father was in his teens. It was the early 1950s. They had fled Pakistan and they had nothing. He and his brothers used to walk round the Connaught Place area in Delhi in the evenings. One day they came upon Noor, which was at that time a newer hotel in the city center. Even from the outside Papa was mesmerized by it. He told his older brothers—now, we don't know if it was a joke or whether he really meant it—that he would own that hotel one day. He

ended up getting into construction and real estate. He bought Noor in 1976. It is one of the most prime locations in central Delhi now.

Noor does not get mentioned in any of our initial meetings, but the story of how the building came to be coveted and then owned is eventually a crucial way for me to apprehend Amritji's oral history. For me, the building is, to a large extent, a symbol of Amritji's life after Partition. The aspiration embedded in the "Noor story" shows me why I must note Amritji's "movement to build," and how this movement—*here* and *here* and *here*—is what (perhaps) leaves me nervous, almost motion-sick. Neither passages, nor pieces, nor memories, this is a different kind of attempt at rehoming/regrounding.[50] A drifting in building. A different kind of rehoming.

(FIRST) PLACING THE ETHNOGRAPHER

We rarely meet alone. But Amritji does not ask for Papa to accompany me. We are always in the presence of his wife, Roniji, and his daughter, Meher. He is a conservative man who, as his daughter says, considers it awkward for a married man and father to be around other women. "A complete chauvinist, but a good man," Meher says resignedly. A devout Sikh, he prays at the Bangla Sahib Gurudwara, a famous Sikh temple in the outer circle of Connaught Place, every single evening of the year. And when we meet, it is always after Amritji's prayer routine. I'm impressed by such devotion. I know he spends his entire day at Noor, which is also the main office for his various construction undertakings, and after the day's work he unfailingly visits the temple before returning home. Curious about this routine, I once ask him, "Do you ever miss a day?" "No, *beta* (child), if I am in Delhi, *pher shaam noo matha teken zaroor janda naan* (then I make sure that I pay my respects)," he replies in a mixture of English and Punjabi. It is peaceful to spend thirty minutes sitting there, he tells me.

   I reach Amritji's palatial bungalow in South Delhi just a few minutes after his return from Bangla Sahib. It is a humid monsoon evening in July 2008. I have visited him before and am directed to his private rooms on the second level of the home. A man of small proportions, a little bent by age, he greets me at the French doors to the bedroom suite where he and his wife lounge with the extended family in the evenings. His son and daughter-in-law have their own suite of rooms on another floor of the bungalow. The rooms are the size of a large two-bedroom apartment. Amritji, who I always refer to as "Uncle" because of my friendship with his daughter Meher, removes his *pagdi* (turban) and reclines on the bed in a cotton *kurta pyjama* (long shirt and loose trousers worn in North India, Pakistan, and parts of Central Asia). His wife, whom I call Aunty, is seated on a divan by the French windows in the corner. An unmistakable air of affluence surrounds them and the home, which is located in one of the prime residential locations in the city. Amritji's words about his elder cousin Kiranji ring in my ears when I am inside the room, "We all made a life for ourselves here, but Kiran, she *became* something." The life *he* has made for himself—having achieved tremendous success as a hotelier, a restaurateur, and a builder—might be the envy of any person. I once ask him, "But, you have done so well, have you not, Uncle?" "Just money, it's just money," he dismisses.

Aunty insists on ordering tea from their large kitchen downstairs, along with snacks, "*Bache* [child], Uncle will eat something too, and I will have some more tea," she says, brushing off my pleas about it being too close to dinner. "Of course, we will have dinner later after you talk to Uncle," she informs me. Uncle tells me to sit on the bed and when I hesitate he says, "Don't worry, no formality here, take off your *chappals* [flip flops], sit on the bed, and let's wait for Meher to get here." Meher is stuck in traffic and he does not want to start without her because "she likes to listen to these things, these stories."

And another wait ritual begins. This is a common occurrence with many of my elderly participants, except Dadaji, who will always chastise me about arriving late for all our meetings. The talk turns to my life in America. There it is again, the same curiosity about how I manage alone. I am the same age as Meher, and Aunty asks me how I run my household without any house help in America. And this question does not just come from the affluent, but from persons in all classes, since domestic help is an intrinsic part of home economy (for better or worse) in most of middle-class India. Having been away for so long, I find it hard to describe how I do this since it is now like a second skin, a habit—a home, a life—here. I start with telling her how I awaken at six in the morning, drink tea, after which I make coffee for my spouse, who gets up later. Aunty cuts in, remarking, "That's early. And then?" I recite my daily rigmarole—I read the paper, tidy up a little around the house, make the bed, empty the dishwasher, and either go to work or, if it is not a teaching day, close myself in my study for four hours until lunch, when my spouse comes home. "What do you do for lunch?" she prompts. Either I make something or we have a sandwich or one of those organic meals, or soup, I smilingly tell her. What about dinner, she continues probing. I cook dinner every other day, enough for two days. Cleaning? I have two cleaning ladies come in every fortnight because the house has too many rooms. We take care of the cooking, laundry, groceries, and other errands between the two of us.

She looks at Uncle and says in Punjabi, "*Kinna ghar daa kum karna painda hai uthe*" (they have to do so much housework there). "It's good, *changa hai, karna chaahida hain*" (it's good, one should work)," he replies. Later on he will tell me how his mother looked after all eight of her children without any help in Rawalpindi and in Delhi, how everyone worked a lot in the house to keep it running.

"*Mainu changa ladga hain kum karna, aadat ho jaindi hai*" (I am used to it and I like working around the house), I declare, also speaking in Punjabi. Uncle and Aunty look at me in shock, as I have spoken in fluent Punjabi, and ask, "You know Punjabi?" "Yes, yes, I can also read and write, Papa worked in Punjab for eight years and I had to learn Punjabi in schools, and half of my family is Sikh, my aunt is married into Sikhs," I inform them. Then with some amount of proud flourish, I take a piece of paper from my notebook and write out their names in Punjabi. Both husband and wife inspect it and when they look up I know it has endeared me to them. Uncle laughs, "My kids grew up in Delhi, even they don't know Punjabi, we speak to them in Hindi or English." Discerning a small note of disappointment in his voice, I am a bit embarrassed at my immodesty and soothingly note, "We had to learn it because it was the language of the state, we were living in Punjab after all." I know that had they continued living in Pakistan, all the children would have learned the language. Who would have thought that Papa's work in Punjab and my linguistic legacy from our stay there would emerge here, pulling me inside this family? From here on, Uncle and Meher will jokingly call me "Bona Fide, the real deal"—the real Punjabi—because I know how to read and write in *Gurumukhi*, I do the *gidda*, I know the difference between *chikki* and *gajak*, and I almost chose to be wed in a Sikh temple ceremony.[51]

Roniji tells me she too "worked in the house" like me, because they lived in Manhattan for some years after the 1984 Hindu-Sikh riots broke out all over North India, following Prime Minister Indira Gandhi's assassination by two of her Sikh bodyguards at her official residence in Delhi. Uncle, Aunty, and the three children moved to America for some years. Of course, their move is anomalous, an indicator also of class; the Suris had the resources to move to the West—they are the most affluent of my participants. For Sikhs living in North India, these riots were a breach of communal relations by the very Hindus by whose sides they had struggled in 1947. Uncle decided to buy an apartment in Manhattan and relocate to the United States, but eventually returned after things settled down.

Ironically, my family was in Punjab during these riots, Papa having taken a job with the multinational Nestlé, which had factories in Moga, a town that was one epicenter of the communal unrest. The unrest, whose roots could be traced to one Sikh group's struggle for an independent nation,[52] lasted over a decade, eight years of which we spent in Punjab. Teased by Sikh students for being a part of the minority Hindu community, my brother and I found ourselves in boarding schools chosen because of the riots *and* chosen also because they would provide us with a proper British-style education. Papa left Punjab in 1985, but we stayed in these schools.

Disparate. Similar. Displacements. For the Suris the riots mean a move to a different continent less than thirty years after Partition, a move that accelerates and exacerbates the shifting and drifting self that Uncle un/settles into in the new India. For my parents, brother, and myself, the riots mean an internal displacement, moving states, leaving home for school/home. For me, the legacy of this dislocation is coming to a realization, albeit years later, that school seems more home than home.[53] The choice of an academic life is perhaps not a choice, but an inevitability following from those movings and rehomings—uprootings as proclivities. I know, of course, that my own mobilities contribute in some way or the other to the nervousness that emanates from (or the nervousness that I sense in) these stories. As we talk of my household chores in Ohio, Meher arrives, and father and daughter start to reminiscence about some of this family's history that is already circulating among us.

In June 1947, the month the Suris leave Pakistan, Uncle is only nine years old; he is the youngest of eight siblings in a devout Sikh family from Rawalpindi. Their father owns a furniture factory, and while not wealthy, they lead comfortable lives. When they decide to leave, they believe (like everyone else) that the stay in India will be a hiatus. Uncle recalls this decision: "My father was convinced that we would return, so we took nothing, we had the furniture factory and two houses, we could have sold them, but we just left them there. We didn't bring money. We didn't bring anything." The belief that the conflict was temporary madness is a sentiment that resurfaces in this oral history record and others. Even so, some came away with gold or money or the promise of a job (as was the case with Labbi Devi, my own grandfather, and Kiranji's husband).

What is also distinct about Anilji, Arjunji, and Uncle is that they came from large families with many siblings. In these families, struggling to feed, clothe, and provide shelter for every member was one of the bigger day-to-day problems; therefore the siblings were often left to their own devices, to make their own ways in the world. The unmarried girls stayed at home for some years, and were married into stable homes. While I have no statistics to support this belief, anecdotal evidence suggests that among many refugee families, marrying within the refugee community was preferred. Kaur too observes, "For the refugees . . . marriage contracts held an array of social possibilities from which they could re/create their social networks."[54] In my own family it is not unusual, even now, to see marriages being arranged among grandchildren of the first-generation families—unrelated by birth, perhaps, but linked deeply by the watershed moment. Unsurprisingly, third-generation Partition refugees have not stayed with the tradition, yet it persists.

BUILDING, DRIFTING

"Uncle, tell me about life after Partition," I ask, gently interrupting our conversation about the escape. He has told me that in June, Kiranji's father, Meher's grand-uncle, a doctor in the army, sent trucks that brought the Suris to the army cantonment, a safe zone whence they took trains to Ambala and stayed with other relatives. "So what happened, where did you live?" I continue. The story he proceeds to tell is one of shifting spaces, places, and occupations—a life set adrift by forces outside his control. Even though Amritji is younger than Anilji and Arjunji, like them he drifts in and out of different jobs, schools, and places of abode—"here and there"—for many years, until he "makes a life for himself." And also like Anilji and Arjunji, even though his family is large and there are many siblings, survival is a solitary experience, remembered acutely.

Amritji: We went to Ambala because my sister was there with her husband, then from there I went to Udaipur with my father. My uncle was an engineer and he asked us to come there because he used to do some work for the Maharaja of Udaipur. We started supplying rations [groceries] to the Maharaja's army. We were there until 1950, then we moved to Delhi. We moved to Delhi because my brother had started a furniture shop in Connaught Place, because we had got some money in exchange for our property in Pakistan. It was called a claim.

Devika: So everyone was not together?

Amritji: No, my father and I were in Udaipur. [The rest of the family was in Delhi.] I was twelve at that time. My father was still in Udaipur and I returned to Delhi, and he used to send some wooden toys from there. So I used to take a *redi* [cart] and take it to Ajmal Khan Road and sit outside Standard Bakery and sell them. I used to make 10, 15 rupees from that.

Devika: Where were you staying?

Amritji: We were staying in Rohtak Road. We just took over the house, it was abandoned by some Muslims. Have you been there?

Devika: Yes, very few times, it is quite far.

The Muslims who had "abandoned" the house were probably among those who fell within the state-created category of "evacuees," Muslims who were "departing, or had departed," and whose "homes and lands came to be classified as 'evacuee property' which was used to rehabilitate Hindu or Sikh 'displaced persons,'"[55] as Zamindar has described. In fact, the house in which the Suris were staying might have been one of the 10,200 Muslim-owned houses in Delhi that were taken into official custody by the Indian state, though many had already been taken over by the time evacuee property legislation became operative in Delhi, thus making official allotments moot.[56]

Amritji: There was a temporary furniture shop next to the house on Rohtak Road. The carpenters who worked there needed three people to clean the cable; I used to do the cleaning of the wood—it's like shaving—then I would fill a sack with the shavings and sell those. I would make 1 or 2 rupees doing that. I used to buy *dal* [lentils, legumes] for one *anna* [one-sixteenth of a rupee] and meat and we would eat that. We put potatoes in everything just to survive.

Other people were there too, struggling. My uncle, all of us, we stayed in one room on Rohtak Road. My mother used to say that we should not feel that only we are struggling because this had happened to everyone, not just us.

Devika: It was one room?

Amritji: No, it was a house, but we were all too scared, so we used to all sleep in one room at night. Together.

Devika: Why were you scared?

Amritji: The Mohammedans used to live close by. My *mammaji* [mother's brother], who was with us, could not deal with the fear. He left for Amritsar. We stayed. There used to be exhibitions, they started in 1955. We used to get some contracts.

Devika: What exhibits?

Amritji: Industry and agriculture. We would get work in the exhibition and we made some money. We fixed the house a little bit.

The exhibitions involve building pavilions in exhibit halls for various companies to display their materials. Uncle recalls working day and night to complete some of these jobs. He is almost fifteen by then and has finished his schooling via distance learning. He does not attend regular school because he feels pressure to contribute to the family income. And besides, he tells me, "Also, I could not go to school because I used to live between Delhi and Meerut at that time to do some construction work there with my father." (Meerut is a city about forty-five miles from Delhi.) He joins college, but hurts his foot at work, so he is unable to clear his exams. School, like everything else, just drifts away: "We were not encouraged to go to school, my parents did not insist, the reason being, there was no food in the house, what could Mother tell us?" There are eight siblings and only one, a sister, is married. He tells me, "We all needed to be settled, that was the main thing."

The exhibition work marks his entry into the world of construction—building houses, schools, and industrial complexes. The first job is to build homes for "slum people." I marvel at the irony of the situation. Still unsettled, still drifting from home to home, from job to job, here he is, an unhoused person, building homes for the homeless. These first buildings are built amid extreme hardship, but he and his brothers make a profit.

> Life was hard. *Beta*, when we ate in the evening, we got dal for 4 annas—250 grams—for ten people. We used to put water in it or there used to be some *sabzi* [vegetable]. Or we had meat, we could only afford to buy 250 grams of it, it was for 5 annas. My mother used to put cauliflower or potatoes in it. She would give us a piece each. There was always *aam ka achaar* [pickled mango] in the home, so if we got hungry we used to eat our *rotis* [wholemeal flatbreads] with the *achaar*. Then things got better, and we had more. But at that time even food was a problem, there was always a shortage. I also remember how we got our first ceiling fan, we had it put in one room. We could sleep inside in the summer, we would all sleep in the same room. Before the fan, we would just sleep on the terrace at night, during the summers. The whole terrace used to be full of people. My father used to feel very hot, he used to put water on the sheet on his *charpoy* and sleep.

I look around his room, point to the house in general, and remind him that he had a remarkable rise to where he now is, as one of the elite builders in the country. "Is it all a memory now?" I want to know. He says, "It took thirty years." "Thirty?" I exclaim. "Yes, slowly, slowly we got settled, people started enjoying things, but it was a long time before that happened."

The construction jobs are intermittent at first, so Uncle finds another job building storage space for food grains and food grain containers. He builds a home for his sister and says, "It was good to do that because I gained experience building a residential property." This is followed by a contract to build a factory. By now he has a partner in the business. They build hospitals. For twenty-five years, from 1974 to 2001, they also build power plants. They also build multiple homes for themselves.

Then, along the way, in 1976, Hotel Noor comes on the market, and Uncle buys it. Owning it is in many ways the ultimate achievement of the life "made" in building. In fact, when I think of the Suri home, I think of Noor. Yet I know from our conversations that he uses it as a place of work and not much else. Noor's value in his life is allegorical. As a young refugee, Uncle seeks affluence, which ultimately comes from constructing buildings, adding more and more property to his name. His activities are a symbolic regrounding. By claiming more portions of the new country he is "domesticating" it, making it his own. But a small, very casual conversation between us shifts how I see his relationship to building, and shows how slippery are my speculations.

Devika: So you think your motivation after Partition, having lost everything, was to be successful?

Amritji: The thing is that we cannot know whether or not we might have been successful if we had stayed back there. Nobody can know that. It could be that if we had stayed there, we would not have done anything because we would have not lost anything.

Devika: So in some ways, the Partition created ambition?

Amritji: Again, how can one prove that? Were people unambitious there? We cannot know. What has happened is that now there is a lot of money and many refugees did very well, but there is selfishness. In Rawalpindi everyone knew everyone, if something happened to someone, people immediately visited. No one does that these days. People were content, people were so involved with each other, there was so much love . . . everyone felt oneness with others. After this success, whatever community there was started decreasing, love started decreasing. . . . See, I have stayed in this house for thirty years and I don't know who lives to my right or to my left.

Devika: But some good came of the Partition? Those who worked hard and gained affluence, created a better life.

Amritji: No good has come of it. Nothing. People are not happy. From inside. They have some problem or the other. *Beta*, earlier all we had was *dal-sabzi*, you ate, you slept, you did not worry about locking your doors. Nowadays, if you have a Mercedes, you want a Porsche, if you have that, then you want the even more expensive car. There is no end to this.

Devika: So why build?

Amritji: One keeps doing what one has to. Making a life.

Noting this relationship between being, home, life, and a livelihood made in building encourages a discussion of Heidegger's classic ruminations, "Building Dwelling Thinking," wherein he explores, among other matters, the root meaning for the word *bauen*, "to build," which in Old English or Old High German usage really means "to dwell." To build, in other words, is in itself to dwell.[57] Architectural theorist Hilde Heynen further expands these ideas, noting that "dwelling is the primary term" as a way of being "whose fundamental character consists of sparing and preserving."[58] Put simply, she argues that if we have the capacity to dwell, then we can build, and that our "building activities are integrally associated with and arise out of our capacity to dwell. In short the forms we build, whether they be material or imaginary, arise out of our immersion in the world—the very homeland of our thoughts."[59] Heidegger questions the very possibility of dwelling within our present conditions (the contemporary metropolis), positing that the manner in which we function as persons intersects with how we make ourselves at home. How we make ourselves at home is linked with space, and "many of the events and communities that shape our sense of self are connected to particular places."[60] In Heideggerian thought there is an entwined relationship between home, habit, and place—human beings live spatially, and therefore spatiality is inherent to life itself. And place, say geographers Donald Conradson and Mckay, "plays a major role in the ongoing construction of identity."[61]

Stretching these ideas, Massimo Cacciari writes, "The problem lies in the fact that spirit may no longer dwell—it has become estranged from dwelling. And that is why building cannot 'make' the Home (Dimora) 'appear.'"[62] Even as Heidegger traces the intricate relationship between home, habit, space, and dwelling, he is convinced that the modern technological-instrumentalist outlook does not lend itself to authentic dwelling and being. Instead, what we have is the "homelessness of modernity," and this would extend, indeed would be amplified, in postmodern, postcolonial, and transnational contexts.[63]

Without complicating Heidegger's position, and taking it quite literally, I return to Uncle's building activities and his success in those endeavors by simply focusing on his emphatic negation of the new life he builds as "nothing" because there is no "oneness" among people. Without "oneness" the building is seen and experienced as an empty, objective process, which forces me to pose a question to him and others, and to myself: "So you think the success is the reason that people have lost feelings for each other?" He replies simply, "Who can say that is the cause, but you know when we had nothing we used to drink tea and eat a samosa in the corner shop and take a walk after dinner, and we enjoyed ourselves, we were together." That's not something I have not heard before. My father laments this loss repeatedly; it unnerves him that his nephews and nieces do not call him even when he has been gravely unwell, as he was in 2010. "I used to go and look after my uncles and aunts, lend a hand if anyone needed help in the family," he grumbles.

This type of care was expected and unquestioned in the past. My grandmother sold every single piece of the gold she was able to bring away, on her person, from Pakistan, so that not only her own children, but nephews, nieces, and even other distant relatives could go to school, build homes, and buy much-needed materials to live. These were not loans. I tell Papa that life is different, people are more selfish. "Yes," he agrees, "those days are over."

Has the oneness been lost as a consequence of affluence, or is oneness impossible to achieve because the Partition rupture stymied any possibility for these persons to be able to dwell, to be at one with the world, or with their own being? Is it a universal condition, or the condition of the refugee? Is the nostalgia brought on by the melancholy of aging? That is, is such nostalgia the universal condition of persons from older generations (anywhere), who, quite consistently, lament the loss of community, of home, of homeliness, brought on by late industrial society's consumerist impulse, so that any sort of dwelling, as Adorno tell us, is now an impossibility?[64] Rather than allowing Uncle a place to dwell, his success leaves him longing for the "way things were" in Pakistan. He thereby joins in yet another constant refrain of my Partition participants—the desire for a simple life in which "home is being-with-other(s)" rather than a place.[65] The homes/businesses that are built are still not experienced as peaceful or stable spaces—in fact, they seem to come across as sites that reinforce loss. Are building and dwelling simply lost causes?

I find myself holding on to two negatives—no dwelling in building, no building in dwelling. I also find myself rejecting the idea of "dwelling-in-travel," so strenuously proposed in studies of migration, home, and displacement.[66] What I find persevering amid this loss is something else—drifting. Anilji stays inside (of the past) in *passages*. Arjunji *wanders* in dreams and memories (of the past). Uncle, while he does not recall home from memory, *constructs* buildings, looking for a place to call home. Each in his own way exemplifies the notion that home refers to the intersubjective relationships that bring a person, a self, and an identity into existence.[67] Each enacts a unique kind of movement. Passages. Wanderings. Constructing. Drifting. Each movement, being and becoming, its own form of nervousness. Each story similar, yet different. Stories and selves that seem to find a resting place. And then, they don't.

Home-Story Fragments

Feeling adrift and nervous in these stories, I considered whether the unplotted, nonchronological, and fragmentary nature of the storytelling was the cause of my narrative lightheadedness. Theories of autobiography offer a few explanations for why some stories remain or seem unsettled (and in turn unsettle us). The fragmented, timeless, and incoherent nature of refugee narratives has been repeatedly discussed in autobiographical work. If the oral histories are attended to as autobiographical narratives (which they rightly are in their telling), the narration in the histories unfolds in different models of narrative telling and creating. Psychologist Jens Brockmeier proposes the concept of autobiographical time, stating that different models of autobiographical time "encapsulate culturally normative views, patterns of experience and evaluation . . . [and] organize the account of a life course; which is to say, their specific function is to order complex temporal scenarios."[68]

The more straightforward models—*linear, cyclical, circular, spiral*—evoke a certain vision of the life course and the direction it has taking in time. They show life as a process, as movement forward into the future, as development. Two other models of autobiographical time that are pertinent here—the *static* and the *fragmentary*—are considered timeless because they ignore and even deny that life has a direction and a goal. They lack the developmental and operationalized trajectory of the other modes and seem to be diminished in form and content. *Static* models of telling are found in stories that revolve around a catastrophic event. When we read such stories we find an immovable picture of the self that is shaped by an all-dominating central experience or by irresolvable conflicts and contradictions, and/or, following another mantra, irresistible force. Holocaust survivors, survivors of other genocides, and survivors of extreme communal and political conflicts illustrate such a model. Stories told by such subjects often involve stagnant metaphors, such as "as if my watch stopped," "petrified," and "frozen in time." This model is easily recognizable in Anilji's words as he describes months when he lived temporarily in his mammaji's house, when "we did nothing, we just wasted time;" in Arjunji's creation of Sibbi as a timeless space/place where all was good; and in Uncle's negation of his monetary success and longing for the days when eating one samosa was pleasurable. Theirs are stories of lives that were interrupted, derailed, that are stationary owing to one event that shifted all meanings about being somewhere and being home.

The other timeless model proposed by Brockmeier, the one she terms *fragmentary*, is a form of storytelling rooted in a postmodern and postcolonial ethos whereby autobiographical accounts are "decentered," "open," and "ludic," and there is an emphasis on the unpredictable nature of life. Such life narratives rely on metaphors such as play, scenes, patchwork, fragments, and so on. What is striking about such stories, for Brockmeier, is that they tend to undermine the foundation upon which identity is located by shifting the frame of reference and exploding the relationship of individual memory to chronology of experience.[69] Visions of time (and so of experience) in these stories show a fragmentary layout and "alternative versions" of the life are told simultaneously, mingling the real, possible, imaginative, and anticipated life courses like equal story lines. Arjunji's visits to Sibbi in his dreams, his longing for his home place and then his refusal to return, place his oral history well within this form of telling. Anilji's story told as passages and pieces, all linked to that watershed event, is comfortably positioned as both static and fragmentary. Each of their declarations that their lives are now "nothing" because there is no "oneness" links their stories within these two potentially evolutionary modes of telling.

I live with the stories for a long time before I consider approaching them via these modes of narration—modes that both mirror and enact the identities of the tellers. I emphasize these two modes *here* (rather than having done so in the beginning) because my arrival into the conceptual idea of drifting is given impetus by the form of the stories—the ways in which they are told and the ways in which I listen to them, and the ways in which I represent (contain) them. After all, representation is a sort of taming, a kind of imprisonment, that brings about a degree of immovability-immobility to a subject, in words, on a page. The persons who emerge from these encounters—the persons that I produce in this text—are figures and people propelled into a physical, emotional, and narrative state of motion. They are people who, in their literal and figurative movements, become reluctant nomads—who roam because there is no choice.

Reluctant Nomads

I call these subjects *reluctant nomads* because I experience them as unmoored and wandering postcolonial subjects, refugees in exile (not exiles) who cannot find a bearing, who are coerced into movement, and live un/comfortably in a constant state of nervous mobility. It is essential to keep in mind the adjective *reluctant* before the noun *nomad*, because I am wary of conflating the movement of my participants (at least the movement that I discern) with that of the romantic figure of the nomad consistently presented to us in contemporary nomadic thought.[70]

In their "Treatise on Nomadology" in *A Thousand Plateaus*, Deleuze and Guattari describe the nomadic as subject, thought, theory, idea, as that which is unfixed, wandering, peripatetic, and drifting.[71] The nomadic are individuals, groups, and societies without a fixed abode, in a constant state of movement. Ronald Bogue notes that such descriptions of the nomadic derive from particular cultural instances. Within the literature on nomadism, there is some consensus that three categories of mobile people can be considered nomadic—pastoral nomads, hunter-gatherers, and gypsies. Outside of these categories there are vagabonds, traveling thieves, migrant workers, bicoastal executives, and "academic-Gypsies",[72] and there are *flaneurs*, who, of course, come to us via Walter Benjamin.[73]

In *Questions of Travel*, Caren Kaplan provides a succinct understanding (and critique) of the three key ideas—deterritorialization, rhizome, nomad—posited by Deleuze and Guatarri. She notes that they theorize "alternative kinds of identities and modes of dwelling that counter the fixed commodifications of capitalist relations."[74] The notion of deterritorialization appears, in Deleuze and Guatarri's collective works, as a form of radical displacement that enables the imagination to "express another potential community, to force the means of another consciousness and another sensibility."[75] The sites of displacement are explained through a reliance on various metaphors, the most critical of which is the rhizome, also ultimately likened to the nomad. Kaplan explains:

The botanical metaphor of the rootlike "rhizome" . . . enacts the subjectivities of deterritorialization: burrowing through substance, fragmenting into simultaneous sprouts, moving with a certain stealth, powerful in it dispersion. . . . [T]he rhizome destabilizes the conventions of origins and endings.[76]

Deleuze and Guattari position the rhizome as a root that is always "in the middle, between things, interbeing, *intermezzo*."[77] The rhizome "constitutes an anarchic relationship to space and subjectivity. . . . Like the rhizome, the nomadic subject symbolizes displacement and dispersion."[78] Rosi Braidotti describes the nomad as "the figuration for the kind of subject who has relinquished all idea, desire, or nostalgia for fixity" and the nomadic consciousness as "an acute awareness of the nonfixity of boundaries . . . and the desire to go on trespassing, transgressing."[79] The nomad is likened by Deleuze and Guattari to the immigrant and the gypsy who live along borders and margins—"becoming minor." However, Kaplan argues:

Becoming minor, a utopian process of letting go privileged identities and practices, requires emulating the ways and modes of modernity's "others." Yet, like all imperialist discourses, these spaces and identities are produced through their imagining; that is, the production of sites of escape or decolonization for the colonizer signals a kind of theoretical tourism. . . . Their model of deterritorialization, like most Euro-American modernist versions of exilic displacement, stresses the freedom of disconnection and the pleasures of interstitial subjectivity. Yet deterritorialization itself cannot escape colonial discourse. The movement of deterritorialization *colonizes*, appropriates, even raids other *spaces*. . . . Deterritorialization is always reterritorialization, an increase of territory, an imperialization.[80]

Theorists in the newly emerging "mobilities" paradigm also criticize this romanticizing of mobility through its association with freedom, and they criticize nomadology for associating the nomad with the ability to evade power.[81] Timothy Creswell elaborates:

The romanticization of the nomad, for instance, is infected with the discourse of Orientalism. It is also the outcome, historically, of deep-rooted ideas about mobility as a progressive force, as a form of relative freedom, as a break from earlier, more confused, space and times.[82]

Deleuze and Guatarri's conceptualizations of nomadism as a condition that stresses the "freedom of disconnection" is not dissimilar to Euro-American modernisms that celebrate "singularity, solitude, estrangement, and aestheticized excisions of location in favor of locale—that is, the 'artist in exile' is never 'at home,' always existentially alone, and shocked by the strain of displacement into significant experimentations and insights."[83] Modernist writers and critics consistently conflate exile and expatriation, thereby privileging distance as the most valuable perspective on the subject under scrutiny—achieving aesthetic gain through/in exile. The modernist "seeks to create the effect of statelessness—whether or not the writer is, literally, in exile. . . . Within this form of modernism, exilic displacement occupies a privileged position."[84]

Interest in nomadism and deterritorialization can be traced back to the "critique of colonial modes of ordering and knowing that informed most of twentieth-century human sciences. . . . Studies of migration, diasporas, and transnational citizenship offered trenchant critiques of the bounded and static categories of nation, ethnicity, community, place, and state, within much social science."[85] Mobilities theorists who focus on migration studies position the latter as having a two-pronged focus. On the one hand, work in the field of migration studies highlights (even celebrates) dislocation, displacement, disjuncture, and dialogism; on the other hand, it foregrounds "acts of 'homing' and 're-grounding' which point towards the complex interrelation between travel and dwelling, home and not-home."[86] Yet another tension over the conceptualization of the nomadic is that the "extreme version of the nomadic turn and the celebration of cosmopolitanism have emphasized almost effortless flux at the expense of exactly how people move."[87] How, why, and where people move is a subject of much discussion in the politics of mobility. Peter Adey proposes two main ideas that undergird the politics of mobility:

> First, that movement is differentiated—that there is a politics to these differentials. In other words, that power is enacted in very different ways. And second, that it is related in very different ways, it means different things, to different people, in differing social circumstances.[88]

Very often *movement*, Nick Gill, Javier Caletrío, and Victoria Mason tell us, "is imposed upon populations that long for stillness."[89] And while constant movement and uncertainty about the future are shared experiences between nomads and forced migrants, for the "refugee and sans papier this is no cause for celebration due to their reluctance to being subjected to these conditions."[90] For some displaced subjects, geographic and cultural stability can be highly coveted. Joining in the critiques of the privileged position accorded to the nomadic, Ahmed says:

> But the subject who has chosen to be homeless, rather than homeless due to the contingency of 'external' circumstance, is certainly a subject who is privileged, and someone for whom having or not having a home does not affect their ability to occupy a given space.[91]

It follows, then, that exile becomes aesthetic gain, and is "completely dehistoricized." Kaplan summarizes: "Normalizing exile, aestheticizing homelessness, the critical mythologization of the 'artist in exile' moves from a commentary on cultural production based on historically grounded experiences of displacement to the production of a *style* that emulates exile's efforts"; and this positive valuation of exile "privileges distance and separation as aesthetic benefits even while simultaneously deploring any political or psychological crises that such conditions might engender."[92]

The "rhetorical conflation" of exiles, expatriates, nomads, travelers, refugees, and tourists in the creation of global cosmopolitanism/s continues to be viewed with skepticism as a dehistoricizing trend in Euro-American modernist writing—a trend that, some argue, includes the conceptual propositions of such postcolonial critics as Edward Said and Homi Bhabha. In his classic essay "Reflections on Exile," following Adorno, Said notes:

> The exile knows that in a secular and contingent world, homes are always provisional. Borders and barriers, which enclose us within the safety of familiar territory, can also become prisons, and are often defended beyond reason or necessity. Exiles cross borders, break barriers of thought and experience.[93]

Said invokes images of refugees for inspiration, thereby linking the solitary/lone exile to a large-scale global experience of displacement. He further names our contemporary era "the age of the refugee, the displaced person, mass immigration."[94] Despite this, Said returns again and again to the mythologized solitary exile of modernist writing, so that in his work the concept of exile "oscillates between the privileged literary reflections of the middle class and the complicated, unexpressed experience of large-scale displacement."[95] Anita Goldman, while not directly referencing Said, reinforces these criticisms of current literary discussions of exile, saying "there has been a rather misleading tendency to use the term metaphorically, so that the experience of exile has come to mean, more broadly, the experience of difference and estrangement in society, and most broadly, an aspect of what is human in us all."[96] Peter van der Veer in "Cosmopolitan Options" levels a resonating complaint at Homi Bhabha's position about the hybrid identities held by postcolonial subjects:

> Homi Bhabha is especially quite exuberant in his description of the possibilities of migrant populations, of subjects "formed-in-between." . . . [His] claim that one can bring newness into the world, that one can reinvent the self when one is writing literature from the cultural interstices, is a conceit of the literature-producing and consuming world.[97]

For some mobility theorists, the in-between place (intersitices) can also be a 'non-place' "of the context of transit where the connections between humans are homogenized and stripped of specificity."[98] Mobility as immobility. Movement as stagnation.

These criticisms notwithstanding, even though the pull of the exile of Euro-American modernity is powerful in his own work, Said provides a key distinction between refugees and exiles, a distinction I find important vis-à-vis the three stories in motion here:

> Refugees . . . are a creation of the twentieth-century state. The word 'refugee' has become a political one, suggesting large hoards of innocent and bewildered people requiring urgent international assistance, whereas 'exile' carries with it, I think, a touch of solitude and spirituality.[99]

Said implies that refugees are undocumentable; they are quite often people without papers, people who must fabricate papers to confirm their origins, people who need to consistently prove their lineage. I am reminded of Anilji's search for his birth certificate, his desire to place himself into an identity through a document. That moment, meant just for me, performed before me, is a reminder that the refugee is forever sensitive over matters of origin. Origins are also about tangible material realities of life for the refugee. I think back also to Kiranji's efforts to secure proof of her departure from Pakistan so she can get compensated in cash for the property left behind. I return to

Arjunji's faking a medical condition and a medical certificate to get discharged from the army, a job he falls into because as a refugee there is nowhere else for him to work.

Papers constantly place us—between here and there, home and away, or the spaces in between. They are always hierarchical, always settling us somewhere, into something, always working for someone, through something. We look to them to prove who we are. Of this need to claim lineage and origins—for ourselves and for the sake of others—the Polish-American writer Eva Hoffman writes, "lineage gives a solidity, a depth that . . . newly minted success cannot bestow; it implies a moral uprightness and the dignity of not having to prove yourself, of being somebody to begin with."[100] The self, the home, and origins *must* rely on each other.

The exile "by choice"—such as the bicoastal professional who moves and lives across a continent, or the writer who wants to write from the space of "statelessness," or the artist whose imagination is fed by the intermezzo, or the anthropologist who is disciplined to go "away" to "other" places, or this ethnographer who leaves home on an intellectual whim—has a different, and unequal, displacement in comparison to the refugee. *Displacement*, Clifford, rightly notes, is a slippery word; "I hang on to 'travel' as a term of cultural comparison precisely because of its historical taintedness, its associations with gendered, racial bodies, class privilege, specific means of conveyance, beaten paths, agents, frontiers, documents . . . I prefer it to the more apparently neutral, and 'theoretical,' terms, such as 'displacement,' which makes the drawing of equivalences across different historical experiences too easy."[101] Displacement, far from being a one-off event—as these stories illustrate—is a process that lasts for years, decades, maybe generations, or a lifetime.

Those displaced owing to economic factors and/or made homeless/stateless via political displacement—conditions that describe the subjects of this oral history work—experience an exile that is, in Said's words, "the unhealable rift forced between a human being and a native place, between the self and its true home: its essential sadness can never be surmounted"; and as he further remarks, "The achievements of exile are permanently undermined by the loss of something left behind forever."[102] The three refugees whose stories I have told in this chapter have had no choice, as I see it, but to make home in drifting. Yet to even say that they "make home" is an interpretive stretch, because I don't sense any of them feeling-at-home as subjects who dwell-in-travel. If we believe that our sense of home and self are deeply entwined, then these selves, here, remain fragmentary, static, and unsettled— immobile in their mobilities.

And even though it is romantic, popular, and trendy to talk about the unstable, the unreliable, and the dynamic self negotiated in everyday experience, here I find no evidence that such "scattered subjectivities" are either welcome or desired. They just are. John Noyes reaffirms this belief, explaining, "It is a miserable plight to be a postmodern nomad, to be homeless, wandering, a refugee, following not a dream of disembodied bliss but a slim hope for survival. . . . [T]he nomadic subject is both the failure of the global order and the fundamental structure of subjectivity upon which this order can build."[103] Gill, Caletrío, and Mason further pronounce, "The message from forced migrants to those who romanticize mobility may very well be one of caution: there is as much un-freedom in mobility as there is in fixity."[104]

The irony is palpable: Partition was the outcome of India's liberation from British rule. It created a citizenry free of colonial rule, but here in these stories, these three reluctant nomads, the free citizens of newly independent India, remain imprisoned in homely mobilities. They suffer from, to offer a literary and anthropological diagnosis, what Eva Hoffman calls *tesknota*, the Polish word for nostalgia, which includes within it tonalities of longing and sadness. The root of the word *nostalgia* is Greek—*nostos* means homeward journey, and *algos* means pain or sorrow. This kind of nostalgia (here) is not romantic. It is not something to celebrate. Like a phantom limb, it hovers, it persists, and it resists erasure.

The experiences of these men could not be more disparate from that of the romantic figure of the exile, the nomad, the traveler, the expatriate of Euro-American thought (also bourgeois, white, male, First World)—a person who has historically found aesthetic gain in being and living in the interstices, in motion. These men's stories find home on the margins of the exile of contemporary thought. They prompt questions such as the following: What kind of self and what kind of home is available or accessible for displaced persons who are outside the romanticized narratives of the exile as a solitary, creative, and appealing intellectual figure of modern thought? When movement and exile cannot be fetishized, how do the subjects of these experiences continue to be home? Are they destined to wander like the men whose stories we have experienced? When movement is forced, then what recourse does the forced traveler have to find roots, seek home, and fashion a self? What happens to us when exile is real, tangible, material, as well as existential? Ultimately, until and unless the displacement is ours, home-in-movement, or drifting, can only be read-in-text as a conceptual idea.

Nervousness is felt. Movement is experienced. Both are hard to pin down. Drifting may be home. But not for everyone.

Hearth Crossings

I walk down the stairs from my study on the second level of my house in Ohio and step into the living room. I pause, as I often do, in front of the painting *Mataji* and wonder who she is, where she is from, and what she is thinking. Does she miss her home in Pakistan? Is she reminiscing or is she in mourning? In my mind, Biji and Mataji have become one person. Not an entirely implausible morphing, because Mataji is certainly a composite visual representation of an older-generation female Partition refugee. She is the grandmother I knew as a child. She is the sum of many of the grandmothers of my generation. Her melancholy echoes a sort of national nostalgia for the past that was. At the same time, one does not know and is not told whether she is a Partition widow or whether she is an abandoned and abducted woman who is living in an ashram because she has nowhere else to go. It is just easier to assume that Mataji shares parallels to my Biji. It is plausible, however, that she was one among many unlucky women who were used as weapons, targets, and instruments of war in the communal riots that coincided with Partition.

The gendered history of Partition, typical of the gendered histories of most communal conflicts, is violent—women from either community were used as targets of torture, rape, and abductions. Children were sometimes taken from parents or were brutally murdered in mob attacks. In their feminist historiography *Borders and Boundaries: Women in India's Partition*, Menon and Bhasin point out that "[t]he most predictable form of violence experienced by women, as women, is when the women of one community are assaulted by the men of the other, in an overt assertion of their identity and a simultaneous humiliation of the Other by 'dishonoring' their women."[1] They provide a comprehensive analysis, via oral histories and archival research, of the plight of women who were violated not only by men from opposing communities, but who also suffered violence at the hands of their own families. Abducted women were either forcibly married to men from opposing communities or abandoned after being raped. In either case, their natal families often refused to take them back, since the women were considered sullied, impure—bodies that had brought dishonor to the family. A vast body of literature (which I will not summon here) on women, honor, and shame has arisen from violent conflicts across the globe. A large part of the work of repatriation of women after Partition involved returning women to their natal families (if they would take them) or rehabilitating them. Many hundreds languished in ashrams and died there, hoping to be invited back home to their natal or marital families. Some refused to return to families who wanted them back because they were too ashamed.

But another kind of violence was internal and occurred within the family itself. Hindu and Sikh women were encouraged by their own families to commit suicide rather than be carried away by Muslim mobs. Menon and Bhasin provide a more detailed explanation of this phenomenon, one that is common in fictional, nonfictional, and academic accounts of the event:

> Very large numbers of women were forced into death to avoid sexual violence against them, to preserve chastity and protect individual, family and community "honour." The means to accomplish this end varied; when women themselves took their lives, they would either jump into the nearest well or set themselves ablaze, singly, or in groups that could be made up either of all the women in the family; the younger women; or women and children. . . . So powerful and general was the belief that safeguarding a woman's honour was *essential* to upholding male and community honour that a whole new order of violence

came into play, by men against their own kinswomen; and by women against their daughters and sisters and their own selves.[2]

Several government-run programs and commissions in both India and Pakistan continued their attempts, until the 1950s, to return these women to their families, or, if the families would not have them, to rehabilitate them in ashrams that sprang up all over North India. While these are estimates, between seventy-five thousand and one hundred thousand women were abducted during Partition.[3] For these abducted and raped women, home and family were often the first betrayers of their identities, their selfhood, and their bodied being in the world and home. The larger betrayal, however, was that they were sacrificed in the name of both religion and nationality by what Butalia refers to as "patriarchal consensus," arrived at "by the men and elders of the community."[4] This consensus is embodied well in the words of a first-generation participant, eighty-year-old Poonamji:

> People were killing their daughters by poisoning them or giving them *pudias* [sachets] of poison, so that they would eat them if they were getting molested, kidnapped, or raped. The whole point was—don't go into the hands of the Muslims. Entire trains were being massacred, and if you got caught you were told that as a girl you were better off killing yourself.

I continue to hold romantic notions about Mataji's life and identity, feelings helped along by the artists' own inscription under the painting, which reads, "She sits knitting in the sun, dreaming of Lahore in the days before Partition." But I have to constantly remind myself that this picture reflects a mere fraction of the experiences of those women who could not be saved, who were forced to live out their lives as converts to Hinduism or Islam with abductee families, or who lived essentially homeless lives because their natal or marital families disallowed their return into the familial fold.

Because when I look at my oral history record and review and re-read and re-listen to the stories of women from the older generation, I find that an/other story about home seems to be emerging. Home is omniscient, home is spoken, and home shapes the stories, yet it is remembered in ways that are quite disparate from how their male counterparts sketch home in memory. While this is not an unusual induction because we know that home is a gendered space[5] experienced in multiple and unequal ways, it still surprises me. I have assumed that since all refugees lost home, they miss it. I have unconsciously dismissed another alternative. It is not so much that these women—the five who speak from these pages—don't miss home, it is the manner in which they dismiss it that lays claim on my imagination. I find in their stories the unfamiliar, the unknown, and the unapproachable homes. Their stories show me, what Bilinda Straight cautions, "the *heaviness of home* for women who must consider many or all of its exclusionary structures."[6]

Home is always there—always missed. Home is (also) always (not) there—often dismissed.

Women Remembering (Which) Homes?

This question is prompted by my contemplation of *Mataji*. It is a question that I must ask even of myself. *Which* homes do *women* remember? *Which* home will *I* remember? And more importantly, which homes are they—which homes are we—*allowed* to remember? Do women remember the homes that give birth to them, their natal homes? And if they remember natal homes, is it the maternal or the paternal construction of home that they hold on to? Or do they simply remember the homes that they make with the families they marry into and/or the families they create? I have not felt it necessary to put memories under such an examination where my male participants are concerned. Why this need, I ask myself, to interrogate the roots of these memories?

A small sociological explanation seems like a good place to start. In spite of urbanization and India's accelerated entry into the global economy, familial structures remain unshaken in the bulk of rural and urban India. Most Hindu women in India share one crucial displacement. As is the case for most of us, Indian women's first homes are their natal homes, the homes of their parents. In the context of the subcontinent, this first home can quite often be a home that is shared with the extended paternal family, or what is known as a *joint family*.[7] After marriage—be this an arranged marriage or a love marriage[8]—a woman leaves her natal family to live with her in-law family. And while these practices are shifting in urban India, the understanding that a daughter will leave her natal home to make a home with her husband's family is still the norm. A married daughter who makes a home with her parents in their home is still considered an anomaly, something of an oddity.

When Asha, Labbi Devi's daughter, tells me that her (married) daughter and son-in-law live in a nested flat in the natal home, I am a little surprised. I know that Asha does not have a son, so I wonder whether the situation would be different had she a son, who would be encouraged to stay on in the home after marriage.

There is an old saying in North India, among Hindus, that daughters are *paraya dhan* (another's treasure, or temporary guests) in the homes of their parents, because ultimately they are expected to marry and make a home elsewhere with another family. Sons, on other hand, are expected and gently encouraged to continue living in the natal home. These everyday practices are tied to caste, descent, and inheritance laws among Hindus. As recently as 1956, Hindu women did not have right to natal or marital property,[9] and were to be cared for by their fathers, brothers, and husbands.[10] The male child was—is—given preference because one needed to beget sons who would light one's funeral pyre, an activity that ensured men a place in heaven, rebirth in the next life as a human being, and the liberation of future generations of the family (what is known as *moksha*). The need for a male heir was, moreover, an economic necessity—he was needed because he alone could continue the family line and inherit ancestral property. Women, under these conditions, were necessary tools to beget a male heir. For these reasons, the Hindu marriage has been discussed as an arrangement that is "male-emphasized,"[11] and, in fact, the word for *wife* in Sanskrit—*grahastha*—literally means "household."

Despite shifts in inheritance laws, inequalities endure. For instance, in my own life-history work in 2003–04 with urban Hindu women in arranged marriages, many of my participants defined marriage as "a chore," thereby echoing the historical and structural continuity of their roles, even though these women, who ranged from professionals to homemakers, had been married fairly recently, between the early 1980s and 2003.[12] This way of defining marriage, what I considered a thematic in those life histories, echoes feminist critiques of home as a patriarchal space that is produced by women, maintained by women, but ultimately claimed by men as a place they are allowed to romanticize, own, and desire. Joshua M. Price's critique of the patriarchal conception of home in Gaston Bachelard's *The Poetics of Space* is worth mentioning here. Using Bachelard's ideas about home as "an example of a proponent of a romanticized, idealized view of home," Price scrutinizes home as a place of danger and terror:

The assumption that the home is safe not only obscures violence. It also obscures the labor that produces the home. Indeed, the labor that produces the peaceful home is often produced under the threat of violence.[13]

He argues that the home as a site of safety and security, produced by the painstaking labor (of women), becomes an ideological given. The victimization of the very women who help produce this home can go unnoticed because violence—physical or symbolic—is not something we normatively associate with the ideal home. He notes "violence against women is abetted, enabled, by the normative ideal."[14] And cases of intrafamilial violence whereby women were encouraged by "patriarchal consensus" to kill themselves can certainly be considered in light of Price's argument. Even though he is interrogating battered women vis-à-vis the traditional constructions of home within North America, Price establishes an idea that requires constant reinforcement—that spaces are generated intersubjectively:

> The position one holds is not solitary or still; it refers to one's activity, one's practices. People are involved in a multitude of practices in a particular place. Hence, one always finds multiple constructions of what the ambiance is within any given physical locale. . . . [H]ow one understands the space one is in, whether it be a space of solace or despair, a space of dreamy pleasure or back-breaking work, depends a lot on who you are, what you do, on whom you are focused.[15]

A site that represents security for men can be experienced as a space of vulnerability by women—an idea consistently reinforced in postcolonial and feminist theorizing and writing about home. Edward Said's notable critique of Bachelard's imaginary and romantic construction of home also problematizes the latter's home spaces as fantastic, more fanciful than lived; Said notes, "There is no use in pretending that all we know about time and space, or rather history and geography, is more than anything else imaginative."[16] Such contemplations echo what has long been discussed among contemporary anthropologists as the "colonial imaginary" that has produced home and field as distinct spaces.

Feminist critics of the home-as-haven idea, such as Julia Wardhaugh and Doreen Massey, among others, have long argued that such an ideology leads to "the creation of homelessness," because those who feel imprisoned, Other, and violated at home feel "homeless at home."[17] Roberta Rubenstein, in her work *Home Matters*, contrasts the received romanticized version of home with how women typically see the home, as a space shaped by the reality of both domestic obligations and confinement.[18] And Ahmed, Castaneda, Fortier, and Sheller note that "much work goes into the making of homes, national and otherwise, and the labour of reproducing them is often designated as 'women's work.' . . . [H]ow women negotiate such genderings of space and labour become part of the story of home and migration."[19] About the domestic, Price notes:

> Domesticity—domus—domain: three cognates that bring one from home to that place of man's dominion. . . . Home promises individual freedom and home is a place of objectified labor braced by authoritative language. Both capture the way in which the ideology of home slides between a description of domesticity as safe, a place of repose, a place where things are at hand for use and disposal, and a prescription that that is how one's home ought to be.[20]

David Sibley reasserts such ideas, calling home a space of "unavoidable tensions surrounding the use of domestic spaces" and domestic practices—domesticity itself, a paradox.[21] And for some women safety, security, comfort, and refuge can be found beyond the reaches of home or "outside" home, [22] as we see in Kiranji's story.

To return to my sociological explanation: Among Hindus, a bride traditionally entered her marital home and life of domesticity aware of the role and duties expected of her. She knew that as a daughter-in-law in a joint or semi-joint family, she would be given an overall subordinate status compared to the men, who were the caretakers of the family. In a typical joint family, formal authority was centered on the oldest male and thereby hierarchically bound by age. Hierarchy was discernable on many levels, with women invariably at the bottom. When a woman married, she would be entering a family in which all the men were related by blood, making wives automatic outsiders, strangers, instant Others. In "Six Ways of Being a Stranger," Lindsay Bremner writes that "a person becomes a stranger when s/he is out of place." In this situation of a joint family, women were literally and figuratively out of place, strangers in their own families. Their status would only rise if they gave birth to a son. If a woman was unable to produce a male child, a second wife could be brought in (the status of wives was given a boost, at least theoretically, with the passing of the Hindu Divorce

Bill in 1952, which gave women some privileges if their husbands chose to marry again).[23] Even so, the preference for male children prevails, as evidenced by steadily increasing rates of female foeticide and female infanticide across India.[24] The first-generation women in this oral history record, many of whom were already married in 1947, were submerged in such types of living arrangements.

Memories (of) Patriarchy

My own memories of home and domesticity are structured by patriarchy. They are, first and foremost, memories of life in my paternal family, because my mother made the crucial displacement and entered a joint family upon her marriage. Not much was spoken (or remembered) about my maternal grandparents and their life. We met them, customarily, once a year, and still do.

As an adult with an interest in family history, I began, unconsciously, gathering fragments of memories from various maternal family members and began to uncover that the mobilities, displacements, and travels of my maternal grandmother's family, Nani's family, were, in fact, quite significant. Nani's natal family, the Sonis, were Punjabi merchants in Mandalay and Rangoon in Burma (now Myanmar) for many generations. I have no specifics, only that this is Nani's father's family history. In 1942, during the Second World War when the Japanese invaded Burma, the entire family stowed away on a large merchant ship and reached India. The facts I have are hazy, because the story has not been repeated to me very often; they either arrived in Calcutta or Orissa, whence they went to join family in the province of Punjab (after Partition, Punjab was divided into two states, one on each side of the India-Pakistan border). In 1947 when Partition occurred, the Sonis were displaced once more and had to relocate as refugees to the Indian part of Punjab, and from there they came to Delhi.

When I ask Nani, who is now eighty-seven, to give me details about these forced movements, she cannot recall them in any depth, but she remembers stowing away on the ship. When I ask her last surviving sibling, a brother, he tells me he remembers Punjab only after Partition. What we know is this:

Nani's father was a wealthy Hindu merchant in Rangoon; Nani spoke Burmese with her siblings; my mother, Amma, tells me that Nani spoke Burmese with Nana, my maternal grandfather, whose family also lived in Burma around the same time; and Nani and Nana were married in what is now Pakistan. Amma too is vague about the histories of both sides of her natal family, yet she knows, almost by rote, her husband's—my father's—family history, the one that she "inherited" from his mother, from Biji. Her own "home" history has been twice suppressed—first by Nani's displacement to another home through marriage at the age of seventeen, and then by Amma's own marital displacement at the age of twenty-two. That history has been subject to a cycle of suppression that is, I believe, a common and inadvertent occurrence (even though patriarchy, overall, is hardly inadvertent). Of course I cannot deny that it was also Amma's fondness for her mother-in-law, Biji, which inspired her interest in the Chawla family story. "I was so young when I married, Biji taught me everything as an adult," Amma often says. I remember many long summer afternoons when Amma and Biji would sit at the dining table with their Urdu tutor and recite the Urdu alphabet. Biji had evinced an interest in relearning Urdu sometime in the early 1980s (she'd forgotten the alphabet), and Amma enthusiastically joined in the endeavor. Amma does not, however, know any Burmese, though her parents spoke it in her childhood home.

Still, I feel more distant from my maternal family story than from my paternal family story, even though the migrations in the Soni family—both forced and unforced—are almost panoramic. It is as if this history has no choice but to stay silent.

Segue: Filling in a Blank

May 3, 2008. A four-hour car ride through soaked rice fields in the northern mountainous region of Chiang Rai, Thailand, gets us to Mae Sai—a small congested Thai town that borders the town of Tachileik in Myanmar (Burma). It has rained all morning and the flora is a sharp, robust green. In my last month in Bangkok, at the end of April, I find myself desperately arranging this trip with my spouse, Anirudh; something is compelling me to travel to the Thai-Myanmar border before I leave. This is the first time

I have been so close to this country that was home for generations to one side of my family.

We have requested that our hotel in Chiang Mai arrange a tour guide for us, since we are driving through rural areas where English speakers are scarce. Pim, a licensed travel agent, accompanies us to Chiang Rai, the Golden Triangle, and some ancient Thai archaeological sites along the route. Our final destination is the border town of Mae Sai. We skip a tour of the main town because we are interested in the human traffic around the large military-guarded gates that separate the two countries. A congested bazaar, not unlike Indian markets, lines the entry to Myanmar. A series of gates separate the two countries. The market is packed with cross-border street vendors selling all manner of goods. A feeling of impermanence looms over the space. As in most parts of Thailand, people here seem friendly, but there is an edge, a tension, a slight strain to the smiles. Borders as liminal spaces can be taut with uneasiness. Not dangerous, just nervous.

Pim asks us if we want to cross over to Myanmar. "You will get a day pass, you can stay for thirty minutes," she says. Anirudh and I know this and have discussed it beforehand. I shake my head and tell her that I am an Indian passport holder, so I do not have permission to enter. I am on a non-immigrant, temporary work visa in Thailand (since I have been teaching here for a semester) and I am the holder of an American green card. Even though I could have applied for a Myanmar visa in Bangkok, I chose not to. I felt that too many explanations would be needed at this small border, here in Mae Sai, to explain my status. My spouse, a naturalized U.S. citizen, with the more preferred passport, or at least one that is accorded more prestige, tells Pim that he will go. We decide to meet in the only coffee shop in the market, just two hundred feet from the border gates.

I walk past cajoling vendors and head to a side *soi* (street) where I see young girls selling jewelry and traditional Burmese coral-colored papier-mâché boxes. As I am browsing the street carts, I hear a polite *namaste* being called out. Not expecting to hear Hindi here, I turn around and see a young Thai-, Burmese-, and Indian-looking teenage girl smiling at me. With fair skin and grey-green eyes, she shares an eerie resemblance to some of my mother's maternal cousins. There is (as I find) no connection, there cannot really be. I walk toward her and ask in Hindi, *"Aap Indian ho?"* (Are you Indian?). Yes, she says. Where from? "Just the town across the border," she tells me. "How long have you lived in Burma?" I ask. "Myanmar," she smilingly corrects me, "We are from here." Her name, Deepa, is a Hindu-Indian name. She is eighteen years old and she crosses the border into Thailand with her wares at 8:oo A.M. every morning because "there is no business in Myanmar," and she returns home to Myanmar by 5:oo in the evening. I tell her about my Nani, that she is from Rangoon, and that we were Punjabis from Rangoon. "There are many Indians here still," Deepa says. She asks me about life in India, and I haltingly inform her that I am Indian, but I live in America. I can feel a gap opening after she processes this information. But we keep talking. "Why are you alone here?" she asks, just as my female Indian aunts, cousins, and friends would. "No, no, my husband, Anirudh, is here, he has gone for a walk around Tachileik," I tell her. "Anirudh is a Burmese name," she informs me. "I know, I know, he was one of the great Burmese kings, was he not?" I ask. She nods. "Yes, but his family has no connection to Myanmar," I laugh.

I buy many papier-mâché boxes from Deepa along with other trinkets that I do not need. When it is time to go, I hug Deepa, we fold our hands in a *namaste*. I tell her, *"Bahut Accha lagaa aapko mil kar, mai apni Nani ko apke bare mein bataoungee"* (I feel so good having met you, I will tell my Nani about you), and I am almost teary-eyed as I say this. I saunter into the Good-Luck Café, where Pim, Anirudh, and I are to meet before we make the drive back to Chiang Mai. I order an Americano and just like that, I have switched to another world in this already border-crossed zone. I could be in any cozy local coffee shop in any small college town in America. Stan Getz's "The Girl from Ipanema" filters in through an ancient cassette player resting on a rickety wooden side table.

Ten minutes later, Pim and Anirudh walk in, looking sweaty and tired. "That was quick, I didn't get a text message," I chide my spouse. "They kept my passport and phone until I crossed back," he replies, rolling his eyes. "Wow, I thought they stamped the day pass on your passport," I quiz. "They do, but they keep the passport," he replies. He says it was an anxious forty-five minutes, "You don't really know what they are going to do, and they have your papers." It is as congested as the Thai side, but the Junta soldiers are a strong presence. There is no visible security on the Thai side save some guards at the gates. "I did not even take out my camera from its case, I thought it might be best," Anirudh laughs.

In a few weeks, I am in Delhi making my customary yearly visit to Nani's house. I present her with two small papier-mâché boxes from Mae Sai and tell her about Anirudh's walk in Tachileik. I tell her about Deepa and how much she looked like some of our cousins. Nani nods and says, "The Punjabis from Burma, we all were more fair-skinned and light-eyed." I don't really know what that means, but I suspect she says it with some pride, because fair-skinned girls are prized among Punjabi families. She does not know where Tachileik is, but she is thrilled with the stories. When we are leaving, she takes out a mother-of-pearl plate and gives it to Amma, who is with me. "You always wanted this plate, did you not?" she asks Amma. Yes, Amma eagerly nods. "Well, here it is," says Nani. The plate is now on display in Amma's living room in Delhi. This is hardly any kind of serious material genealogy, but it is the closest we can get to one, for now.

I have not returned to this border for four years. In 2011, the military leaders of Myanmar institute reforms and announce elections. The opposition leader, Daw Aung Sun Suu Kyi—who went to the same college in Delhi as Amma, around the same years—is released from a two-decade-long house arrest. Her party wins substantial seats in the parliament. Times are changing. I am hopeful. I am now a naturalized U.S. citizen; this border will be more permeable. I will make the crossing again one of these years.

Where Did Home Go?

So, I ask again, *which* homes do women remember? Which homes *can* we remember? What are the memories of those days in Lahore, for Mataji, in the painting? What are the memories of my Nani, memories she rarely shares with us? For we know that even the memories we inherit come to us via structures over which we have no control. How can we keep history and memory close to us, within our folds, also to be inherited, to be passed down, dispersed equally?

These dilemmas are, of course, not new. For many decades now, feminist historians have reminded us that "hardly ever, and hardly anywhere, have women 'written history.'"[25] Anthropologists consistently observe "how the expression of women's unique experiences as women is often muted, particularly in any situation where women's interests and experiences are at variance with those of men."[26] Urvashi Butalia tells us that she learned to recognize that there was a gendered telling of the Partition by the way in which women located, "almost immediately, this major event in the minor key of their lives . . . from the women I learned the minutiae of their lives."[27] Kathryn Anderson and Dana Jack note that

> [a] woman's discussion of her life may combine two separate, often conflicting, perspectives: one framed in concepts and values that reflect men's dominant position in the culture, and one informed by the more immediate realities of a woman's personal experience. . . . To hear women's perspectives accurately, we have to learn to listen in stereo, receiving both the dominant and muted channels clearly, and tuning into them carefully to understand the relationship between them.[28]

This space too is a continued quest to listen, to look, to feel, to see, and to sense in stereo [29]—to take in the anecdotes, the dismissed incidents, the sideways conversations, the feelings, the activities, the said and the unsaid, the corners, the crevices, and the vestiges; because often, rather than a thought or an idea, home is a doing and a feeling.[30]

I don't immediately begin to notice that there is something un/familiarly missing in the women's stories. It is only after I have interviewed enough male and female family members that I start to discern an absence in the women's stories, something that I noted in Kiranji's narration of her life in Rawalpindi—"absence/presence, it's there, but not there." I cannot say that absences in *all* the women's stories share similar motivations or that they are equal, because in Kiranji's case, I posit that the life she builds outside home—in school—is how she folds in the intricacies of the lost place, how she memorializes the paternal home.

But here, in *these* absences, home is spoken as places, traces, as objects, as escapes, as scenes, as Other relationships—of strangeness, of un/home. I tell it here like a montage of active memories.

Absences

RESTRICTIONS

Eighty-year-old Poonamji[31] is Anilji's sister. Our families have known each other for years—Biji and her mother were friends. As an adult, I am meeting her and her husband for the first time. When we ring the bell, through their wire mesh front door we can see that they are searching for something under tables, sofas, and a dresser in the central covered courtyard of their small one-story home in Patel Nagar. She unlocks the front door and laughingly informs us that they spend most mornings like this, searching for things they misplaced the day before. Looking at each other fondly, they tell us, "We are old, you see, this keeps us busy, we are never bored, always searching for lost things." Memory is, in some ways, a search for what has been lost, a search to find something, isn't it? This moment seems apt, destined. As if it has been awaiting my arrival.

Houses such as theirs are typical post-Partition homes, wherein the bedrooms, kitchen, living area, and bathrooms are built around a covered or open-air courtyard. My childhood home in Rajouri Garden, which I only remember from pictures and faint images, was a larger replica of this house. We sit awhile talking. Papa shares news of common friends and acquaintances; he is seeing them after five years.

I look around me and realize that I must interview Poonamji in her bedroom because it is the only private space where it seems unlikely that her husband will interrupt us. Papa shoos me into the room and closes the door, saying, "I will talk to Bhapaji [Uncle], you go in, and start." Poonamji nervously asks, "We can call them in here, can't we? He [her husband] was also born in Pakistan." "No Aunty," I tell her, "I want to just talk to you because I am following your side of the family, for now." After five minutes, she settles into the moment. She seems like a very subdued person, a woman who has spent most of her life inside the home, keeping her husband and family comfortable. As our conversation continues, I find her more honest, more forthcoming, more reflective than I have expected. She replies simply when I ask her to tell me about life in Pakistan, her home, and her school.

> *Poonamji*: There were a lot of restrictions on our lives, especially for us girls. My grandfather used to allow us to go to the verandah, but he used to tell us to sit down. He did not like girls to stand outside just like that. So even for school, we used to go to school and we used to come back, we were not allowed to go anywhere else in between. One day I went to a political meeting of the Janta Party—they used to be called *Shakas*—and I went with my friends and was late in coming home; I was yelled at even by my older brother.

Devika: Did you go to many Shakas?

Poonamji: No, *beta* [child], just that one. It was something to do.

Devika: How was your home?

Poonamji: The house? *Beta*, for those days it was a nice house, for that time it was a good house.

Devika: What was it like?

Poonamji: It was a good house.

Devika: Your school, do you remember it?

I am prodding because her brother, Anilji, has given me vivid descriptions of home in his two "passages" between Pakistan and India.

Poonamji: No. Now it is boring. It has been so many years. Now I do not have the energy and I don't even know how I spoke with you so long. It is finished. What can one gain from remembering these things? That time is over and this time will also be over. I don't even remember how we came here and stayed in this house. All I remember is that this is now my home.

Poonamji's daughter, Anisha—whom I meet for a very brief time because she is willing to give me and Papa only an hour one afternoon—echoes, eerily and also naturally, her mother's sentiments about home, both here and there:

Anisha: Yes, we have heard all the stories about our life in Pakistan, but this is our life now, this is my house, I have a son and a husband and this is where we live. What is the point in remembering those times? Life was different. This is what it is now. You talked to my mother, even she is not so interested in all that.

A house restricts, as much as it protects. A house imprisons, as much as it encloses. A house just is. So why remember home?

TRACES

Mrs. Chopra is Amritji's older sister, older by almost by thirteen years. She is the only female participant who never gives me her first name, and asks me to address her as Mrs. Chopra. I cannot see her alone. Her husband, a retired air force officer, is always present and holds forth in her reminiscences. In fact, all our conversations get filtered through his-story. Even memories of Mrs. Chopra's home are recited by him.

Mrs. Chopra: My father's house? We had a big gate? Did we not? [She asks her husband]

Devika: This was your childhood house before you married? You don't remember it?

Mrs. Chopra: Yes. There was a big gate and all the houses were inside the gate. There were ten, fifteen houses inside and the Muslims lived across from us.

Mr. Chopra: Her father was a contractor. Mainly he had furniture shops and furniture. We have that bed still here—one there and one in that room. That bed has traveled all over India, because wherever I went, I took them.

A sprightly eighty-three-year-old, Mrs. Chopra springs up from the king-sized bed where we are all seated, takes my hand, walks me through the house to show me some furniture, and confides, "See this table and this cupboard, and this bed, they are so old, they're from Lahore, but my daughters—and none of them have even been to Pakistan, they were all born here—they won't let me throw these away." She laughs, "These are so old, I don't know why they like them."

Devika: You don't?

Mrs. Chopra: They are old. I don't know why they want to keep them. My daughters don't even live in India. They don't even have Indian passports anymore. Only one of them does, and she says she is the "real" Indian in the family [laughs]. They want to keep these things. So I have them.

Home, objects of home, almost set aside. Home—almost un/remembered.

HOUSE

Sarlaji, Anilji and Poonamji's paternal aunt, agrees to meet Papa and me on a rainy monsoon afternoon in July. A widow for many years, she lives in a very small ground-level flat in a former refugee colony in West Delhi. The bedroom is the only air-conditioned room in the house, and she insists we retreat there. I begin as I usually do, with asking about life there before the Partition.

Devika: What was family life like in Pakistan?

Sarlaji: What life?

It is only the beginning, and I pause for what seems like a long time, wondering what she means by this question in response to my question. I linger over the question, afraid to commit interpretive excess there and then (and here and now), yet too surprised to let it go. In living with her oral history for years, I continue to wonder what is behind "What life?" Was that life [in Pakistan] not her own? Is it that she feels no agency in this life? Is it that she rejects the way she has to live this life? Who owns this life that she is living? I mull over all these thoughts, but there in that ethnographic moment, I simply ask, "What was life like there?"

Sarlaji: What do you want to know?

Devika: The house? The home? The school? Do you remember your home?

Sarlaji: Yes, yes, I remember the house.

Devika: Which house?

Sarlaji: The house in Quetta, my father's house. I was small, but I remember it being a big house. My father had it constructed. There were tenants, but we lived downstairs. My father-in-law had a house made in Karachi, it was a nice house. We had to leave it. Anil's father (my brother-in-law) had a house in DI Khan. I saw it. That was a good house too. All the Sikhs used to live closer by so there was a *gurudwara* [Sikh temple]. They used to go there. We used to go out in the evening.

Devika: Where?

Sarlaji: *Babuji* [Father-in-law] used to allow me to go out for a while with women my age.

Devika: Just outside? Or the to gurudwara?

Sarlaji: No, just outside.

Home is memories of stepping outside home. Home is an enduring restriction. A house, which is just there, just nice, just big.

Shielaji is a reluctant participant. Recalcitrant might be a better word to describe her. She is both forthcoming and evasive about her experiences in her hometown of Ferozpur, a border town fifty miles from Lahore that became a part of India after 1947. Even though its location would not have required its Hindu inhabitants to move away, many of the residents migrated into the interior of the country voluntarily, becoming refugees. As Hindus, Shielaji's family members felt unsafe and forced themselves to migrate more inward into the country—perhaps not an enforced migration, but one forced by circumstance.

Like that of many North Indian women her age, in her eighties, Shielaji's summer wardrobe is made up of starched printed pastel-colored cotton saris worn with sleeveless cotton poplin blouses. Today she wears a pink and white paisley print. Her hair is almost all grey and she walks with a bit of a limp. In all the hours we spend together, I never see her face break into a smile. Yet she does not seem melancholic. Her tone, about everything, is matter-of-fact, almost angry. Still angry. I am used to nostalgia, sadness, loss, but this is new for me.

Shielaji: We lost a lot of property on that side [in Pakistan] and then we lost the property we had in Ferozpur. We had to sell our Ferozpur house in a distress sale (whatever you call a distress sale). But more than that, you know, coming away from Ferozpur did a lot of damage to my mother and even to us children because we lost a home. She was very unhappy. She never got over it. She came to Ferozpur as a bride and that is where she was all her life. She had children there, a wonderful life. She lost all of that. When she came here to India [even though Ferozpur was in India], she was a nobody. . . . My father was a lawyer. He was very well-thought of and even my grandparents, they were known, nice people, and known in that small town. My mother never got over it. There she was a somebody and here she became a nobody. It is normal to feel bad about it.

Devika: Yes, of course.

Shielaji: But a lot of bad things happened. I had a cousin in Montgomery, which went to Pakistan. My cousin felt he was safe there, he stayed even though his other siblings left. The mob came, they killed my cousin. My cousin's wife had just delivered a baby, so when she heard all this commotion going on outside the house, she put the baby under the bed because she knew she would die; she wanted to save the baby. They came in, they cut off her breast, they beat her up, and they thought they had killed her. Now my cousin had a Muslim *chawkidar* [watchman] who was very loyal to him, he found her, picked her up, took her to the hospital and left her there. Two days later, my sister-in-law regained consciousness and asked for her baby. She told the doctors she had hidden it under the bed. They went to look for the baby and found her alive.

Devika: That is a nice memory, though, yes? That she was saved by a Muslim man?

Shielaji: Yes. But, to be honest, I have no pleasant memories of that time. I don't talk much about it and even if it does come up then I talk in a noncommittal tone. Some of my friends who had good experiences there, they went and visited their old home or they go on a jaunt or they ask me to go to Lahore. My grandson is a golfer and he was interested in organizing a tournament there. He was invited to go there and when he went he tried his level best to convince me to go with him. I didn't go. His father and mother, my son and daughter-in-law both went. Because I do not have any pleasant memories to talk about, I didn't want to go there.

I try to prod further, but Shielaji has rejected the old home. After telling me that she is noncommittal about the Partition, her tone turns noncommittal. Taking the cue, I ask about Delhi, coaxing her to speak a bit about how they got here to this city.

Shielaji: Well I was already married in 1947 and he [her husband] was in the army, so we lived all over the country. After my husband retired, we got this piece of land and we built a house and started living here. Otherwise we had no love or affection for Delhi as such. We had never lived in Delhi. We didn't know Delhi. I didn't want to return to Ferozpur, even twenty-five years after Partition (in '72) because it is not like it used to be before Partition. Now that we are here, we are here.

Devika: So you never went back?

Shielaji: Yes, we did go back once because there was a celebration of my grandfather's birthday. He was a very active member of the Arya Samaj temple.[32] Try going somewhere and not staying in your own house (because by then our house was sold in the distress sale) and see how you feel. After that I just did not go.

Devika: Your grandson is, of course, interested in history. So, does he ask you lots of questions?

Shielaji: If he asks, I answer, but I am not so interested in remembering those days.

Home is an unmemorialized space. Home is a refusal to speak of home. And a refusal to return home.

MEMORIES OF ESCAPES (FROM HOME)

Departures. Arrivals. Escapes. The most remembered, rich points in my oral history record—by those who experienced Partition as well as by those who have inherited the memories. A plot focus that is inevitable when one's life is so deeply entwined with a watershed event in history. I hear and sense and am told of the departure as a leaving, a fleeing, an escape, an adventure, and a sorrowful goodbye. Its intricacies are well remembered and untiringly repeated. I am interested in the way that women narrate these travels, because the departure was the first time most of them traveled alone, without chaperones, sometimes with other women, and often without the presence of any male family relatives. These departures are first travels outside the confines of the natal or marital home. I sense fondness and I see humor in how these travels are remembered. A foil, in a way, to the experience of home.

Poonamji travels to India with another female member of her family, a paternal aunt. Her memories of the journey are distinct. It is the first time she is "outside" unaccompanied by male relatives.

Poonamji: We took a steamer from Karachi to Okha. We were sick all night on the deck, sea-sickness. We were in bad shape. The steamer was overflowing with people. That was the most terrible part of the journey.

Devika: How many hours did this take?

Poonamji: One night. We were there the next morning. From here we had to go to Kanpur. It took us one month to get to Kanpur.

"Why?" I ask in a surprised tone, because Okha and Kanpur are not that far from each other:

Poonamji: Sometimes on some days we used to get some space on trains, then from there they used to drop us . . . at *dharamsalas* [hostels for Hindu pilgrims] and camps and the food used to be taken care of. Food was free. They did not take money and we did not have to buy tickets for the trains.

Some of the official history fills in these blanks; these dharamsalas were being run by Hindu communalists, who might have been responsible also for instigating riots against Muslims in the very parts of the country where they were helping the Hindu refugees.[33]

Poonamji: But there was no place on the trains. We walked, got on trains, got off, and stayed in these free places.

I think those trains were running for refugees so you could not find space in those. I don't remember exactly why they used to leave us. They would leave us in small, small stations. Then we would lie there for days hoping that the train would come [laughs] and there would be space on it.

Devika: Was it hot?

Poonamji: Yes, it was the summer.

Devika: Were you scared?

Poonamji: *Beta*, at that time, it was a time when I was naïve. I was immature. I did not have much sense. [Laughingly continues.] We were thinking, we are roaming around. We didn't feel scared of anything.

Devika: Why not?

Poonamji: First of all our life in Pakistan both in Karachi, and especially when we lived in DI Khan, was restricted. We girls were hardly allowed outside the house, as I told you. My father's job was in the frontier and our home there was attacked by the tribes consistently even before Partition, so we were always afraid. So when we knew we were moving to Delhi, we were excited. We thought we would go to Delhi, we would see the Lal Quila [Red Fort], Jama Masjid, we will see the Qutab Minar.[34] When we got there, my brother, Anil, used to take us two sisters on his bicycle all over the city. One sat in the front, one in the back [giggles]. We saw many things. We went to Birla Mandir, Lal Quila, Qutab Minar. He took us to the Lal Quila when August 15th happened and Nehruji [Jawahar Lal Nehru] gave his speech for India's independence. We watched with so much passion.

She is quiet for a few moments remembering those jaunts with her siblings. Then she clutches my arm eagerly, gushing, "I wanted to tell you a story,

I almost forgot to tell you this." "Please, tell me," I urge, pressing gently on her fingers.

Poonamji: When Gandhiji died in January 1948, when he was assassinated, we kept a fast all day. We did not eat all day and then we knew that his body was being taken to the Jamuna-ji [River Jamuna] for the cremation. We brothers and sisters went by foot. There were so many people there. It was a very long walk from the refugee camp in Tibia College. We could not stop crying. And until his cremation was complete, we did not eat anything. I saw the cremation with my own eyes. In those days there was so much love for Gandhiji.

These escapades, I point out to her, were only possible because they lived not-at-home and at the refugee camp, a place that ironically allowed more freedom of movement than home. In the old country, such expeditions with her brother and sister would have been shunned, disallowed. She replies, "Of course, in the camp, we did anything, there were no rules, and yes had Partition not happened, Gandhiji would be alive. We loved him so much."

And then I ask a question that I wish I had not asked, because her answer solidifies my sense of how home was never home. My contemplations about which homes women remember or are allowed to remember or permitted to claim as their own is given form in this small exchange.

Devika: When you had children, you talked about this with them?

Poonamji: Yes, sometimes, not too often.

Devika: What do you tell them?

Poonamji: That we came here this way. My grandchildren sometimes tease us and tell us that we are "Pakistanis." I tell them there was no Pakistan, we were all Indians. Even now I remember the streets and the roads of DI Khan. They are still in my head. Just recently my brother [Anilji] went there. I also wanted to go.

I told them I wanted to go. But my husband, he did not want to go. He is from Quetta and my brother was not visiting Quetta, so he did not want to go and so I could not go.

Devika: Why not?

Poonamji: Well, if my husband could not see his home, what would be the point?

Devika: But you could?

Poonamji: No, you know how it is.

I know and do not know how it is. I know that Poonamji's desire to see her home is not as important as her husband's wish. I know that she has acquiesced because her natal home will never be as important as her marital home. How can she be allowed to visit her old home, if he can't visit his? He forces this sacrifice and she complies without complaint. I want to believe that telling me of his refusal, albeit in passing, is a sort of complaint that she allows herself to make. An (un)complaint that finds me resenting her husband's refusal, even when she won't. She will not and must not permit herself to go home alone. And so, yet again, home's inequities stay consistent, repetitive, encompassing, and pervasive.

Mrs. Chopra too made the journey to India unaccompanied by any male relative, with her sister-in-law. Her memories of the movement, of leaving, are full of adventure and mirth because, she says, "We were lucky, we never saw any violence." Even as I write this, my intention is not to underplay the loss of home, but to show a few ways that the rupture is remembered differently.

> *Mrs. Chopra*: My sister-in-law and myself were brought in a military train from Lahore to Ambala. It was a special train and they closed it up. It was not opened until we reached Ambala. In a way we had a terrible time on it because my sister-in-law kept shouting, "*Bhabhi* [brother's wife)], they are coming, they are coming." Naturally, we were both scared. My mother-in-law wanted us on that train, she wanted us girls away from the violence. So we left for India alone—just us two girls.
>
> Before we left, it was so hot. It was so hot that day. You cannot imagine that heat. But we were funny. My sister-in-law and I—that was the funniest thing we did—she told me, "Bhabhi, let's put on more clothes, you know?" We put on four *salwar kameezes* on top of each other and we wore sweaters.

Mr. Chopra, who is reclining on one end of the bed, smilingly says, "In summer these girls were wearing sweaters." We all laugh. Mrs. Chopra continues:

> We laughed and laughed after doing that. A lot of people were wearing four or five sets of clothes on top of each other because we could not take anything

with us. What an exciting adventure it was. We left at night. At two or three in
the morning, we went to a house where other refugees were being kept and
that's how we were saved. [She laughs again].

Home can be an experience located in a space beyond the reaches of home.[35]
Here, it is a place of wandering, of mirth, and of freedom. Resisting stable
locations, it announces itself as activities performed outside of itself. An it-
eration that forces me to ruminate—where did nostalgia for the home go?
And moreover, who can be nostalgic for the lost home?

HOMING IN THE "CONVERSATION OF STRUGGLE"

The only person from my field record who is introduced to me by my mother,
Amma, is Veeranji. My mother has known Veeranji for almost five decades.
Their families were neighbors in the small government colony of Moti
Bagh in Delhi during the 1950s and 1960s. The first time she hears of my
project, Amma announces, "You must meet Veeri Aunty." "Who is she?" I
ask. "Did I never tell you about her? I was so fond of them," Amma exclaims.
No, I shake my head. Of course, since she belongs to my mother's natal past,
I am unsurprised that she had been left unmentioned all these years. Amma
has not met them for almost twenty-five years, but the families were very
close, as neighbors often were.

Why she is fond of them is the story before the story. In 1967, Amma is in
a serious committed relationship with Papa, but no one in her family is aware
of it. She has been keeping it a secret because in those years it is unacceptable
(and common generally) for women in my maternal family to find their own
spouses. When Amma turns twenty-one, Nani begins receiving offers of
marriage for her. Amma is worried that things will get out of hand and that
my Nani will fix her marriage. She confides in Veeri Aunty and her husband, and they offer to intervene. They meet Papa and "interview" him, as
Amma laughingly puts it. They are the ones who talk with Nani about his
prospects, telling her that he is responsible and marriage-worthy. Nani trusts
them. She agrees. They are married in 1970. Would they have been wed
without Veeri Aunty? Perhaps they would. But she has a place in Amma's
heart, and when this field-homework begins, she takes me to Veeri Aunty
because Amma must see her too.

How I get to people, who accompanies me to them, the anecdotes, the events, the incidents that lead me to someone's oral history remains as interesting as the story itself. Every step to a story is a kernel of the story, every step a link to how stories are connected. Veeranji is twenty-one years old and unmarried when the Partition occurs. She remembers the riots, the terror surrounding her neighborhood. She witnesses a killing on her own street:

> *Veeranji*: A Muslim man was murdered right in front of me, I was so shocked. We all did not eat for days. We were very friendly with Muslims in our neighborhood. It was the Hindus, us people, who never ate in their homes, they did. They ate and drank in ours.

The chasm that was is now being recalled. The inevitability of Partition, yet another refrain. She chooses not to dwell on the sadness and instead tells me how they got on. "The house in Rawalpindi?" I ask.

> *Veeranji*: Of course, we were very sad. We came to Delhi from Srinagar. We just locked the house. I think my brother brought some jewelry. I brought my clothes and my books. I was supposed to take my final exams for my B.A. degree. I did take them, but the results never came. Then when we came to Delhi, we were allowed to sit for the exams again through the camp college. We just wanted to carry on with our life. Do something.

"So what happened in the years following 1947? How did you carry on?" I probe. Side-stepping the old home, Veeranji describes how they relocate from Delhi to Allahabad and back to Delhi. In between all of this, her older sister helps her to get married to a "simple" man, "who is quite encouraging about my getting a job." "So you were allowed to work?" I question. "No, I was not, not by my in-laws, but my husband was adamant and told everyone that it was difficult to make ends meet on one salary," she answers. "It is because we both worked that we have all this, it was a lot of hard work," she points to her three-story house in a very respectable middle-class neighborhood in an area of Delhi known as trans-Jamuna (meaning, literally, across the River Yamuna)

The rest of her story, and most of her story—like Kiranji's, like Labbi Devi's—is "the conversation of struggle." I consider it an/other story of home, a story about the labor of making new lives—of homing in the new country. This labor in the men's stories, what we see in "Adrift," is more public, more related to the work outside the home. Of course with Kiranji's story this thematic too, falls apart. Among these women, this labor is the work of home both inside and outside as they become, and are often welcomed, as partners in the struggle to remake home. For these women, in doing this labor some remnant of home (coming) is achieved:

> *Veeranji*: In Pakistan, we had a simple life. I would have finished my degree and would have been married to someone and would have not worked. I started working here. My husband's family was against it, but we could not have survived. Our standard of living changed. We really struggled. We moved from home to home. We made new houses. We bought this land where we build this house.
>
> Also, we changed with the times. We became more progressive, you see, because I was working *outside*. Because of us (me and my sister, who also worked), the younger girls in the family are all educated, they all work. There is now not a single girl in the family who does not have a job. I retired from the U.S. Embassy. I get my pension. My husband is no more, but I also get his pension. I have no financial worries because I worked and he worked. And we built this life.
>
> Before Partition, we were nothing, there was nothing. We became something, we got all this, we have this life because of the Partition. Otherwise we would have just spent our *poori zindagi* [entire lifetime] there in the same old street in Rawalpindi.

And just like that the old street, the old home, the old self is set aside and apart from the story. "We were nothing, there was nothing," speaks of the simplicity as well as the emptiness of the old country (for some women). It is dissimilar to Kiranji's story, because I argue that she memorializes her home in the life she creates (yet another thematic that disintegrates). But the idea that a loss of home and the struggle to rebuild a life forges new selves is the simple plot that brings these stories together.

Just as I have felt with Kiranji, here too, I feel a sisterhood with Veeranji, a woman as old as Nani, who also struggles to be someone in a new country. Links are inevitable, and I cannot but think of my own leaving for here, the United States just four days short of fifty years after Partition. I find that I must ask myself the same question as Kiranji, "Would I be where I am, would I be who I am, had I not lost that home?" The answer does not require much thought. I would not be who I am, had I not left home. Ironically, I would not be here talking to these women had I not left home. Leaving creates an attunement, of sorts, to other departures. Leaving home and struggling—willingly and unwillingly—to make a life, is the rehoming that emplaces us in these elsewhere places.

Homing—a struggle between self and home. Homing—a conversation of struggle.

HOME WITH THE "HUMANIZED" OTHER

The Other/Musalman/Mohammedan walks along as a recurring character in this oral history record. He is invoked as a friend, yet never fully embraced. Even as my participants lament the loss of their friendships with Muslims, they continue to position them as Other. Very few make any attempts at reigniting relationships. Women's stories embody this Other differently. The Others in these stories are persons, real, tangible, vulnerable human beings—a piece of and a bridge to home.

In the midst of the chaos of Partition, Sarlaji and her husband are stuck in their home in Karachi. He has contracted typhoid and they cannot leave until he recovers. The Hindus in their neighborhood have already left for India and the area has "become full of Muslims, who had arrived from India." It is after August 1947, the Partition has been officially finalized, and India and Pakistan have become independent nation states. The men in the family caution Sarlaji to stay inside the home and away from the Muslim women in the neighborhood. She does not heed their advice.

> *Sarlaji*: There was our building and there was another building adjoining ours. They looked similar. A Muslim family had moved into the house from Agra, which was given to India. Our building was called Sena Niwas and the adjoining one was call Narayana Niwas. The woman of the family, a Muslim woman, used to sit on her balcony at night and I used to sit on mine. We used to chat late into the night. We used to talk about anything and everything, whatever was in our hearts.
>
> She told me that she was her husband's third wife and that he used to drink a lot and had sold all her gold jewelry for his alcohol. She also said that the Hindus really troubled them in Agra, which is why they moved here. She used to say, "You should leave here because the Muslims will start

troubling you." She used to say, "Go, go, leave or they will harass you, I don't know what they will do to you; I will feel bad if you leave, but I think you need to go."

Hindus and the Muslims are invoked, but placed outside of this friendship that evolves amid and despite the bloodshed that is taking place right under their noses, outside their homes. Sarlaji continues:

> *Sarlaji*: My husband was unhappy that I had befriended her. He used to tell me that my Muslim friend would get us killed. We were making plans to leave for Hindustan, but he had made me promise that I would keep it a secret from her. I felt bad, but I kept it a secret. Then one night our plans were finalized and we were to leave the next morning. That evening on the balcony she asked me, "There is a lot of noise coming from your house, are you all going somewhere?" I told her that we were just moving some furniture. In my heart I used to feel she is my friend and we talk so much every night, and if I did not even meet her before we left I would feel really bad. We had made a local bell with a rope and she had tied one to her side and I had tied the other end to my side, if we moved it a bell would ring. We had bamboo blinds on the doors and she used to peep from her side and I used to peep from mine. I rang that bell in the morning and she was surprised because we only met at night. I told her to come outside and sit on the balcony. I told her we were leaving. We both cried. She told me to wait, ran inside her house and got me a *pudia*, a cotton pouch, with something in it. I said goodbye and went downstairs to the tonga that was waiting to take us. In the tonga, I opened the pudia and saw that she had given us three *paans*,[36] since we were three of us. My husband and his brother pushed them away and threw them on the ground saying they would not touch them, what if they were poisoned? By chance, one *paan* was still in my hand. They wanted me to throw it, but I quickly put it in my mouth and ate it. I said to them, "She will never do this to me, she is my friend." I ate it. They were angry with me. It was fine. I am alive, no? [Laughs, pointing to herself.]

I recall a phrase oft repeated by many participants, "They ate in our homes, but we never did, Hindus never ate with Muslims." Sarlaji's disobedience in eating the *paan* is a minute show of camaraderie, a miniscule act of resistance that erodes, albeit marginally, the spaces in between. In taking that bite and telling me the story she makes a visceral link with the Other. She crosses a border even before she crosses the literal border to

India. When I ask her why she did it, she simply answers, "She was my friend."

Shielaji will not return home because her home-on-the-border is lost to the terrors of her memories. She shuns it, she wants to disremember it. She will not even speak of home to her grandchildren. Her home story is best understood as a resistance to home. So I am expecting Shielaji to be non-committal about any relationships with Muslims, just as she is about home. But she surprises me with the memory of an encounter that she wants to relate:

> *Shielaji*: There were bad, bad things that happened. But so many nice things also happened in the middle of all of it. We had already moved away from the border and were living in Meerut. There was a carpet dealer in Meerut. One day he came over in his usual way, he always brought a tonga full of carpets. He just walked into the house and said, "Ma'am, I've brought you carpets." I told him that I did not need carpets, but he said he was still going to give them to me. He put his carpets all over the house, and I pled with him, "Look, what are you doing?" He said that he would probably be shunted out from here, he said, "Hindus will come and kill me, what if they come and set fire to all these carpets, I am going to leave them in your house, you like them, you appreciate them, if I die at least I know you will be enjoying my carpets." So he left them with me. He ran away from Meerut. But he came back after three months or so. The carpets were all there. He told me, "I knew I would find them all intact in your house, that is why I left them with you." He tried very, very hard to give me one carpet as he was taking them. I just said, "You left them in good faith, and you take them all back in good faith."
>
> One can think of all these things as silly incidents. But this is what I would rather remember.

Instances of trust and distrust between the two communities abound; they not only populate these field discourses, they are also very much a refrain throughout the literature on Partition. Indeed, there isn't a single oral history here that is devoid of this paradoxical bond. Among men, the post-Partition Other, the state-created category of Pakistani, comes to subsume any earlier iterations of the ties between the communities. Yet these women, even while they enact the uneasy ambivalences, seem to humanize the Other, wanting to preserve the "good things," the "silly incidents."

Perhaps humanizing the Other is a kind of (re)homing. Julia Kristeva proposes that recognizing our own differences allows us to transform foreignness into commonality, "promoting the togetherness of foreigners that we all recognize ourselves to be."[37] Or perhaps it is I, the ethnographer, who wants this to be a kind of homing? Perhaps it is easier to believe that humanizing is a gendered habit—more feminine than masculine. It is quite possible that this is a fiction I have created and want desperately to believe. To allow the Other to become the story, to give the Other the story, is an "act of identity," a performance of self that one can live with.

Contemplating, Inhabiting, Unhomely Homes

The homes sketched here tell a gendered story of home spaces—who stays inside, who moves outside, who authorizes movements, and who submits. What is notable about these anecdotes is that instead of narrations that provide us with (much needed) critiques of domesticity, alternative versions of home as un/home are shown to us. The unhomely home is not a new against-the-grain story. It has been long embraced by feminist and transnational scholars as a variant story of home spaces and places.[38] Home has, as we know, long lived in the romantic imagination as a place, space, idea, and feeling of safety and refuge. Home has also been long articulated in the postmodern and postcolonial imagination as a place where Freud's *unheimlich* (uncanny, unfamiliar) might be experienced.[39] The uncanny is "an experience of the unfamiliar in something that should otherwise be quite familiar;" "the home, which is something that should feel most comfortable and familiar" can become "a space where the uncanny is experienced."[40] In "Reading the House: A Literary Perspective," Kathy Mezei and Chiara Briganti explain:

> Freud's investigation of the German word *unheimlich* led to the discovery of the coincidence of homely and unhomely, his elaboration of the sinister transformation of the familiar into the unfamiliar, and the return of the repressed through the unhomely, the uncanny.[41]

The unhomely is a repetitive theme that permeates conversations about home. The unhomely reveals "the forgotten but familiar strangeness of home as a site that elicits enigmatic longing, control, or outright violence,"[42] and it is a state of the unfamiliar strangeness or "foreignness within" discussed by Kristeva in *Strangers to Ourselves*. This uncanny nature of home and the unhomely condition can also be seen in Theodor Adorno's critique of bourgeoisie society in *Minima Moralia*,[43] wherein the private space of the conjugal family that cultivated subjectivity is now a nostalgic impossibility. A dwelling space is no longer the home of childhood memories, and to remain homeless is now one's home.[44] This kind of homelessness is quite different from the valorization of the state of homelessness and the destruction of home espoused by Deleuze and Guattari, who value the exhilaration that comes from movement.[45]

There is another reading of the unhomely wherein the artificial division between home (as inside) and world (as outside) is placed under scrutiny. In his strategic interpretation of *unheimlich*, Homi Bhabha positions the unhomely as a postcolonial space that relates the "traumatic ambivalence of a personal, psychic history to the wider disjunctions of political existence."[46] The unhomely, he notes, "Captures something of the estranging sense of the relocation of home and the world in an unhallowed place." Bhabha marks a distinction between unhomed and homeless, noting that the unhomely is not easily accommodated "in that familiar division of social life into public and private spheres." It is not as if the "home" is the domestic domain, and the "world" is its social and historical equivalent. Rather, says Bhabha, "The unhomely is the shock of recognition of the world-in-the-home, the home-in-the-world."[47]

Even though his ideas veer too close to bourgeois notions of the ease with which we can travel across worlds and identities, I consider Bhabha's reading of *unhomely* important because of his description of the tensions between world-in-the-home and home-in-the world; in these tensions is where I see some of these stories finding an explanation. Even while there are criticisms of the normative notions of home and domesticity, women continue to be positioned as persons who labor in the private sphere, and domestic space still "implies the everyday, the rituals of domesticity in their cyclical, repetitive ordinariness."[48] How a house—the domestic—might limit and oppress the construction of feminine subjectivity comes under constant feminist critique. While such critiques continue to be essential, many feminists offer other routes to envision the nexus of home, domesticity, and the feminine, urging us to "discover more about the place of home in the woman."[49] The domestic, in this sense, "is seen as a modality that is contained both in the house and spills outside of it."[50] It can stretch from world-in-the-home to home-in-the-world.

Let me end by suggesting that the five women in these stories speak homes that spill outside of the traditional renditions of home spaces and places. Their stories allow us to look to the "elsewheres" as viable topographies shaping home and selves. Each woman narrates a home space or lack thereof into existence, a home space that is neither inside nor outside the confines of home and world, that is both familiar and unfamiliar, that is both spatial and existential. These are narrations that I find curious, given their narrators' already-outsider position in the natal and marital homes. They are "outsiders" inside the family, and the homes they speak and want to remember are located in a liminal space—the membrane that links the inside with the outside, home with unhome. Or more simply, home for these women is built upon the activities (and the memories of the activities) that occur in (and away from) the place.[51] Speaking different, even unhomely homes, these women show how home might be imagined as its antithesis—outside, away, alongside—the interior place of domesticity.

SEVEN

Remnants

An Autobiographer

Delhi, July 2008

The monsoon rains arrive, providing some respite from the blistering heat that seizes Delhi every summer. This July it has rained almost every day, thankfully lowering the temperatures, making it bearable to step outside. Papa and I walk the ten minutes it takes to get to Mohanji's home. He lives just a street away from ours, and they know each other through their morning walks in the neighborhood park. Some days I join Papa for his walks in the park that adjoins my parents' home. That is where I meet Mohanji. He is hard to miss with his loud recitations of "Hare Ram" and "Om," as well as the clicking of the thick walking stick that he carries. Sometimes Papa and I walk with him. A few weeks later, we decide to meet formally, for what Mohanji calls "in-depth talking."

We find him seated at one end of a mahogany dining table that has seen better days. He waves at us to sit down and tells us that he is waiting for his breakfast, which is cooked by his daughter-in-law every morning. It is easy to see that he is the presiding patriarch of this home. At eighty-seven years of age (now, as I write, he is ninety-two), Mohanji eats a heavy, customary Punjabi breakfast of *ghee paranthas* with buttermilk every morning.[1] "I have eaten this since I was two years of age, all this talk of low-fat food is nonsense, I walk for an hour everyday and I do all my own work, it gets digested," he declares. His daughter-in-law has put generous blobs of homemade white butter in the centers of the thick *paranthas*. She offers us water, chai, and breakfast. "Just water," we tell her. "*Thoda sa kha lo, beta*" (eat a little bit, child), Mohanji cajoles. "No, no, Uncle, I just ate breakfast," I reply. Papa announces that he is leaving. "*Tusi ni sunoge kahani?*"—You won't listen to the story?—Mohanji asks Papa in Punjabi; Papa grins and replies, "*Mainu kum haiga ajj, tusi mainu walk vich suna dena*" (I have some work this morning, but you can tell me these stories when we walk). Mohanji nods and again invites me to eat. I refuse again.

He calls out to his daughter-in-law, Menu, who is in the kitchen, and requests her to bring us his autobiography. Surprised, I ask, "You wrote one?" "Yes, I wanted my children to know about my life, how I got here from Pakistan, how we made a life here," he explains. She hands it to me and joins us at the dining table, saying, "I also want to hear what he says." Of course, please do, I reply. He invites me to look at it, saying, "You can also photocopy it." I do.

I start glancing through it. It is a seventy-page-long spiral-bound document typed on white paper. "I had it typed and bound," says Mohanji. "You can read it at your leisure," he adds. I will and I do. This is another layer of his story, one that can be a bonus (or not) because it can fill in blanks about incidents, events, memories that we don't cover in our conversations. Since he is the only person I meet who has written his life out in a chronology, I wonder if he will compose his oral history with me by aligning it to the story that has already been told in text. Will the oral history, which is already always a repetition, become a rehearsal—scripted by itself? The writer Rebecca Solnit muses over the displacement that inevitably occurs in writing down memories of her childhood:

Most of them have grown fainter with time, and whenever I write one down I give it away: it ceases to have the shadowy life of memory and becomes fixed in letters; it ceases to be mine; it loses the mobile unreliability of the live.[2]

My Life Career

1. Childhood
2. School/College Career
3. Married Life
4. Education & Marriages in the Family
5. Service Career
6. Retired Life
7. Conclusion

Preface

This small booklet has been written not with a view
to give publicity in the general public but with the
object of bringing home to my children the way of life
led by me during my life time. I had a strong desire to
write it in Urdu because I can express my feelings much

An excerpt from Mohanji's typewritten autobiography.

Even as I worry about this objectification (or solidification) of memories—yet another accompanying crisis of representation—I find myself distracted by Mohanji's autobiography. The very act of writing this autobiography, even though it is quite chronological, is a poetic and critical act, and a decision to write one's life in words shows both awareness and a desire for an awareness of self. And autobiographical contemplations, in the words of Paul Eakin, are "both an art of memory and an art of the imagination."[3] I skim through the brief, one-page preface that follows the table of contents, where Mohanji states (and I reproduce his words verbatim):

> This small booklet has been written not with the view to give publicity in the general public but with the object of bringing home to my children the way of life lead by me during my lifetime. I had a strong desire to write it in Urdu language than in English. But because my children do not know Urdu, I have attempted it in English. Here & there, I have quoted Urdu verses to express my feelings about my life . . . Here I quote below a Persian couplet:

Een Bazor-e-bazooaye naist
Tana Bakshad Khaidai Bakhshinda

Meaning thereby that it (life) is not possible with the strength of anybody until and unless God Almighty showers his Mercy on him.

"Why did you not write your entire story in Urdu?" I ask even after reading the explanation in the preface. "*Beta*, it is easier for my children and grand-children to know about my life in the language they can read," he explains. I tell him how much I love to listen to Urdu being spoken. "Of course, for you youngsters it is poetic, but it was our language, we spoke the same language as the Muslims, when we came here we started calling it Hindustani," he ex-plains. Hindustani, the coupling of Hindi and Urdu, is the language we all speak in Delhi, what I consider my mother tongue. It is the language that I speak with my Pakistani friends and colleagues in America—they joke and tell me that I speak Urdu, and I insist that *they* speak Hindustani. Almost the same, but not quite. Meanwhile, it is English that I consider my first lan-guage, what I speak and think and dream in, and what I write with.

I flip through the booklet and find Urdu verses on almost every page. He has thought through his life, mingled it with these verses, and what I have in front of me is a very interesting chronological, yet poetic account of a pre- and post-Partition life. For me, Urdu is the language of verse, song, and poetry—not a language that is spoken every day. Many third-generation participants such as myself are perhaps attracted to it because of what Mar-ianne Hirsch calls the aesthetics of postmemory, what she describes as "a diasporic aesthetics of temporal and spatial exile that needs simultaneously to (re)build and to mourn."[4] Urdu had now become the language of the Other, spoken over *there*, in Pakistan. But in these pages of Mohaniji's auto-biography, it is the language of emotion, the natural language of the self. I stop at page 15 of the autobiography and giggle. He smiles and asks, "*Kaun sa para pada?*" (Which paragraph did you read?) I recite:

I exactly remember our history professor Mr. Behl was very jovial and roman-tic. He used to start his Lecture in the class by an Urdu verse which he asked a student named Sultan to recite. That verse is as under:

Mohabbat ik majboori hai warna
Mujhe tujh se koyee matlab nahi hai

"You didn't translate this here?" I question him. "No, this is an easy one, just means that loving you is a necessity, if not for love, why would I need to bother with you?" he translates. I chuckle. We move on to more sonnets that he has written into the autobiography. There is even English poetry toward the end when he writes about the death of his wife. I point to page 65 and ask if he remembers the name of the poet. "No, *beta*, I don't, but I remembered it from college" he replies.

> Nothing begins and nothing ends
> that is not paid with a moan
> For we are born in another's pain
> and perish in our own.

I search for these verses online, and find that the poet who composed them is the Englishman Francis Thompson. It is the last stanza of a poem called "Daisy." The next time I see Mohanji I tell him about my find. He says, "I am sure that I read it somewhere in college when I was in D. A. V. [Dayanand Anglo-Vedic] College and Gordon College in Rawalpindi, I just remembered the last two lines," he nods.

We stay with the verses, and I find a medley of Urdu, Punjabi, and English poetry interspersed with his life story. Of course, I complete formal recordings of our conversations and there is a lot he tells me about his life in Pakistan and his struggles after Partition. He is yet another remarkably self-made man who made a life for himself and his family after Partition. With three children who are all medical doctors, he seems satisfied. The trajectory of his rise to middle-class status aligns with that of many of the participants. By now, I am inured to this narrative trajectory, I anticipate it, and mostly, it follows. But here, with Mohanji, what I (want to) remember and what enters my notes are these small moments with him and the poetry he uses to describe his feelings. As if in verse, he feels at home.

The Sufi Singers

Nizammudin, August 2008
I feel an elbow poke under my ribcage and quietly curse the stranger-culprit in the jostling crowd. It is the evening holy hour of Maghrib in this Muslim

neighborhood and I daren't use any expletives. Iqbal tells me that the street is less crowded than normal because it is prayer time and *namaz* is being read in the large and small mosques close by. We are in a market inside the *basti* behind Nizamuddin. *Basti* is the general name for working-class localities surrounding the famous tomb of Nizamuddin (among other places) in New Delhi. There is also a posh end to Nizamuddin, where upper- and middle-class Punjabi Delhites live in palatial homes and large apartments. Today we are on the other side, the economically depressed one where mostly Muslims live—there are furniture makers, locksmiths, jewelry makers, *zardozi* embroiderers[5]—*karigars* (craftsmen) who supply their goods to some of the upscale stores in the city, who in turn sell them to rich customers—mostly upper middle-class and wealthy Punjabis (both Hindus and Sikhs)—for many times the manufacturing cost. The bastis outside Nizammudin are glaring examples of a deeply communalized Delhi, spaces that are shunned by Punjabis, who otherwise romanticize (even fetishize) Urdu poetry, music, and performances, and yet are deeply discriminatory against the Muslim community.[6]

I can see that some shopkeepers in the bazaar have put their shutters half down for the evening salutations to Mecca. I am trying to make sure I don't lose sight of Iqbal, who is leading the way to the *qawwali* singing—the singing of Sufi devotional music—that takes place on Thursday evenings. It is him and his cousins who told me about this weekly event. We keep our ears tuned for the lively sounds of qawwali singers with their variations of Sufi poetry. We have been walking the streets for some time and don't see or hear anything.

We enter an embroidery shop and ask for directions. The owner, an old Muslim man wearing a white *kurta pyjama*—a long loose shirt and matching trousers—with a *taqiyah* (the Muslim prayer cap) on his head, his myopic eyes hidden behind thick spectacles, says, "It does take place on Thursdays but they might have canceled today because it is quite hot, otherwise you would have heard them." "You think they will be here next week?" I ask. *"Bitiya, garmi par depend karega"* (Daughter, it will depend on the heat), he replies. We thank him and walk ahead for another ten minutes, give up our search, and walk back the winding streets to Iqbal's parked taxi. *"Didi, agle hafte ya uske baad aa jayenge"* (Sister, we can come back next week or later), he tells me consolingly.

We return one more time on a Thursday, but don't find them. Fieldwork continues, and my pursuit of the *qawwals* (the qawwali singers) remains unfulfilled. Mostly, it is a matter of finding a free Thursday evening—I cannot cancel meetings with my participants for this indulgence. Mohanji is one among many of my older male participants who have quoted love verses from Sufi poets like Rumi and Baba Bulleh Shah amid our conversations. Labbi Devi's husband, Lalaji, who suffers from Alzhiemer's, remembers two things from the past—his house in Lahore, and *shairs*—Urdu sonnets—learned in college, also in Lahore. When I decide, on a whim, to search for the Sufi singers that the taxi drivers from the Bhoore Khan Taxi Service often mention, Papa finds my search amusing. He is also a bit perturbed about my going into an economically depressed Muslim area, but he does not volunteer to accompany me.

Papa: It's too crowded in that area, who will go in this heat?

Devika: You like *ghazals* . . . *ghazals*⁷ are rooted in Sufi poetry, how come you're not interested in seeing these guys sing? You made us listen to them all the time.

Papa: Well, I can listen to them on the CD player. I am sure the sound will be better anyway.

Devika: But it's not live.

Papa replies, a bit cheekily, "You can listen to the live recordings." I roll my eyes. I am a bit puzzled that he does not want to accompany me. When we were children, it was Papa who fed us heavy doses of *ghazals* and *shairi*—both Indian and Pakistani—by such singers as Abida Parveen, Begum Akhtar, Jagjit and Chitra Singh, Talat Aziz, Farida Khanum, and Mehdi Hasan. I have fond memories of awakening to this music being played in the living room and of long weekend afternoons in Punjab spent lazing in the lawn while my parents and their friends hummed to this music. I still know most of the lines from these *ghazals* by heart.

There are many more field and home trips to Delhi, but the Sufi singers remain elusive. Either I am not determined enough or just unlucky. Eventually, unexpectedly, I see them elsewhere.

The Accidental Fieldnote

Chattar Pur, February 2012

The stage is purple and creamy white. Thousands of white flowers, sewn closely together, form a lacy backdrop to the singers, who are seated cross-legged in a semicircle on a low stage covered with white cotton sheets and purple cushions. About fifteen *qawwals*, including a small boy, no more than seven years of age, are tuning their musical instruments and humming. Since it is a cold night, small portable wood-burning stoves are spread across two lawns with chairs in a semicircle around each—all facing the stage. Amma and I join a group of three women and seat ourselves on cushiony outdoor chairs quite close to the stage. "The little boy must be family, right?" I ask the woman sitting next to me. Yes, she replies, "He's getting trained, these singers are generational." In a minute or so, one of the older singers begins to chant to the sound of a slowly beaten *tabla*—a pair of small hand drums—and the melodious harmonium. The Urdu chorus is easy enough for me to follow:

> *Dil ke Bazaar me daulat nahi dekhi jati.*
> *Pyar ho jai to surat nahi dekhi jati.*

> (In the marketplace of love, one does not look for wealth. And when you fall in love one does not look at physical looks.)

We grin over the meaning. One of the women points to her husband, who is standing a few yards away, a middle-aged portly man with a receding hair-line, and remarks, "Or in other words, in English—love is blind as you age." We laugh aloud.

I flew into Delhi four days ago. I am here just to meet Amma and Papa. My fieldwork has been over—to the extent that any fieldwork is ever complete—for a year. Yesterday Meher called and invited my parents and me to a "Sufi evening," with love poetry being sung by *qawwals*, to celebrate her tenth wedding anniversary—an indulgence not many of my participants can afford, but hers is the most affluent of the families in this record. The party is being held outside, on the lawns of her father's country house. I am still a bit jet-lagged, but she is persistent. Papa begs off, saying the night air is too cold for him to be outdoors. So, on a Saturday evening in early February, Amma and I find ourselves in a cab going to Amritji's country house in the affluent area of Chattar Pur near Qutab Minar. "Come dressed appropriately for Sufi music," she says. I've not packed any of my saris or *salwar kameezes*, so I arrive quite unsuitably attired in a black dress and a winter wool coat.

Meher, dressed in a dark green silk *salwar kameez*, walks briskly toward me with her husband by her side. We all hug. She looks me up and down and admonishes, "Dressed in Western clothes? Could you not have borrowed a sari from your mom?" she asks. "Lazy, just laziness, it is such an effort to wear them, and besides I did not bring a blouse and petticoat either, how to wear them without those?" I counter smilingly. She clicks her tongue at me, "You Americans, anyway, have you had something to drink?" "We'll take care of ourselves, relax, no worries." I tell her to carry on with her other guests. I walk over to the food stalls that are on another lawn right behind the seating area for guests and get everyone in our semicircle a glass of hot soup.

In a few moments I spot Meher's father, Amritji, sitting on a loveseat near the singers, who are still singing quite softly; the evening is not yet underway and it is already 10:00 P.M. I walk over to greet him. "*Baithen raho tusin* [please keep sitting], Uncle," I insist as he gets up to hug me. Like all the men in the Suri family, he too is dressed for the occasion; he wears a black *sherwani* and fitted *chooridar pyjamas*,[8] with a maroon pashmina shawl. His turban matches the maroon of the pashmina. "You look so royal, Uncle," I tell him admiringly. "*Beta jo Meher ne pahenenne ko kahaa, wo maina pehen liya*" (Child, whatever Meher asked me to wear, I wore), he replies, chuckling. Always hospitable, he asks, "Have you eaten something?"

Devika: I will in a bit.

Amritji: The food is very good. It's Hyderabadi cuisine. Meher wanted to keep it authentic.

Devika: I wonder why she decided on having a *qawwali* evening.

Amritji: We all understand it. We all like this music. These singers are from Nizammudin.

Still raw from my failed attempts to hear and watch the singers on their home turf in Nizammudin, and now, incredulous at my good luck, I ask, "Really? Are these the singers who play there every Thursday?"

Amritji: They must be. They also gave the music for some Hindi films. But see they are a simple group, all are from the same family. That small child must be getting trained.

Devika: Did you listen to this music when you lived in Pindi?

Amritji: Of course. We lived in such proximity to the Muslims. That is why we know so many of these poems. Even my children know them, don't you?

Devika: Yes, they are familiar. I feel like I have heard them all my life. You know all these songs?

Amritji: I don't know all, but I have heard all of them over the years.

To see these performers that I was unable to find in Nizamuddin, here, at this party, a gathering that I almost bypassed, on a trip to Delhi that is a visit home, over a year after my official fieldwork has concluded, can only be serendipitous. Or fortuitous. But here, in this space, amid these verses, home and field converge (yet again), showing me that I was meant to witness this— four generations of Sikh Partition refugees—celebrating a family event in songs and poetry, in a form that the parents and grandparents knew in the old country, a form that their children (and I) want to resurrect—another/ our aesthetic of what Hirsch calls postmemory.

The singing seems to have begun in earnest. The *qawwals* are calling out to Meher and her husband because they want to sing special verses for the couple celebrating their wedding anniversary. Meher and her husband dance a little in front of the stage. As is customary, people applaud and fling rupees in the direction of the dancing couple. The money is intended for the singers, who walk to the front of the stage to collect the notes each time there is a pause in the songs. I look in amazement at the Sikh youngsters—some are swaying with their eyes closed, some are standing close to the singers, some are sitting and watching intently—engrossed by this ancestral form. When a verse is about to come to an end on a refrain, many of them complete it for the singers.

For Sikhs, the traditional Punjabi *bhangra*, their folk dance, is the more favored form of entertainment. It is the preferred mode of entertainment at such festivities, in fact it is almost a staple in North and South Indian family gatherings. Yet here these thirty-something adults are humming, singing, and dancing to Sufi music that their grandparents knew and loved.

Anecdotally, I also know from media reports from the last few decades that Pakistanis have embraced Bollywood films and Indian cinema. An aesthetic refusion, because many of us—members of the third Partition generation—never have and probably never will visit Pakistan, but we welcome the old country in these sonnets, a safer way, perhaps, to be home, and another way that we perform postmemory, which brings with it "its own narrative genres and aesthetic shapes."[9]

Much has been said about the power of art, poetry, and music to bring people together. And even more has been written, for over five decades, about migrant characters in Partition fiction, who resort to and reside in the poetic.[10] I am wary of literary analysis here because my focus is on the ordinary legacies of Partition, and I have consciously stayed close to the stories of my participants. Witnessing this evening is a reinforcement of the theme that aesthetic bonds were (and are) inevitable counterbalances to the fragmentation of the nation. They were bound to hold firm. Unfortunately, one must acknowledge that they hold firm because it takes less physical and psychological effort, less courage, to maintain aesthetic bonds than it does to overcome political, religious, and personal estrangement. Seemingly borderless, but bordered.

A Poet, a Singer

When I am least expecting it, some participants, mostly men, break into verse, like seventy-three-year-old Roshanji, who starts talking to me by reciting the line, "*Hum log sub hum hai*" (We people are all a "we"). We are seated in the large sunlit living room of his South Delhi home. His three-year-old granddaughter sits on his lap on an unseasonably pleasant summer morning in June 2007. "You wrote this?" I ask.

> *Roshanji*: Yes, and I have written hundreds of poems in English, Hindi, and Urdu. [He opens the notebooks and shows me the poems.]
>
> *Devika*: Did you ever get them published?
>
> *Roshanji*: No, no. I just wanted to write these for children. I used to be very involved in the Rotary Club and I would read these at children's events. Listen to this:

Is Navyug ki Pehchaan ho tum
Manavtaa Ka Abhimaan ho tum
Tum ho bhavivashya is dharti kaa
Mere Bharat kee shaan ho tum.

(You are the face of the new country
You are the pride of the people
You are the future of this earth
You are the pride of Bharat [India].)

When I was growing up in a small village . . . I don't remember the name of this village anymore. It was in Sargoda District. Anyway, I used to walk to school, almost a three kilometer walk, can you imagine? I walked with three friends—one was Hindu, one was Sikh, and the other was Muslim. We were four of us. I was the Hindu, there was a Sikh boy, Attar Singh. There was Barkat Ram, another Hindu. And then there was Gulam, my Muslim friend. We called him Gulu Gulu. His mother was very fond of me and so was his big sister. They would make delicious *paranthas* for us on our way to school in the morning. So I still remember . . . and these are the types of memories that are etched in my mind.

He calls out to his daughter-in-law, who brings out three thick notebooks that have his handwritten poems in the three languages—Hindi, Urdu, and English. The poems are of varying length, and at first glance they seem to focus on the theme of communal unity. I wonder if the childhood cross-communal friendship is an impetus to writing poetry in these three languages.

Devika: So, is this the reason that you write in three languages?

Roshanji: Maybe [and chuckles], but I don't write in Punjabi, since I never learned how to write in Gurmukhi [the Punjabi script]. So listen to this, it's simple, but I like to read this small line to people.
   Main Hindu hoon na Muslman hoon, ek mamooli sa insaan hoon.
   (I am neither Hindu nor Muslim, I am an ordinary human being.)

Devika: You wrote this?

Roshanji: No, I did not. This is from some other poem that I read and liked, so I noted it down here. But this is how I feel, you see. Sometimes I just write to show my *khayaals* [thoughts], they are not always poetic. We are all the same, we are caught in the arguments of politicians. We were divided because of them, but we are all the same.

Devika: So the poetry, since when did you start writing it?

Roshanji: I have always been writing it. I feel equally in all three languages.

Devika: Even in English?

Roshanji: Yes, why not? I feel no different. I was small when Partition occurred, but I started writing these in school and then I continued.

Devika: What made you start? The friends?

Roshanji: As I said, maybe it was my memory of them. There is unity in poetry, *beta*. I feel this. They are my *khayaals*. We are not so different from each other. If only we could all understand that. If people would really look at how we were, how our lives were, we were the same. That is what I try to write. To understand that. We *all* must understand that.

The impetus is different, but the search for poetic meaning is similar among these men whose stories of Partition and home are filtered through this mode. In these trilingual poems—these unpublished, even unseen words, these *khayaals*—there is an aesthetic re-homing. A conscious and unconscious mode and a means to live in the absence of home.

And poetry continues to arrive.[11] This time it comes in the form of ninety-two-year-old Dadaji, who is not on my list of participants. For many months, Meher urges me to meet the grandfather of her friend. What is his name, I ask. "Dadaji," she says. "Just Dadaji? That just means grandfather, so whose grandfather?" I question. "Just meet him, he's from Lahore, everyone calls him Dadaji, he's ninety-two, what else can anyone call him?" she counters. Of course, I chuckle. I ask her if the two subsequent generations of his family live in Delhi. "No, just one son is here I think," she replies, "but meet him, he is worth meeting, trust me." Curious, I set a time for our first meeting and find my way to his home on a weekday morning in June 2007.

"You are late!" Dadaji pronounces, peering at me with strangely clear but myopic eyes. He has been waiting at the gate for over fifteen minutes. He has turned ninety-seven as I write this. A tall man, who must have been even taller in his youth, he is dressed in a crisp white starched *khadi* (silk) *kurta pyjama*. There is a walking stick in his hand, but he does not seem to be leaning on it. "I am sorry Dadaji, this traffic is terrible," I apologize. "I am a stickler—isn't that what the British say?—I am a stickler for time," he announces. As we walk into the home, he gives me a breakdown of his daily routine. He awakens at 5:00 A.M., takes his morning walk at 5:30, and brews chai for the entire household by 6:15 A.M. "I love it when everything is on time," he declares. I smile sheepishly and tell him that I will be careful in the future. I try and fail—repeatedly. There is a gridlocked bridge that separates his neighborhood from my parents' locality, with a perennial traffic jam that seldom dissipates.

Dadaji's name is Kedarnath Seth. He spells it for me, but says, "It is pronounced like k-e-d-a-r-n-a-t-h." I nod, indicating that I am familiar with the phonetic pronunciation. We drink tea and talk about this and that; he is curious about my life in the United States and says that he is "happy to meet me, I don't go anywhere much you see, since I am over-young." "Over-young, what is over-young?" I grin. "I am simply older than young," he bursts out laughing. I join in and we walk toward the living room and seat ourselves. His daughter-in-law, a fifty-something woman in a comfortable pale pink *salwar kameez*, breezes in and introduces herself. "Dadaji was waiting for you, he must have told you," she remarks. "Yes, yes, sorry I was late." "Are you going to start?" she asks. Yes, I nod. "Okay, let me leave you, but I might peep in off and on to listen to you both, I will also bring some tea," she calls out as she leaves the room. "I won't drink tea," Dadaji tells me, "but I will have lemonade and say cheers with you." I laugh and nod.

"Over-young, you thought that was funny?" asks Dadaji with a twinkle in his eye. Of course, I answer. "Let us start wherever you want, but *beta*, tell me your name" he invites. "Devika," I reply. "Beautiful name, beautiful, unforgettable," he praises. "My father named me after the 1920s actress, Devika Rani, you must have seen her films," I reply. "Yes, yes, she was a great actress," he agrees. He names a few of her films, some that I have seen, other that are new to me. "You must, you must watch all the films of your namesake," he insists. I tell him about the project and we enter his story about Partition. His trajectory of departure and arrival into India was smooth, "Nothing happened to any of us," he says. "We were very lucky." How, I ask.

Dadaji: My wife, who is no more, was a doctor. She was almost immediately given a transfer to Delhi and I worked for an insurance company and I was also transferred. She worked for a government hospital, we were given a four-bedroom house. It came with the job. We were also able to accommodate a lot of our relatives because we had space in our house. And I was already familiar with Delhi because I used to travel here from Lahore to record in the All India Radio studios. I was an artist, you see. My insurance job was just a day job.

This is news to me, so I ask, "What kind of an artist?"

Dadaji: Yes. I sang. Ghazals, in Urdu and Punjabi. [He breaks into a song that I am unfamiliar with, but I can hear the professional singer's training in his voice.] I had plenty of friends since I was an artist. I used to have concerts. I had wonderful friends. I had wonderful Muslim friends and I stayed in touch with them even after Partition. In fact they helped me to move from Lahore. I was an artist, I was very well liked.

Devika: Did you return?

Dadaji: No, but many of them would come to see me here. Some would stay for weeks.

Devika: Really?

Dadaji: It was hard because we were already two countries, but there was always some sort of cultural exchange.

Curious about his singing career, I ask many of my older participants about Dadaji, giving them his full name. Many of them recall his singing and are shocked to hear that he is still alive. "He must be one hundred," Anilji notes. "No, no, he is ninety-two; he was thirty-two in 1947," I correct him. That he was famous is clear from the number of people who have heard his name. He was a household radio name in the 1930s and the 1940s. For Dadaji to say that he was "well liked" is certainly an understatement.

Dadaji is not so much interested in the Partition and its aftermath, but wants to talk about poetry and song. His memories of Lahore and Pakistan are secondary to the concerts that he was invited to sing and the life that he lived as an artist. Any bitterness, sorrow, or loss that I anticipate from him over the Batwara is overshadowed by the art, which I think has sustained his sense of himself and is a secure bridge between the old and new country.

Dadaji: I write *shairs*. I make them even now.

Devika: Even now?

Dadaji: I used to sing on the radio until five years ago. I stopped because my voice is not strong anymore.

Devika: You still sound good.

Dadaji: But it's weak. Let me tell you a *shair*:
Yeh Maana ke hai umr mein budhapa
Magar hazoor tabiyat mein abhi jawaani hai.
(It is true that I am getting older with age, but Sir, my temperament is still young.)

Devika: *Wah wah!* [Hear hear!]

Dadaji: There is another charm in old age. Just another charm. Now all I need is love, nothing else. See, you want to talk to me, you come here and are sitting with me, that is all I need.

That I am both charmed and delighted by his demeanor cannot be denied. I laugh my way through our conversations, evidenced in my recordings, where I can hear my own peals of laughter instigated by some poetic joke, or *shair*, or general observation about life by this aged celebrity.

Dadaji, the oldest amongst my participants, is also the most unusual. His story does not align with any of the other oral histories that I have recorded. If there is a common thematic, it is that he is a singer and a poet like some of the other men. Exhibiting neither regret nor nostalgia for the old country in any of our moments together, he repeatedly tells me, "I was an artist, I sang, I was not so interested in knowing anything else about politics or what not." He also puts me under scrutiny:

Dadaji: I like you as a person. You have done a very good interview with me. From all angles you have interviewed me and I am very happy to meet you and pray for your good health, long life, and family life. Hear this, it is from Kabir Sahib [the famous poet and saint]:
Aisee banee boliye
Man ka aapa khoye
Auron ko sheetal kare
Aap bhi sheetal hoye.
(You should talk in such a way that your mind is pure; your talk should calm you and calm others.)

As I am about to leave, Dadaji asks his daughter-in-law to look for the invitation from the Queen of England. In a month, his son, a surgeon who lives in England, is being awarded Most Excellent Order of the British Empire for his service to medicine. As the only surviving parent, Dadaji, is invited by Buckingham Palace. He is flying to attend the ceremony. "I never saw the Queen when she ruled us, but I get to see her now," he beams. We all admire the invitation and exclaim over how proper it looks. Dadaji has lived out his life in poetry and song, and I think he belongs neither *there* (Pakistan) nor *here* (India). Yet I sense that this visit to the mother country, to England, is some sort of a homecoming. In Dadaji, the nostalgic thematic dismantles. And yet another one holds.

Trains, Fictions

"We know more about the train journey . . . than we know about their home" announces Kavi, Labbi Devi's granddaughter, a third-generation participant who has come to my parents' home to meet me. We've been talking about her grandmother Labbi Devi's train journey to India. The train is a symbol, a metaphor, and a reality in the way the movement across the border occurred in the violence-ridden months of 1947. The train, the last material connection to the old country, was a membrane between the past and the future. As the most commonplace and affordable means of travel, it was the official mode utilized by the newly formed Pakistani and Indian governments for the transfer of populations. It is now common knowledge that hundreds of thousands could not get on these very trains owing to lack of space or limited financial resources and made the journey across by foot, and many perished along the way. Only *one* of my participants, Kiranji, flew to Delhi, and that was only because of family contacts in the Indian Air Force.

Trains trail as conduits between nations, containers of lives and of memories. These very trains were also the harbingers of death. Trains departing from each side of the border often reached their destinations with only dead bodies on board. These trains full of dead were used as weapons to incite more communal violence. A death train would arrive in India, and Hindu rioters would massacre a train full of Muslins in retaliation; they would spare the driver, who was asked to take the train back to Pakistan. Muslim rioters would retaliate in a similar fashion. So many of my older participants have memories of having witnessed these death trains. "It is a good thing I was young because to see something like that stays with you, but over the years I forgot the image," says Anilji, who witnessed such a train near the refugee camp in Delhi where his family lived for years. Kiranji, who saw both a killing and a death train at a train station in Delhi, simply asks, "Now to have seen that? To have seen that?"

Returning me to the moment, almost becoming an oral historian herself, there in my parent's home, Kavi questions me:

> Did you not read Khushwant Singh's book *Train to Pakistan*?[12] I think that was my first introduction, outside of the family—to Partition and to the way that it took place, the violence. In a way it was what I knew about the Partition. I cannot forget Mano Majra.

Mano Majra is the fictional village in Punjab where the novel is set. Yes, even as Biji's stories during our walks were my entry into the Batwara, it was *Train to Pakistan* by Khuswant Singh that was my first foray into Partition fiction. Published in 1956, it was probably bought by Papa and was a fixture on the family bookshelf as long as I can remember. I read it as soon as I was allowed, sometime after I turned thirteen. I don't remember what I felt, but the death train central to the story is unforgettable.

Writing in 2002, literary critic Suvir Kaul notes that *Train to Pakistan* remains "one of the most popular accounts of the impact of the political partition of the subcontinent on the small villages and communities of the Punjab."[13] Literary critics evince surprise at how a novel so "thin in character and event" appealed so strongly to the popular imagination, but Kaul rightly proposes that that book, set in 1947,

> invites us to think seriously about border communities ripped asunder by Partition and about the cultural and social values that enabled mass violence. . . . The novel opens by describing a time when people's identities had been polarized into a simple, murderous, opposition: you were Hindu or you were Muslim, and you "belonged" to India or to Pakistan.[14]

In these ways the fictional domain of Partition literature resonates with historiographies like Zamindar's *The Long Partition*, which continue to emphasize that the Partition led to the creation of fixed communal categories that have troubled the subcontinent since 1947.[15]

The storyline of *Train to Pakistan* is fairly simple. In summer 1947, the Partition is underway, but it means very little to the Sikhs and Muslims of Mano Majra, a village that lies on the border of India and Pakistan, where people live in relative communal harmony. But strange incidents begin to occur. A local moneylender is murdered, and suspicion falls on Juggut Singh, the Sikh village gangster who happens to be in love with a local Muslim girl. Local trains have always functioned like the village clock, allowing village residents to carry on their daily routines based on the trains' arrivals and departures. Then one day, quite suddenly, the trains start running irregularly. Soon after, the first train carrying the dead bodies of Sikhs arrives, and Mano Majra's residents witness, for the first time, the communal violence that has so far not touched their village. This moment transforms the village into a battlefield, and neither the magistrate nor the police are able to stem the rising tide of violence.

While there are many more nuances to the novel, what seems to have captured and stayed in our imaginations are images of the death trains. Labbi Devi, a survivor of such a train, a first-generation refugee, nonchalantly tells me in Punjabi, *"Agge pichhe lashaan hi lashaan sigian"* (there were just dead bodies in the front and back and around us). And so perhaps it is no surprise that Kavi, her granddaughter, remains tied to these images.

Surat, another third-generation participant, talks to me not so much about what his father, an older Partition refugee, remembers, or what stories about the family have sustained its memories, but more about the fictive terrains that have sustained an entire generation's curiosity about the event. Surat also addresses the Partition via *Train to Pakistan*. He asks me if I have seen the 50th anniversary edition. Shaking my head, a bit puzzled, I question him, "What about it?" I own a few editions of the novel, bought over the years because new prefaces were added, and the original stays in my parents' home in Delhi. "The edition has pictures by Margaret Bourke-White, the *New York Times* photographer who documented the Partition," he replies. He walks to the bookshelf in his living room and brings it over to where I am seated on a divan. I start looking through the book; it is the novel interspersed with black-and-white photographs that provide the human face of the transfer of populations. These are difficult pictures to look at. The first picture is of Muslim women in *burkas* (full body veils), trying to get into a train that would take them to Pakistan. The last image is that of a small Sikh boy who takes a last look at Punjab before he crosses over into India.

I make a note to myself that I must buy this edition. And I do. Surat continues, "This is what I think of when I think of Partition; even though my father took me to see the places that they lived in Old Delhi when they first came here as refugees, for me, this is the Partition." In hearing this, again and again, from participants my age and my generation, I realize that the fictional terrain of Partition is inescapable. In the end, that is "our story" of this continuous watershed moment. This is a matter well explained by Suvir Kaul:

> Literary texts, cinema, and other creative arts bear witness to the entire 'business' of Partition, to the feelings of bewilderment, loss, and dislocation, to the horrific experiences to which entire communities were subject, to the cultural and economic insecurities and aspirations that motivated socio-political elites and subaltern groups in their search for new homelands.[16]

And I have expected that participants in my age group will engage a different Partition narrative, because much of what they know about Partition has come to them via fictive memorials—poetry, film, and song. Confirming what I already know, Surat asks, "Did you read *Ice Candy Man?*"[17]

Devika: Of course.

Surat: Yes. What about the film? Did you watch it?

Devika: Yes, I did. I watched it. *Earth*,[18] right?

Surat: Right. I mean that is how I know more about Partition. I know some stuff from my father. But most of what I know is from these stories. Now I know that they are not all real, but I guess it is the closest to the daily life of my grandparents that I could ever get. They are more concrete, you know? Of what life was like over there.

That the old country is realized in fiction and that home is also largely a fiction is a legacy of anthropology's colonial encounter. A complex idea, which Surat articulates in this simple manner, reminding me that the real, the imagined, and the remembered may all be fictive terrains. Surat's words also emphasize the force of how *here* and *there* remain local, contingent, and ultimately undefinable.

Every few months I receive the occasional phone call from a third-generation participant (and sometimes from the sibling of a participant) asking me whether I have watched *Khamosh Pani* or *Pinjar*,[19] or if I have read the latest book released about the Partition. If I have already seen the film or read the book, then an inevitable discussion about its merits ensues. Since I am neither a literary nor film critic, I do what I can do best as an ethnographer and an oral historian—I take note of what they note, I ask them why the films seem more evocative than the stories their parents and their grandparents tell. They tell me—again and again—that these spaces are their only way of knowing that life, that old home. They consume literature and art as aesthetic vehicles that return them to their ancestral homes, homes that they did not know to begin with—homes that will always be fictions in one form or the other. In writing about similar experiences shared by children of the Holocaust, under the framework of postmemory, Hirsch explains:

> None of us ever knows the world of our parents. We can say that the motor of the fictional imagination is fueled in part by the desire to know the world as it looked and felt before our birth. . . . How much more ambivalent is this curiosity for children of Holocaust survivors. . . . Theirs is a different desire, at once more powerful and more conflicted: the need not just to feel and to know, but also to re-member, to re-build, to re-incarnate, to replace, and to repair.[20]

And I too travel home in these very ways. In bringing the print of *Mataji* to my home and placing it in the center of my living room here in this Appalachian portion of Ohio, in treasuring the "English Make" Taj box, in repeatedly reading Partition fiction, in this very oral history record, I add my own aesthetic of postmemory to this story.

And still others, like Shielji's grandson, Tarun, bypass all of these poetic dimensions and just continue to physically return to the old country. I never meet Tarun. I hear about him from his grandmother, who subtly disapproves of his passion for Pakistan—a country she associates with the terrors of communal violence, a lost home that she does not want to recover. I don't meet him, because every time I am in Delhi for fieldwork and attempt to see him, he is in Lahore, participating in a golf or bowling or cricket tournament. He stays busy arranging more "Indo-Pak activities," as his grandmother resignedly calls them. These *crossings*, another kind of return, home.

EIGHT

My Father, My Interlocutor

Gurgaon, March 2009

The scowl on Papa's face is deepening. For almost an hour now we have been driving in circles looking for the house of Arjunji's daughter Rekha, in Gurgaon. We keep going past identical, dust-laden high-rise construction sites that have become near-permanent eyesores in this Delhi suburb. A big dry cloud of dust with no infrastructure—that is what Papa calls this afflu-ent locality. Our dilemma is our own fault; we were given a landmark that we forgot to note down, and a phone number that we forgot to feed into our mobile phones. I start to regret not having asked Arjunji to accompany us, but he lives almost three hours away and the travel would have tired him out.

We are meeting Rekha in her home, on the first level of which she runs a pre-kindergarten playschool. It is a weekday, she is busy, but she will talk to us in between working the entire afternoon. "My house is on the top level of the school, so we can go there after you've spent some time in the school, you will like the children, they cheer everyone up" she says on the phone. Arjunji has proudly told us about her school and that "we must tour it, Rekha is a great Montessori teacher."

Ahmed and I catch each other's eyes in the rearview mirror. I give him a small smile. I see the irritation growing on Papa's face—the stage of furious-thunderous frowning, the precursor to a full-blown outburst. He wants to berate me for leaving behind the information, but he knows I will point out that it was he who spoke with Rekha before we left, and only he knows where the note was kept. Thirty minutes later we are greeted with a front-lawn full of some thirty laughing children who are celebrating five birthdays—there are five big balloons and five mini–birthday cakes. Innocent sights and sounds that, thankfully, restore Papa's mood.

Déjà vu

Two days previously, on our way to meet Aniliji's aunt, Sarlaji, we lost our way. We had directions and her phone number, but Abdul took a wrong exit. Papa was angry with him, and I tried to neutralize the situation, to keep it calm: "It's fine, she's not in a rush, we will get there." Not the best tactic to use, because Papa turned to me, and speaking in English, accused me of "siding" with the driver over him, and that too in front of the driver! "I am not taking any sides, and this is ridiculous, and why be mad at him, he made a mistake," I tell him. "These days these guys don't know how to drive, they are just interested in making quick money," Papa announces. Of course, this is another reminder that "these" people, who work for those of us who can afford their services, are constantly set aside. Spoken over. Made un/present. Here, it is Abdul's working-class status that makes him invisible; elsewhere, it is his Muslim-ness. I am as guilty of such behavior as my father. I recognize these middle-class traits, and I am also quite sure I perform them unconsciously. The only difference is that my movement to the West has, among other things, made me more sympathetic to how we labor in our daily lives.

But to start giving Papa a lecture here would only exacerbate the situation. We reach our destination half an hour later than planned. Papa is calm as we spend the afternoon with Sarlaji, but I know I have not heard the last of it. That night after dinner, he replays my so-called disloyalty to Amma, telling her, "She does not know how to deal with these people anymore," and looking at me, he accuses, "You all live in America and forget that there is a way of working and dealing with people here." I roll my eyes sarcastically, remarking, "I did live here for twenty-three years, you know? I know how it works. A mistake is a mistake." As always I am also placed as Other, from another location, when I do anything contrary to the norm. My un/belonging "self and home" are repeatedly centered, and thus I am repeatedly reminded of the breach I have committed in leaving.

I retire to my room for the evening. Amma tries to calm Papa down, saying *"Chod do ab"* (Let it be now). After he is asleep, she comes to my room as she does every day after dinner, mostly to gossip about the day and watch some television with me. Amma says, "Your father always needs someone, something to 'run' or 'organize.'" I tell her that we are also probably getting on each other's nerves; we have been doing this work for over two years now, and besides, I say, "He does not need to go with me to interview the younger people." Amma giggles, "Well, you've got him involved in a project, hard to stop him." "But the fieldwork will be over at some point, I hope he gets that?" I ask Amma, whose only response is a resigned, "Well this is how your father is, right now this is *his* project."

Flashback

My father is a sprightly, slight, grey-haired bespectacled man with deep reserves of daily energy, a quality that he used well in his job as a human resources professional until he retired in 2002 after thirty-five years of work. The years after his retirement are difficult—both for him and for Amma. For many men of his generation everywhere, retirement, the end of their working years, is the end of their longest-worn identity. Homebound for the first time in his life, Papa is aimless, depressed because there is nothing for him to do, no place to routinely visit, no one to call him "Sir," no one who needs his expert advice. He eyes the running of Amma's household as a potential place to expend his energies. "He has nothing to do, so he wants to interfere and run this place like his office," is Amma's constant complaint in those years. "He thinks everything is disorganized, it's not, this place runs just fine, he has nothing to do so he wants to institute a new system," she wails to me on the phone one morning. Her domain—that of the domestic—is being encroached upon, and Amma vehemently resists. We try to coerce Papa to take on some part-time work, but he is adamantly opposed to it; "I have worked too long to get back into that again."

Papa just wants to be home, but for years we wonder whether the family and household will survive his homeboundness. Five years go by, and my parents' postretirement life settles into some modicum of normalcy. Papa volunteers for the neighborhood welfare association, they travel here and there, the bickering ebbs and flows. They divide daily tasks in such a way that Papa is out of the house for a few hours before lunch. It is still strange to wake up in the mornings to find Papa busy at work in the kitchen, still in his *khadi* (homespun cotton) *kurta pyjama*, cooking fresh *dhaliya* (steel-cut oats), heating milk, toasting bread, and generally shepherding everyone to the breakfast table—a task that was Amma's for the first thirty years of my life.

During these years, Papa builds himself a separate suite on the terrace where he keeps his books, computer, paperwork, and even a futon. We call it his terrace-room. He spends almost half the day there, and we rarely disturb him, save for winter afternoons when we force ourselves into his space to soak in the afternoon sun. It's the domain within the domain, a somewhat neutral zone, because the home "proper" continues to be fought over. But in this small way in this space (or because of it), outside the main home, a tenuous peace continues to hold.

Father: Informant, Interferer, Interlocutor

In early 2007, sensing my vacillation and insecurity in starting this oral history work that I have discussed for years, Papa gently admonishes me, "Well, even if others have studied Partition, you will have something else to say, and I can help you find the families—almost all the people we know in Delhi are refugees." Yes, we do not have to go far. I remember a moment during my wedding in Delhi in December 2005 when a guest asks if the big crowd in the banquet hall is all family. I simply reply, "Yes and no—they are all somehow linked with my grandparents—friends, relatives, neighbors from Pakistan—Papa does not even know whether they are family or friends, and I do not know most of them." For some, Partition ties have stayed strong, deep. Even though we only meet during ceremonial family gatherings such as weddings and funerals, the old country is a strong link, yet one that is fast eroding. For my generation, which is dispersed within India and spread across continents, these punctuated moments are more frequently skipped owing to the vagaries of transcontinental travel.

May 2007 is the start of my field-homework for *Home, Uprooted.* I make seven more such trips home—long and short—in the ensuing three years. Papa eagerly jumps into the project. His enthusiasm amuses us all, especially my mother, who thinks this is a "fine" opportunity to get him out of her hair and out of the house. I need him for the fieldwork. He is my family's last link to the old country, but I wonder if it is too much to ask of him. I'm sure he will soon tire of both the travel and the talk. I am proved wrong.

He carries a little notepad in which he organizes our schedule. Every morning, after he makes bed tea for the entire household—he has done this for at least two decades, ever since the passing of my grandfather, Pitaji—we go for a walk in the park and plan our day. Every place, including the park, becomes a field site for him. Here, he finds me a few older participants, such as ninety-year-old Mohanji, who takes his morning walk leaning on a thick wooden cane. We know he is somewhere in the park when we hear loud yogic throat-clearing sounds in between recitations of Hindu *bhajans* (hymns). He lives a couple of blocks down from our home, and Papa arranges for us to meet over a few Sunday brunches of *paranthas.*

Every day after he has served us breakfast I hear Papa on the phone as he arranges meetings with participants, describing my "book" and telling people, *"Meri beti aayi hui hai America se, wo wahan professor hai, Wo bas aapse thodi dair ke liye baat karna chahti hain, wo apnee book ke liye research kar rahi hain"* (My daughter is here from America, she is a professor there, she wants to talk to you briefly, she is gathering research for her book). I resist.

Devika: Papa, you are misleading them by calling our conversations brief.

Papa (cajoling): *Arre bacche* [Oh, child], if you tell eighty, ninety-year-olds that you are going to talk to them for hours, they will get scared and not let you come over. They don't know it is informal.

How can one counter that? I don't. I have not worked with an elderly population and I must take his word for it. The project is in its infancy and my "book" has not even been conceived, but when I reach my participants' homes, the family members promptly ask when my "book" will become available in stores. I cannot embarrass Papa, so I tell them that once the interviews are complete, I will be working on it. The truth, just without a timeline.

When I insist that I cannot meet just our friends and family as potential participants, Papa finds many more, but wisely reminds me, "You do not know most of them because you did not live close to them, because of my jobs and your school; for you they are all strangers, and anyway this is a family history study, why leave them out?" He's right, and in so many ways we are slaves to our academic field training, and mine has taught me to keep some degrees of separation from my participants.

Other small, practical, and consistent doses of fieldwork advice flow from him. One of the questions I ask my participants is, "What is your understanding of the Partition?" Having heard many older women and men struggle to answer it, Papa directs me to revise it, "You need to change that question to—*Aap batware ke bare mein kya soonchata hain?*" (What do you now think about the Partition?). He thinks my original question too ambiguous, and old people, he adds, like things to be simple; "they are tired, why make them struggle over this." It is a small semantic restructuring that does indeed change the way the question is answered, because many refugees take the opportunity to simply tell me, "I don't want to think about the Partition, I hate thinking about it." This is a response my own question would not have elicited, an answer that tells me that Partition wounds run deep, that many refugees would rather shut out the memories than remember them. It is a reply that also shows well how uneven memories of home and memories of the political rupture will always be.

"You must try to meet as many people from one family at one time [as you can], because people get involved in their lives, they forget, and don't really give you time later; focus on one family for a few days," Papa cautions. I take it lightly at that time, but in subsequent trips I start doing just that—I meet as many members of one family as possible over a few days. People forget. They travel. Older participants fall sick. Their children are busy. Their grandchildren are the most difficult to schedule, since they are mostly in school or in new jobs. I am not a priority in these rushed lives.

Our fieldwork (at home and in homes) is another kind of beginning for this father-daughter relationship. I call it a beginning, because even though he is my father, Papa—with his habits, his personality, his moods—is still a stranger to me. As children my brother and I saw him for a few hours a day before or after dinner. After we left for our boarding schools in the early and mid-1980s, we became more distant. Even now, I make it a point to mention to Papa that he wrote us once a year and that, too, a letter dictated to his secretary and signed by him. We make light of it, but he defends himself: "I knew what you were doing, your mother kept me posted." At the peak of his corporate career, when I moved to America in 1997, my departure was but a small moment in Papa's otherwise busy life.

But after he retires in 2002, everything changes. We cannot *not* meet because he is always "at home" during my trips to Delhi. He is keen to know us—my brother and me—what we do, what we like, how we live, what we want to do. One day in 2002, when I am almost halfway through my doctoral program, he asks, "What did you do your master's degree in?" I burst out laughing. Yes, indeed we must begin at the very beginning. I am a few years short of thirty then (in 2002), but as the cliché goes, it is never too late (for anything).

With the Partition work, we are together for more hours than we have been in my thirty-something years—car rides, people's homes for tea, lunches, dinners. East, West, North, and South Delhi. Sometimes lost and often disgruntled as we stray into unknown *galis* and *chaurastas* (four-way crossroads) of innumerable neighborhoods. It is a serendipitous kind of getting lost, because it forces us to be together. In these meanderings I begin to notice Papa's attention to detail, his almost natural affinity for research. Everyone in our family knows that he started Ph.D. studies in social work, only to realize that supporting a family on an academic salary, in India at that time, would be difficult. What I don't know and what one of his fellow refugees, a very distant cousin who is not a part of this record, mentions to me, is that Papa's master's thesis focused on a migrant labor population.

One night in Delhi I scour the web, knowing that Delhi University has recently placed its theses and dissertation titles online. I find that his 1965 thesis, "Study of the Immigrant Workers in the Textile Industries at Faridabad," is listed in the Archives of Indian Labour. The next morning during our walk in the park, I interrogate him:

Devika: Why did you choose this topic?

Papa: Well, it was something that interested me. These people had left their homes in the villages to work under really difficult conditions and, you see, so had we. The conditions under which they worked were difficult. Long hours, they lived in huts with their families.

Devika: The website does not say what kind of study it was. What methods did you use?

Papa: It was sociopsychological. They lived in slums outside the factories. I spent months there. I interviewed them. We were trying to understand how they coped with migration.

He pauses, suddenly chortles, and bursts out that his friend who was also writing his thesis manufactured all his project data. I am shocked and I ask if the friend (whose name I daren't mention) was ever found out. He doesn't know. "My major professor wanted to use my data to publish; at first I was hesitant, but I let him because I had decided not to continue onto a Ph.D.," he ends. So he leaves research behind at the age of twenty-four, joins the corporate sector, and works in personnel and human resources for thirty-five years.

Finding out about his thesis at this juncture, in these moments, through another refugee means something. Or it is the inverse? Is it that the moment finds us? An anticipation. Forty-five years after Papa wrote those stories about labor migration, I, his daughter—this ethnographer—attend to and anticipate home, travel, and forced migrations.

A serendipitous legacy. Some things come full circle.

There is no doubt that my fieldwork is smoothed by Papa's active involvement, and sometimes just by his mere presence. It is also not an exaggeration to say that there would be a very thin oral history record without him. When my older participants hesitate about talking to me alone, they ask for Papa, who is only too eager to step in. As he accompanies and participates in the conversations, he starts to worry, as only as a father can, about my listening to many of these stories, both there and here. "They are too sad," he says, shaking his head. After I am back in the United States transcribing and living with the stories, he advises me to avoid working with more than one first-generation story in one day, "Space them out even more if you can, otherwise you will feel depressed," he cautions. I listen to what he says. I space them out. And when I don't, true to his word, they give me the blues for many days. Yes, it is true that father knows best.

That he is my father, who is concerned for my well-being, is steadily evident. He is upset when an older-generation participant, Vermajii, does not even offer us water, let alone tea, in his home—a breach of hospitality that is sacrilege to Papa, and to many of us who are from the subcontinent. My being "away" has lessened such expectations and I try to brush it off, but Papa insists that I drop him from the "sample" altogether. We argue. I don't intend to, but eventually I have to, because his family is not very accessible. Vermaji dies of a cardiac arrest in the subsequent years. And Papa is a bit humbled, reframing his impression of him, giving in to the generosity that someone's passing inevitably occasions: "Well, he was an old man, he is no more, maybe he was already sick when we met him."

When I find it hard to control my own tears when Mrs. Sachdeva breaks down as she remembers post-Partition days in Delhi, Papa, who has been sitting a little apart from us in the family room of her small flat, walks over and consoles her. After we have both composed ourselves, he goes to her kitchen to make us some tea. During this break, he asks her to show us the flat, which she has recently moved into. Mrs. Sachdeva is glad for the distraction and gives us a tour that ends in her prayer/meditation room—since she was widowed she has become a devotee of a Hindu group in that locality and spends much of her day in their ashram. It is Papa who gently takes us back to the kitchen table so we can resume talking. Shifting back to becoming interlocutor, he takes over for a while and questions Mrs. Sachdeva more about Delhi after 1947, until she is talking as freely as she had been. In between he tells her a little about his own parents, pointing out that they were all from the same general area, and our families knew each other well. Their families organized outings and picnics together. He reminds her:

We used to go for picnics every few months, maybe sometimes with your family too. My father and his brothers used to hire a large truck and we would all sit in the back. It was a good life. A comfortable life. A simple life.

Yes, Mrs. Sachdeva nods, "Not complicated." And sometimes the field of memories shifts from Mrs. Sachdeva's to his own when, with a faraway look in his eyes, Papa starts reminiscing.

Papa: I was studying in a convent. It was called Sacred Heart.

Devika: I never knew this. I thought you went to the Hindu High School.

Papa: No. That was a school started by my maternal great-grandfather. He became an educationist later on in his life. He started the Hindu High School in Dera Ghazi Khan.

The school I went to was a convent. We had British nuns. There were Muslim, Hindu, and Sikh students in the school. I used to go to school in a *tonga* every morning. I still remember the faces of my classmates.

We lived in a very big house. My paternal grandfather was a landlord who owned one hundred acres of land. It was a very well-built house. Maybe a thousand square yards. There were eight or ten rooms, I think. All the rooms were carpeted and there were small fireplaces in each room. In the winters, we used to gather around the fireplace to eat dinner.

It was a nice street and mostly Muslims lived there. Our neighbors across were Muslims, I was in their house all the time. Their son was my closest friend—Nawab was his name. In summers, I used to almost eat all my meals there.

Devika (a bit surprised): You were allowed to eat there? So many people told me that they never ate in the homes of Muslims because for Hindus their kitchens were considered unclean, because they ate meat [beef].

Papa and Mrs. Sachdeva: No, we ate in their homes. We didn't think they were any different from us.

Any tidy thematic, any sort of pattern that I anticipate is once more, quickly, dismantled. This break, a constant redundancy.

The conversation related here, and many others, generate Papa's own memories of moments, faces, incidents, names, objects, persons—things that have stayed in the recesses of his mind. It is not unusual for him to interrupt my interviews to ask the participant to clarify some things, as he does with Anilji when there is some confusion over where exactly they all lived. In all honesty, sometimes I am disconcerted by his rapport with some of the older refugees, even when he does not know them. It makes me feel less in charge. But in charge of what? I ask myself. This field of memories is under no one's control. When Kapurji addresses his entire interview to Papa with only occasional glances in my direction, and when Prakashji recites a small sonnet that only the two of them recognize, I feel bereft of my own field, homeless in the field-home. But maturity prevails; I learn to shake off the feeling, because the field would feel barren but for Papa's presence.

When I ask him about the Partition in everyday conversations, Papa is quick to insist that he was only six years old and it is "just a story" for him. But in moments such as the ones with Mrs. Sachdeva, the story is real. He is and was there. It is his story too. If not put to use, stories just hibernate inside us, awaiting the right moment to arrange themselves. Sometimes, such as here, they are helped along by generative, dialogic encounters as co-recitations of family history.

Performance artist and scholar Bryant Keith Alexander refers to this process of dialogic recall as "generative autobiography," wherein audience members (Papa and I—listeners) become active collaborators between that which they experience and their own life-scripts.[1] Alexander discusses "generative autobiography" as a genre that is steeped in Victor Turner's notion of "performative reflexivity," understood as a "condition in which a sociocultural group or its most perceptive members, acting representatively, turn, bend, and reflect back upon themselves."[2] In the context of autobiographical performance—and here I address oral history as autobiographical performance—Alexander considers the reflexive turn on the part of the audience to be a "critical move of making sense of lived experience triggered by a performance of bending the critical eye inward."[3] The audience does not mimic, it reflects and refracts—almost the same, but not quite. And in the context here, there is one more movement at work, owing to two layers of audiencing—my father and I, as audience to the oral history; I, as audience to my father's generative reflections. I must reflect on him reflecting on himself as he participates in the oral histories.

Performances are generative—among other things, they make us reflect and sometimes act upon the world around us. My critical move is to make the decision to formally include Papa as part of the record. I remain hesitant, as is my habit—I fuss, I vacillate. Refugees who know Papa and knew my grandparents keep asking, "*Apne Papa kee interview nahi karogi?*" (Will you not interview your father?), and I find my qualms fading. I do wonder what new information would be elicited in a formalized interview—we have already been talking about our family story "alongside" the interviews. Most of the stories of my family that emerge in these pages have been gathered along with the other oral histories. I am skeptical. I feel and I know there will be redundancy. But I decide to do it anyway, choosing a day on a winter afternoon in December 2009 as the "interview day."

Father: Participant

We pick one midmorning on a weekday, because with so many family members who live in Delhi, the house gets busy on weekends. I ask Papa to forgo his errands for the day and we retire to the terrace room after breakfast. We make ourselves comfortable on the futon. And even before I turn on my recorder, Papa cautions, "I was just six, the Partition is more a story that my mother and father told us." "It's okay, those are the stories I am interested in, let's start with anything," I urge.

> *Papa*: Well you see, Partition is now just a story. That is how I remember it. It has been so long. We moved to India in May, before independence.
>
> *Devika*: Why did you move early?
>
> *Papa*: Pitaji had opted to stay in Pakistan. The rioting was already on, and so he wanted to send us away to Shimla-Solan for a few months, and he would call us back when things settled down. We left everything, and of course we never went back.

I have already told the story of Pitaji's being given refuge by his Muslim boss. This decision to harbor a Hindu earned his boss the wrath of the Muslim rioting mob, which threatened to kill them both. What I did not know is that it was the boss who arranged for Pitaji to leave for India in an army convoy that was headed to Amritsar. It was the boss who packed our household goods into a train wagon, a railroad car, that unfortunately, never made it past Lahore—the train was looted. I ask Papa what happened to the boss. "Nothing, he helped Pitaji to get a transfer within the Indian Railways, so when he came to India, Pitaji had a job," he explains. I am also curious about the contents of the wagon—what was in it? "Furniture, carpets, kitchen utensils, our clothes, the whole household," he replies. Papa fills in some more blanks:

> We were in Solan, we knew Pitaji was going to arrive, but we did not know when.
>
> We used to just spend afternoons at the station—this went on for one month and then he finally arrived.

He remembers quite clearly all the homes and places they lived in India in the few decades after Partition. Biji is central to many of his memories, the "one who kept things going." Her presence as the matriarch, and her willingness to help both close and distant members of the Chawla clan, kept things afloat. Her gold—she brought 200 grams from Pakistan—helped educate children, wed them, and build homes. "Any time something was needed, she would sell a piece of gold; if someone was getting married, she would give gold for the bride," Papa furnishes. She was the only child; her father doted on her.

Devika: Do you remember him?

Papa: I never saw any of my grandparents, but I know that my Nana, my maternal grandfather—Chokhanand Taneja—lived with us when he was older and he died in our house. All I know is what Biji told us. He was a very well-known man. When he rode his carriage across town, people used to stand up and salute him. He owned a British-style carriage with two horses. He was the first graduate from his district in Dera Ghazi Khan. The Britishers had given him a title, knighted him, they had different titles for people in India, he was "Rai Sahib." He entertained the British in his homes. So you know, meat was cooked for them in the house. The women never joined, but the British were a normal presence in the house.

The pride in Papa's voice is unmistakable. His descriptions of my grand-nana are so vivid that I can see him being saluted. This description has survived two generations. And so have colonial longings. Even now, sixty-two years after their exit from the subcontinent, the English and their Englishness define how we think of success, of being "someone."

A lot of what is said that afternoon is a revision, just as oral history, as a genre and a mode of historicizing, is sociocultural-personal history revising itself in repetition.[4] It is a repetition that constantly makes real the everydayness of political events. Della Pollock notes:

A performance-centered account of oral history understands the oral history as a critical repetition among repetitions; liminal truth—truth stories "in the in-between of all regimes of truth"—as at least complementary to "the hierarchical realm of facts" conventionally favored by the social sciences; the teller as authorized by prior tellings; and the interviewer as directly implicated in a narrative environment that precedes, surrounds, and defines his or her conversations.[5]

With this revision-repetition, new memories inevitably emerge, showing me, and showing Papa, how stories too have their own generative potential.

Rai Sahib Chokhanand Taneja with his mother (seated, name unknown) and wife (name unknown).

In between talking about his convent school, his Muslim friend, and the Muslim family across from his house, Papa mentions Ram. "Who is he?" I ask, and even as the words leave my lips, I can hear his name being whispered in hushed tones by Biji and her elderly friends.

> *Papa*: He was my first cousin. A few years before Partition he fell in love with a Muslim girl on our street. His father, my uncle [Pitaji's older brother] was upset and did not want Ram to marry her. He forbade him.

"Why? You said you were in and out of Muslim homes? You ate with them," I sputter accusingly. Calm, almost as if speaking to a child (that I am), he replies:

We never intermarried. Anyway, Ram did not listen, my uncle threw him out of the house. He converted to a Musalman and married her. They say he was a very handsome man.

Devika: So what happened to him after 1947?

Papa: He stayed there.

Devika: No one has ever been in touch with him?

Papa: No. But one other cousin of mine went to Pakistan in the 1950s. He was a pilot and he was sent to—I forget the city—maybe Quetta, to work on the machinery for some aeroplane. He went to Ram's house, he knew the address. He saw two children playing outside and they resembled Ram. They looked like him. The people outside the house told him that Ram was out of town, but his wife was home. This cousin did not know the wife, so he declined to see her and just came back.

Devika: Wow. So his father never asked for him?

Papa: No. But when Ram died his wife had his death announcement printed in the *Times of India* Delhi edition, so that we would all be informed of his death.

This anecdote has an uncanny parallel to the family story with which Urvashi Butalia begins her oral history work, *The Other Side of Silence*. It is the tale of her journey to Lahore to meet Ranamama, her mother's youngest brother, who stayed back in Pakistan with the family property, eventually marrying a Muslim woman and converting to Islam. Butalia's essay "Blood" recounts her journey to Pakistan to meet him, to try to understand why he stayed behind. She writes:

> The way Ranamama described it, the choice to stay on was not really a choice at all. In fact, like many people, he thought he wasn't choosing, but was actually waiting to do so when things were decided for him. But what about the choice to convert? Was he now a believer? Had he been one then? What did religion mean to him then—after all, the entire rationale to create the two countries out of one was said to have been religion. And, it was widely believed—with some truth—that large numbers of people were forced to convert to the "other" religion. But Rana?
>
> "No one forced me to do anything. But in a sense there wasn't really a choice. The only way I could have stayed on was by converting. And so, well, I did."[6]

How strange religion is, I observe loudly to Papa. "Yes, it is, isn't it, he was their son, but lost to them because he converted," he agrees. There is another story here, and maybe it will be resurrected in another time. Those children are my relatives—second cousins—whom I probably shall never meet. I keep quizzing Papa on the Muslim issue, "I don't understand it, how can one eat in their homes, work with them, grow up with them, and then disown a son because he marries one of them?" That is how it is, how it was, says Papa.

When we were children, there were Partition stories at home—of the lost home, the life, and the old country. There was also another parallel and opposing story. In moments of anger over the Partition, Muslims were be-rated and Pakistan was held accountable for not only the family's own problems, but all the broader national problems. Papa and his relatives were often derisive of Pakistan and its people. Some of this anger has seeped into my generation—Pakistan survives and lingers in the national imagination as a bitter enemy, a troublesome distant cousin, a foil that must exist in order for us/India to feel successful. Kiranji is bemused by it, and in our talks wonders aloud, "I am surprised by folks younger than I, who did not see Partition, they seem more bitter about it than us, it is what you are fed by politicians."

But here, on this winter afternoon, with the shining sunlight flowing unevenly through the shaded windows of Papa's terrace room—a metaphor or a reflection perhaps of the unevenness of the ways we want to or are taught to remember—Papa speaks a reframed story of Pakistan and home, a more practical story.

Papa: If Partition had not taken place there would be more opportunities. We would not be so poor.

Devika: How? Pakistan is not exactly a giant producer of anything, so how?

Papa: We would have had more water, more cultivable land, more fruits—Pakistan has all these resources and we have the population. They have good mines, all these would have been and were a part of the greater India. It was a loss to the subcontinent, not just to India. But it might have been difficult to manage a big country.

Devika: How should it be remembered?

Papa: What?

Devika: The Partition?

Papa: It was a sad thing. It should not have happened. It was and is the fanaticism of the politicians. People did not want it. Partition was never meant to be a transfer of populations. That was bad. If it had not happened, we would have just stayed there. Delhi was not an important city—the big important cities were Lahore, Bombay, and Calcutta. Delhi was considered a backward city, it was all Old Delhi, all merchants, no art, no culture.

Devika: A lot of people have said this. Kiranji said, "We taught these people how to live." [We both laugh.]

Papa: There were Hindus and Muslims, yes, we were two communities, but as far as I remember there was never a communal divide, there was never such a feeling that one day we will be enemies. Now it is worse.

Devika: Why?

Papa: Now there is an even bigger divide because of terrorism. Because of a few people who are terrorists and who happen to be Muslim, there is another divide. But the terrorists are a minority, something we never want to comprehend. We just want to blame them.

Even a few years ago, Papa would not have said this. A few years ago when the Indian Parliament was attacked by Islamic terrorists, all we heard was outrage against Islam and Pakistanis. When the Mumbai attacks occurred, the bitterness resurfaced—nationally. But by then Papa and I were already inside these stories, and he uttered not one ill-word, for any Muslims or Pakistanis. And now, here, he carves out an Other space for the terrorists, showing me that in being with these stories, in listening to other refugees speak of their lives, something in him has shifted. Something that makes him more empathetic, and at the same time, more rational about who continues to be responsible for the violence. It is the terrorists who "happen to be Muslim" who are now shunned, not the Pakistanis, who have always been us.

If fields and homes make us, they also—inevitably, naturally—remake us. The stories they produce teach us more about ourselves than we want to acknowledge, more than we would ever know any other way. Fields-homes—bridges between old and new selves, homes, and ways of remembering. And Papa, a second-generation refugee, who has always maintained that Partition is "just a story" for him, is now reluctant to depart from this field, a space that has become a bridge to his memories, a link to his early childhood. There is a trace of a memory he keeps repeating/reliving every time I see him now:

> *Papa*: I can see myself standing by the piano singing with the nuns in my school. I can picture the *tonga* rides to my school, the faces of my classmates—we were little, four, five years old—I can see those faces.

And what makes *me* return, what makes *me* make this home my field—again and again? Friends, cousins, even neighbors in Delhi tease me for deliberately choosing to come home for fieldwork. It's convenient, they banter, how you always choose to do your research here. I deny it, vehemently. I argue that there is very little written about the interior lives of Indian middle-class families. That everything about India is speculative, that we need some analysis. I resist their jests, but I know there is truth in them. As it is for Papa, for me too this field-home is a bridge, a space to understand where I can (*not* where I do, or should) belong. Every field visit brings a new piece of home. Every home visit brings a new piece of the field. This movement—being there, coming here, going back there, and writing back here—is an unruly waltz that tangles further the notion of what it is to be home and what it is to dwell. That nothing shatters in the crossing in-between is a mystery. Or maybe it does and I do not notice. That too is a mystery.

Gurgaon, March 2010

I am alone in a taxi, on my way to Gurgaon. It is 7:00 on a Monday morning. I flew into Delhi ten hours ago. After spending half of what is left of the night at a friend's home, I take a metered commercial cab to the Medicity Hospital. For two months now (and three months since his recorded interview) Papa has been undergoing tests for his heart—the verdict is severely blocked arteries. A heart bypass surgery—a quadruple bypass—is critical. I hear of the surgery on Saturday morning, at home in the United States, and I am on a direct fourteen-hour-long flight to Delhi the next day. I must see my father before he is rolled into the operating room at 8:00 A.M., which is why I am asking the cab driver to step on it, "*Bhaiya, jaldi chalao, mere Papa ka operation hain aath baje*" (Brother, drive faster, my father is being operated on at 8:00 A.M.). The driver is unsure of the directions, but I am not. I rattle them off. The years of fieldwork in this area have familiarized me to the roads. I like to think that everything is linked. All that wandering has been a preparation for this moment. Here. Every road, traveled for a reason.

I arrive on time. It is a large multifacility hospital that caters to patients who are now called "medical tourists": medical nomads who cannot afford healthcare in their own countries travel here for surgeries that cost one-tenth of what surgery and postoperative care cost in the global North. Trust Papa to choose this fancy place; at least his insurance covers the costs. I have been waiting less than five minutes in a lobby that is a mile long when I see Amma lightly running down a long flight of stairs that lead to the cardiology wing. We hug and she whisks me up to Papa's room. He is lounging on a very modern red leather couch in the room, and I reach across to give him a kiss on his cheek. He asks me how the flight was, whether I was cheated by the cab driver, and how I like this hospital—"It's supposed to be like a five-star hotel, well, we will see." He pulls up his *kurta* and shows me his chest—"A barber came in and shaved my whole body at 5:00 A.M.; I mean can a man get some sleep around here? And then they bring me this terrible food, are they charging me all this money for such inconvenience?" I give a loud shout of laughter and quip, "Spoken like a true Punjabi, you want to get your money's worth." He frowns, "Well, I spent a week researching this place and its doctors—they are the best." Amma and I grin at each other and shake our heads. A new project is underway.

We spend an hour chatting. He is wheeled into surgery. It is a long and difficult day mostly because we are waiting outside the intensive care unit (ICU). My brother has taken charge of the guests—relatives, friends, refugees—who arrive and want to wait with Amma. I sit with Amma and her kitty friends, handling all the phone calls, many from persons whom Papa and I have met over the last three years—our participants. By the end of the evening there are some fifty visitors who are here just because they heard of his surgery and decided to drive over. Not one of them will be allowed to meet him. But they want to stay.

He is wheeled out into the ICU at 5:00 P.M. after an eight-hour-long surgery. Amma, Samarth (my brother), and I are allowed to see him one by one. It is interesting what eight hours of surgery can do to a human body—it makes one look smaller than oneself, almost as if the ventilator, even as it gives life, sucks out most of the person's weight—my father's already diminutive, five-foot-six-inch small frame made smaller by the surgeon's scalpel. I hold back the lump in my throat as the doctor explains that Papa's status is normal, and he will be out of the hospital in a week and "be a new man" because the surgery was proactive—conducted to open the blocked arteries, not as a response to a heart attack.

The recovery is long and slow. In 2012, it is still underway. After his surgery, I don't think about the Partition work for many months. When I interviewed him in December 2009, Papa and I still had a few people on our list that we thought we should meet. Our plan was to finish by that May. Summer 2010 arrives, I just return home—to father. Winter comes along and I return home again—to father. We don't mention the Partition. It is almost as if we have banished the field from home.

In January 2011, during one of our weekend phone conversations, Papa impatiently asks, his voice booming, "Are you writing?" Surprised, I reply, "Yes, I am trying to figure out how I want to do this, I am listening, and trying to decide how the book will be done." "I did not think you needed to talk to any more people," he says. Yes, I reply, "We have a lot here, the question is, how to tell the stories." "I trust you can do that on your own?" he chides. Yes, father, I can. Admonished, I begin my homework. Here.

A Segue: An Oath, February 3, 2011

I awaken at 5:00 A.M. having barely slept. I spend the entire night surfing the weather application on my mobile phone—checking and double-checking to make sure that all snowstorms stay at bay, outside of the Ohio Valley, just until 10:00 this morning. By the time Anirudh, as unrested as I am, leaves the bed at 6:00, I am dressed and already outside, scraping ice from the car windshield. Coffee cup in hand, he watches me from the front door, shaking his head at what he calls, my "compulsion" for time. Mostly I laugh it off, but today we cannot and must not be late. At 8:00 A.M., along with dozens of others, I am to take the oath to become a citizen of the United States. And the Supreme Court in Columbus, Ohio, where the ceremony will take place, is seventy miles away.

February in the Ohio Valley is a bitter month, not so much for the snow or the cold, which often bypass us, but for the clouds that stay around like permanent, unwanted winter guests, preventing the sun from peeping up from the horizon for weeks on end. This winter ennui, as I like to call it, lifts only in the last weeks of March, when spring finally bullies her way in. We leave as planned at 6:30, picking up a friend along the way—an anthropologist who wants to be there for the experience. These ceremonies are not open to the public, just to family and friends of those being naturalized. The event remains something of a novelty.

We reach our destination on time. We are together until the security checkpoints to enter the court, after which I am ushered into a large hall where I find myself sitting with fifty-three other hopefuls—Argentinians, Iraqis, Canadians, Afghanis, Turks, Greeks, Armenians, Somalians, Ethiopians—America's global face, seated in neat rows. There is a Mistress of Ceremonies (MC), a Department of Homeland Security official, who asks us to fill in some more forms, show more papers, and relinquish our Green Cards. She plays the "Faces of America" on the television screens in the room, and cajoles us to sing along to a song that I have neither heard nor know the lyrics to. We are then shepherded by her into the courtroom where the ceremony proper is to begin.

We sit facing the judge's bench, in the same order as in the last room, something to do with the order in which the naturalization certificates will be distributed. Today a group of about fifty elementary school children from the Columbus suburb of Bexley are here to watch and witness a citizenship oath ceremony as part of their experiential learning. They are chaperoned by two teachers who are struggling to keep them quiet and seated. The judge enters and we all rise. The Mistress of Ceremonies presents our case, and the judge asks that each of us stand up and announce our name and the country we represent. Some of my fellow oath-takers add flourishes to their introductions—My name is XYZ, I am from ABC, and I am proud to be an American. My turn arrives and I find my throat closing; I search for something appropriate to say, but this is all I manage: "Good morning, Sir, I am Devika Chawla and I was born in India."

My memories are now a blur and so is the chronology of events. "The Star Spangled Banner" is played. We recite the Pledge of Allegiance after the judge or along with him. I remember that our names are individually called so we can receive the certificate from the judge. People cry. They take pictures with the judge. Anirudh has also brought along his camera and takes the customary photograph. The schoolchildren have brought us American

The author's Indian passport, cancelled.

flags. By 9:30 A.M., we are filing out of the courtroom with our certificates in hand. February 3, 2011. I am naturalized. Here.

By 10:00 A.M. we are back on U.S. 33, making the drive home. Papa calls, demanding a description of the ceremony. I comply. He gives the phone to Amma, who greets me by asking, *"Ban gaye American?"* (Have you become American?). I repeat the description of the ceremony. She gives a resigned laugh and mutters, *"Ab waheen ke ho gaye tum log"* (You both belong there now). It is a paper, Amma, it makes travel easier, I insist. I joke that giving up my Indian citizenship is one small way of helping India's population epidemic. I am Indian, how can I be anything else, I laughingly ask her.

In the evening friends call; they ask if I want to celebrate. We do. We have dinner. We drink to one more new American. I raise my glass to *my* old country that now has one less Indian.

Lost Landscapes—Fieldnotes from Here

Driving on U.S. 50, past the belching smoke stacks of Belpre, along winding roads that take us in and out of the hilly, dense, and sometimes ominous terrain of the Appalachian mountain range, we cross the massive industrial bridge on the Ohio River just outside and over the city of Parkersburg. The bridge is a point of separation between West Virginia and Ohio, its $.50 toll the only indication that we are crossing state borders. In a few minutes we are back on winding roads, and the scenery repeats itself. Borders are, after all, human-made; terrains flow organically, resisting human interference.

I take in the hushed silence of the mountain forests that are a deep, deep green owing to the heavy spring rain. I smile, remembering that we say this every year, "Things are much greener this year, because there was so much rain in the spring." The moment repeats itself, annually. Once in a while, I spot a few houses at the foot of the mountains—in the *hollers*, as they call them here. It astounds me to see how the homes seem to sink into the hill-sides, becoming both undergrowth and overgrowth. And their inhabitants, by extension, seem to flow out of the land. People here tell me that they feel lost outside this terrain. What home means here—in local folklore—is the eighty-mile rule. People go to any means to stay, to live out their lives within an eighty-mile radius of their homeplace. When I ask around, they often say that they are so used to the landscape that living without moun-tains and hills makes them feel naked. As if the landscape were a blanket that wraps them.

They describe the trees, the woods, the roads, and the animals with a de-tailed eye—they know what bug populates the forest during what month and which birds are migrating over the skies as we speak. Even the teenagers, who work in the local bakery a few blocks from my home, know more about flora and fauna that I would have ever imagined knowing at their age. They know the trails in the woods around the county like the backs of their hands. I am, quite frankly, envious. When they ask me what tree is native to Delhi, I stumble. Neem, I think aloud. I call Papa and ask; his reply proves no more helpful, "Who knows, and why; just Google it," he mutters, irritated by my quite innocent question. I do eventually Google it and find that imlis and amaltas were native to Delhi before the British planted nonnative spe-cies such as neem, jamun, and arjun, as part of their planning for Delhi as the colonial capital in 1911.[7]

When I begin to attend to home in these oral histories, I also start to pay more attention to what people *here*, in *this* place that I have called home for nine years, say about the landscape. *Their* visceral link to the topography that holds/homes them also gives shape and form to an *overarching absence* both in the oral histories that speak from these pages and in the manner in which *I* speak and story home. *Here*, in *this* space, I finally find a thematic about *them* and *there*, one that holds, steadily. The homes of *Home, Uprooted* are remembered, recalled, resurrected in memories. Even when field and home slip in and out of each other (in-situ, cum landscape, cum terrain), Papa, our participants, and I never really speak of, view, or consider home's physical landscape, its tangible terrains. No one describes the grass, the trees, the hills, the valleys of Pakistan. No one summons the birds, the animals, or the grazing farmlands of the Punjab and Sindh provinces. Many of my elderly participants lived in villages surrounded by farms and the country. Many, like Papa, lived close to the frontier. I lived for eight years in the Indian Punjab—the rice bowl of India, the mother of all farming states. And my boarding school, Waverly, was nestled in the foothills of the Himalayas. Yet none of us has attended to topographies left behind. And before this writing, I did not even know what trees are native to Delhi—the greenest of India's metros.

What happened to the physical landscape? Where did it go? I read, re-read, and in fact over-read my field stories, finding nothing. I read my own writing about them and find that landscape is peripheral, a tinge of scenery here and there—I/we just roam in memories. My homes, our homes, Papa's homes are as bereft of physical landscapes as these person's lives *here* are immersed in them. I consider the terrain only because the people *here* continue to remind me that *their* hills are guardians that stand around them, keeping trespassers at bay. Home, for them, extends outside of home—in a different way—into the veins, the roots, the undergrowth, and even the natural gasses that hold together these mountain ranges. Home is here, present. It lives, it breathes, it is an extension of the self into the physical world.

For the subjects of *Home, Uprooted*, for Papa, for me, home is not *here*, it will always be *someplace else*—a border that cannot be crossed as easily as the one between Ohio and West Virginia, over a toll bridge. Home is a field of memories. Of stories told and those that I tell here. Home is an attempt to write a loss of landscapes. Consider these words one such attempt. Here.

Memorials/Words

It is an unsurprising outrage that no physical memorial exists to acknowledge the lives of those lost and those who lost their home in the catastrophe that was Partition, the Batwara. In my own outrage, I wonder, where it would be built? What would it say? Who would it depict? Which landscape could it evoke? I am unsure of and uninterested in the political history behind this absence, yet the absence echoes the national amnesia about the Batwara that was encouraged—so that a new nation, independent India, could be forged. Every memorial to the Partition lives on in discursive, imaginary, and fictive terrains—poetry, novels, films—mostly in words and recalled images about what home was and what it might have been. Consider *Home, Uprooted* another memorial in words. Neither *here* nor *there*.

anna A currency unit formerly used in India, worth one-sixteenth of a rupee.

bache Child; like *beta*, often used as an affectionate form of address in speaking to younger persons.

bastis Working-class neighborhoods.

batwara Partition. Like *the Partition*, the phrase *the Batwara* refers to the division of British India into the independent, separate countries of India and Pakistan.

beta Child; like *bache*, often used as an affectionate form of address in speaking to younger persons.

bhajans Devotional songs.

charpoy A type of bed commonly used in India, consisting of a wooden frame strung with tape or rope.

chummery A type of accommodation similar to a boarding house, originally meant for single men.

dal Lentils, legumes.

dupatta A long scarf, typically worn with the *salwar kameez*.

galis Narrow side streets.

Gita Short for the Bhagavad Gita, a 700-verse philosophical poem and scripture that is part of the Mahabharata, the Hindu epic.

gurudwara A Sikh temple.

-ji An honorific addendum to a name, commonly used in North India as a sign of respect for older persons or persons of higher status.

khayaals Thoughts.

kothi House, bungalow.

kurta pyjama   The long loose shirt (*kurta*) and trousers (*pyjama*) worn by men in North India, Pakistan, and parts of Central Asia.

mataji   A grandmother.

maulvi   A Muslim religious man.

Musalman   An Urdu word for a Muslim.

namaste   A customary greeting, accompanied by a slight bow with hands pressed together, widely used in India and Nepal.

namaz   The ritual prayers observed five times a day by Muslims.

paranthas   Homemade flatbreads eaten buttered and warm, often as breakfast, in many homes in northern India. They are often stuffed with cheese, meats, and different vegetables.

qawwali   Sufi devotional music, popular in South Asia.

qawwals   Singers of *qawwali*.

sabzi   Vegetable.

salwar kameez   The long shirt (*kameez*) and trousers tapering to the ankle (*salwar*) worn by many South Asian women, and particularly by Punjabi women.

shairi   Urdu sonnets.

tonga   A horse-drawn cart or carriage.

NOTES

I. BEGINNINGS—IN HEADNOTES

1. Devika Chawla, "Walk, Walking, Talking Home," in *Handbook of Auto-ethnography*, ed. Stacy Holman Jones, Tony E. Adams, and Carolyn Ellis (Walnut Creek, Calif.: Left Coast Press, 2013), 162–72. These pages are a very small excerpt from a contributed chapter in the aforementioned volume.

2. FIELDWORK/HOMEWORK

1. The names of elderly participants are followed with *ji*, which is an honorific addendum commonly used in North India as a sign of respect for older persons or persons of higher status. Participants' names and all information that would identify them have been changed to comply with the directives of the Ohio University Institutional Review Board with regard to research with human subjects.

2. See David Carr, *Time, Narrative, and History* (Indiana University Press, 1986); Mark Freeman, "Mythical Time, Historical Time, and the Narrative Fabric of the Self," *Narrative Inquiry* 8, no. 1 (1998): 27–50; Mark Freeman, "Charting the Narrative Unconscious: Cultural Memory and the Challenge of Autobiography," *Narrative Inquiry* 12, no. 1 (2002): 193–211; and Paul Ricoeur, *Oneself as Another*, trans. by Kathleen Blamey (Chicago and London: University of Chicago Press, 1992). My understanding of identity is borrowed from the ideas of these narrative scholars who argue for an entwined relationship among time, narrative, and experience. Human beings organize their lives into temporally meaning episodes that are composed of events that are narrativized. We understand what time "is" because we experience it narratively as events with beginnings, middles, and ends.

3. See Mikhail M. Bakhtin, *The Dialogic Imagination: Four Essays*, ed. Michael Holquist and Vadim Liapunov, trans. Vadim Liapunov and Kenneth Brostrom (Austin: University of Texas Press, 1981); Bruce Mannheim and Dennis

Tedlock, "Introduction," in *The Dialogic Emergence of Culture*, ed. Dennis Tedlock and Bruce Mannheim (Bloomington: University of Illinois Press, 1995), 1–32; Elaine Scarry, *The Body in Pain: The Making and Unmaking of the World* (New York: Oxford University Press, 1985); and Kathleen Stewart, *A Space on the Side of the Road* (Princeton, N.J.: Princeton University Press, 1996). These thinkers view a narrative life as a life-in-culture that is lived historically. They share the notion that the value of narrative lies in its idiographic orientation, in that, the primary unit of analysis is always the individual life.

4. Devika Chawla, "Performing Home/Storying Selves: Home and/as Identity in Oral Histories of Refugees in India's Partition," in *Identity Research and Communication*, ed. Nilanjana Bardhan and Mark P. Orbe (Lanham, Md.: Lexington Books, 2012), 103–18.

5. See Homi K. Bhabha, "The World and the Home," *Social Text* 31/32 (1992): 141–53, and *The Location of Culture* (New York and London: Routledge, 1994); Julia Kristeva, *Strangers to Ourselves*, trans. Leon S. Roudiez (New York: Columbia University Press, 1991); Tyson Lewis and Daniel Cho, "Home Is Where the Neurosis Is: A Topography of the Spatial Unconscious," *Cultural Critique* 64, no. 1 (2006): 69–91; and Bilinda Straight, ed., *Women on the Verge of Home* (New York: State University of New York Press, 2005).

6. Bilinda Straight, "Introduction: Women on the Verge of Home," in Straight, *Women on the Verge of Home*, 2; G. C. Spivak, "Can the Subaltern Speak?" in *Marxism and the Interpretation of Culture*, ed. Cary Nelson and Lawrence Grossberg (Urbana and Chicago: University of Illinois Press, 1988), 271–313.

7. Bhabha, *Location of Culture*.

8. Kathleen Stewart, *Ordinary Affects* (Durham, N.C.: Duke University Press, 2007), 2.

9. Stewart, *Ordinary Affects*, 2.

10. I refer to individuals who were at least ten years old in 1947 as *first generation*; individuals born approximately between 1945 and 1957 as *second generation*; and individuals born after 1970 as *third generation*.

11. *Charpoy* is an Urdu, Persian, and Pashtu word. This type of bed, commonly used in India, consists of a wooden frame strung with tapes or rope, often made from coir. In Punjab the same object is called a *manji* or *manja*.

12. I refer here to popular media discussions of the painting.

13. Marianne Hirsch, *Family Frames: Photography, Narrative, and Postmemory* (Cambridge, Mass.: Harvard University Press, 1997), 22.

14. Hirsch, *Family Frames*, 23.

15. Elizabeth V. Spelman, "Repair and the Scaffold of Memory," in *What Is a City? Rethinking the Urban after Hurricane Katrina*, ed. Rob Shields and Phil Steinberg (Athens: University of Georgia Press, 2008), 11.

16. Katie Walsh, "British Expatriate Belongings: Mobile Homes and Transnational Homing," *Home Cultures* 3, no. 2 (2006): 123.

17. Vazira Fazila-Yacoobali Zamindar, *The Long Partition and the Making of Modern South Asia: Refugees, Boundaries, Histories* (New York: Columbia University Press, 2007).

18. Kathinka Sinha-Kerkhoff, "Partition Memory and Multiple Identities in the Champaran District of Bihar, India," in *The Memory of Catastrophe*, ed. Peter Gray and Kendrick Oliver (Manchester: Manchester University Press, 2004), 146.

19. Ravinder Kaur, *Since 1947: Partition Narratives among Punjabi Migrants of Delhi* (New York: Oxford University Press, 2007); Zamindar, *The Long Partition*.

20. Urvashi Butalia, *The Other Side of Silence: Voices from the Partition of India* (Durham, N.C.: Duke University Press, 2000); Kaur, *Since 1947*; Yasmin Khan, *The Great Partition: The Making of India and Pakistan* (New Haven, Conn.: Yale University Press, 2007); Ritu Menon and Kamla Bhasin, *Borders and Boundaries: Women in India's Partition*, 2nd ed. (New Delhi: Kali for Women, 1998).

21. Butalia, *The Other Side of Silence*.

22. See, for example, Ajit Bhattacharjea, *Countdown to Partition: The Final Days* (Delhi: HarperCollins Publishers India, 1997); P. N. Chopra, chief ed., *Towards Freedom: Documents on the Movement for Independence in India, 1937–47*, vol. 1, *Experiment with Provincial Authority, 1 January–31 December 1937*, ed. P. N. Chopra (New Delhi: Indian Council of Historical Research and Oxford University Press, 1985) and vol. 5, *1943–44*, ed. P. S. Gupta (New Delhi: Indian Council for Historical Research and Oxford University Press, 1997); Mushirul Hasan, *India's Partition: Process, Strategy, and Mobilization* (New Delhi: Oxford University Press, 1993); Ayesha Jalal, *The Sole Spokesman: Jinnah, the Muslim League and the Demand for Pakistan* (Cambridge: Cambridge University Press, 1985); Khan, *The Great Partition*; and Zamindar, *The Long Partition*.

23. Dipesh Chakrabarty, "Reviews: History and Historicality," *Postcolonial Studies* 7, no. 1 (2004): 125–30.

24. Ranajit Guha, "The Small Voice of History," in *Subaltern Studies: Writings on South Asian History and Society*, vol. 9, ed. Shahid Amin and Dipesh Chakrabarty (New Delhi and Oxford: Oxford University Press, 1996), 1–13; Ranajit Guha, *History at the Limit of World-History* (New York: Columbia University Press, 2002).

25. Chakrabarty, "Reviews: History and Historicality"; Manu Goswami, *Producing India: From Colonial Economy to National Space* (Chicago: University of Chicago Press, 2004); Gyanendra Pandey, *Remembering Partition: Violence, Nationalism and History in India* (Cambridge: Cambridge University Press, 2002); Gyan Prakash, ed., *After Colonialism: Imperial Histories and Postcolonial Displacements* (Princeton, N.J.: Princeton University Press, 1995).

26. Maulana Abdul Kalam Azad, *India Wins Freedom* (Delhi: Orient Longman Ltd., 1988); Mushirul Hasan, *Legacy of a Divided Nation: India's Muslims since Independence* (New Delhi: Oxford University Press, 1997); C. H. Philips

and M. D. Wainwright, eds., *The Partition of India: Policies and Perspectives* (London: Allen and Unwin, 1970); H. Bhaskar Rao, *The Story of Rehabilitation* (Delhi: Department of Rehabilitation, 1967); Sumit Sarkar, *Modern India, 1885–1947* (Madras: Macmillan India Ltd., 1983); and Tai Yong Tan and Gyanesh Kudaisya, *The Aftermath of Partition in South Asia* (London and New York: Routledge, 2000).

27. See, for example, Alok Bhalla, *Partition Dialogues: Memories of a Lost Home* (New Delhi: Oxford University Press, 2006); Anita Desai, *Clear Light of Day* (New York: Harper and Row, 1980); Priya Kumar, *Limiting Secularism: The Ethics of Coexistence in Indian Literature and Film* (Minneapolis: University of Minnesota Press, 2008); Amit Majumdar, *Partitions* (New York: Metropolitan Books, 2011); Salman Rushdie, *Midnight's Children: A Novel* (New York: Knopf, 1980); Bapsi Sidhwa, *Cracking India: A Novel* (Minneapolis, Minn.: Milkweed Editions, 1991); and Khushwant Singh, *Train to Pakistan* (New York: Grove Press, 1956).

28. Suvir Kaul, ed., *The Partitions of Memory: The Afterlife of the Division of India* (Bloomington: Indiana University Press, 2001).

29. Kaur, *Since 1947*.

30. Butalia, *The Other Side of Silence*; Kaul, *Partitions of Memory*; Kaur, *Since 1947*; Menon and Bhasin, *Borders and Boundaries*; Zamindar, *The Long Partition*.

31. Menon and Bhasin, *Borders and Boundaries*, 16.

32. Furrukh A. Khan, "Speaking Violence: Pakistani Women's Narratives of Partition," in *Gender, Conflict and Migration*, ed. Navneets Chadha Behera (New Delhi: Sage, 2006).

33. Khan, "Speaking Violence," 103.

34. Butalia, *The Other Side of Silence*.

35. For more oral history work on women and Partition, see Kamla Bhasin, Ritu Menon, and Nighat Said Khan, eds., *Against All Odds* (New Delhi: Kali for Women, 1994).

36. Ian Talbot and Darshan Singh Tatla, eds., *Epicentre of Violence: Partition Voices and Memories from Amritsar* (New Delhi: Orient Longman Ltd., 2006).

37. Bhalla, *Partition Dialogues*.

38. Kaur, *Since 1947*, 4.

39. See Devika Chawla, "Between Stories and Theories: Embodiments, Disembodiments, and Other Struggles," *Storytelling, Self, Society* 3, no. 1 (2007): 16–30.

40. Zamindar, *The Long Partition*, 2; 3.

41. Zamindar, *The Long Partition*, 19.

42. Kaur, *Since 1947*, Khan, *The Great Partition*, and Zamindar, *The Long Partition* were all published in 2007.

43. Ruth Behar, "Foreword," in Straight, *Women on the Verge of Home*, ix–xi. See also Arjun Appadurai, *Modernity at Large: Cultural Dimensions of Global-*

ization (Minneapolis: University of Minnesota Press, 1996) and *Globalization* (Durham, N.C.: Duke University Press, 2001); James Clifford, "Traveling Cultures," in *Cultural Studies*, ed. Lawrence Grossberg, Cary Nelson, and Paula Treichler (New York and London: Routledge, 1992), 96–117; Richard G. Fox, "Introduction: Working in the Present," in *Recapturing Anthropology: Working in the Present*, ed. Richard G. Fox (Santa Fe, N.M.: School of Advanced Research Press, 1991), 1–16; Akhil Gupta and James Ferguson, eds., *Anthropological Locations: Boundaries and Grounds of a Field Science.* (Berkeley and Los Angeles: University of California Press, 1997); Caren Kaplan, *Questions of Travel: Postmodern Discourses of Displacement* (Durham, N.C.: Duke University Press, 1996); Gayatri Chakravorty Spivak, "Subaltern Studies: Deconstructing Historiography," in *Deconstruction: Critical Concepts in Literary and Cultural Studies*, ed. Jonathan D. Culler (New York and London: Routledge, 2003), 4:220–44; and M. Trouillot, "Anthropology and the Savage Slot: The Poetics and Politics of Otherness," in Fox, *Recapturing Anthropology*, 17–44.

44. Kaplan, *Questions of Travel*, 7.

45. Michael Jackson, *At Home in the World* (Durham, N.C.: Duke University Press, 1995), 4.

46. Arjun Appadurai, "Place and Voice in Anthropological Theory," *Comparative Studies in Society and History* 30, no. 1 (1988): 39. See also Appadurai, *Globalization*.

47. Kirin Narayan, "How Native Is the 'Native' Anthropologist?" *American Anthropologist* 95, no. 3 (1993).

48. C. Despres, "The Meaning of Home: Literature Review and Directions for Future Research and Theoretical Development," *Journal of Architectural and Planning Research* 8, no. 2 (1991): 96–115; Shelley Mallett, "Understanding Home: A Critical Review of the Literature," *Sociological Review* 52, no. 1 (February 27, 2004): 62–89; and Peter Somerville, "The Social Construction of Home," *Journal of Architectural and Planning Research* 14, no. 3 (1997): 226–45.

49. Sara Ahmed, "Home and Away Narratives of Migration and Estrangement," *International Journal of Cultural Studies* 2, no. 3 (December 1, 1999): 329–47; Sara Ahmed et al., eds., *Uprootings/Regroundings: Questions of Home and Migration* (New York: Berg, 2003); Clifford, "Traveling Cultures"; Kaplan, *Questions of Travel*.

50. Ahmed et al., *Uprootings/Regroundings*, 2.

51. Straight, "Introduction," *Women on the Verge of Home*, 1.

52. Mallett, "Understanding Home," 71.

53. Dorinne Kondo, "The Narrative Production of 'Home,' Community, and Political Identity in Asian American Theater," in *Displacement, Diaspora, and Geographies of Identity*, ed. Smadar Lavie and Ted Swedenburg (Durham, N.C.: Duke University Press, 1996), 97.

54. Straight, *Women on the Verge of Home*. In chapter 1, the introduction to the anthology, Straight discusses the fraught relationship between home and travel as well as field and home.

55. Witold Rybczynski, *Home: A Short History of an Idea* (New York: Penguin, 1986).

56. Mallett, "Understanding Home," 66.

57. Martin Heidegger, "Building Dwelling Thinking," in *Poetry, Language, Thought*, trans. Alfred Hofstadter (New York: Harper and Row, 1971), 143–61.

58. Gaston Bachelard, *The Poetics of Space* , trans. Maria Jolas (Boston: Beacon Press, 1994).

59. Heidegger, *Poetry, Language, Thought*, 147.

60. Daniel López and Tomás Sánchez-Criado, "Dwelling the Telecare Home: Place, Location and Habitability," *Space and Culture* 12, no. 3 (August 1, 2009): 349.

61. See Mallett, "Understanding Home," for a review of the literature that takes this stance.

62. Bachelard, *Poetics of Space*, 4.

63. Mallett, "Understanding Home."

64. Bachelard, *Poetics of Space*, 6.

65. Lopez and Sanchez-Criado, "Dwelling the Telecare Home," 351.

66. See Behar, "Foreword"; Bhabha, *The Location of Culture*; Biddy Martin and Chandra T. Mohanty, "Feminist Politics: What's Home Got to Do with It?" in *Feminist Studies, Critical Studies*, ed. Teresa De Lauretis (Urbana and Chicago: Indiana University Press, 1986), 191–212; Straight, "Introduction," in *Women on the Verge of Home*; Smadar Lavie and Ted Swedenburg, "Introduction," in *Displacement, Diaspora, and Geographies of Identity*, ed. Smadar Lavie and Ted Swedenburg (Durham, N.C.: Duke University Press, 1996), 1–25; Jonathan Friedman and Shalini Randeria, *Worlds on the Move: Globalization, Migration, and Cultural Security* (London: I. B. Tauris, 2004); and Yi-Fu Tuan, *Cosmos and Hearth: A Cosmopolite's View* (Minneapolis: University of Minnesota Press, 1996).

67. Julia Wardhaugh, "The Unaccommodated Woman: Home, Homelessness and Identity," *Sociological Review* 47, no. 1 (1999): 91–109.

68. Straight, "Cold Hearths," in Straight, *Women on the Verge of Home*, 102; K. E. Zirbel, "Concerning the Travels and Transgressions of a Southern Egyptian Woman," in Straight, *Women on the Verge of Home*, 71–88.

69. K. H. Adler, "Gendering Histories of Homes and Homecomings," *Gender and History* 21, no. 3 (November 1, 2009): 455–64; Betty Friedan, *The Feminine Mystique* (New York: W. W. Norton, 1963); Mallett, "Understanding Home"; Ann Oakley, *Housewife* (London: Allen Lane, 1974); and Somerville, "Social Construction of Home."

70. Hilde Heynen, "Modernity and Domesticity: Tensions and Contradictions," in *Negotiating Domesticity: Spatial Productions of Gender in Modern Ar-*

chitecture, ed. Hilde Heynen and Gülsüm Baydar (London: Routledge, 2005), 1–29.

71. Ahmed, "Home and Away Narratives."

72. Bhabha, *The Location of Culture*, 11.

73. Bhabha, "The World and the Home," 141.

74. Straight, "Introduction," in Straight, *Women on the Verge of Home*, 2. See also Appadurai, *Modernity at Large*; Bhabha, "The World and the Home"; Danielle Sears Vignes, "'Hang It Out To Dry': Performing Ethnography, Cultural Memory, and Hurricane Katrina in Chalmette, Louisiana," *Text and Performance Quarterly* 28, no. 3 (2008): 344–50; and Danielle Sears Vignes, "Hang It Out To Dry: A Performance Script," *Text and Performance Quarterly* 28, no. 3 (2008): 351–65. All of these writers approach the uncanny nature of home in their work in their own varied contexts.

75. Theodor W. Adorno, *Minima Moralia: Reflections from a Damaged Life*, trans. E. F. Jephcott (New York: Verso Books, 1996).

76. Hilde Heynen, "Architecture between Modernity and Dwelling: Reflections on Adorno's Aesthetic Theory," *Assemblage* 17 (1992): 78–91.

77. Gilles Deleuze and Felix Guattari, *Anti-Oedipus: Capitalism and Schizophrenia*, trans. Robert Hurley, Mark Seem, and Helen Lane (New York: Penguin, 2009); Gilles Deleuze and Felix Guattari, *A Thousand Plateaus*, trans. Brian Massumi (Minneapolis: University of Minnesota Press, 1987).

78. Lewis and Cho, "Home Is Where the Neurosis Is."

79. Kondo, "Narrative Production of 'Home,'" 97.

80. Mallett, "Understanding Home," 79.

81. Avtar Brah, *Cartographies of Diaspora: Contesting Identities* (New York and London: Routledge, 1996).

82. Kaur, *Since 1947*, 181.

83. Kondo, "Narrative Production of 'Home'"; Martin and Mohanty, "Feminist Politics"; Straight, *Women on the Verge of Home*.

84. Straight, "Introduction," in Straight, *Women on the Verge of Home*, 9.

85. James Agee and Walker Evans, *Let Us Now Praise Famous Men* (Boston: Houghton Mifflin, 2001), 9.

86. Bakhtin, quoted by Michael Holquist in *Dialogism: Bakhtin and His World* (London and New York: Routledge, 1990), 69.

87. Holquist, *Dialogism*, 89.

88. James Clifford, "Introduction: Partial Truths," in *Writing Culture: The Poetics and Politics of Ethnography*, ed. James Clifford and George E. Marcus (Berkeley and Los Angeles: University of California Press, 1986), 305.

89. Clifford, "Traveling Cultures."

90. Clifford, "Traveling Cultures," 108.

91. See, for example, Kwame Anthony Appiah, *Cosmopolitanism: Ethics in a World of Strangers*, annotated ed. (New York: W. W. Norton, 2006); Carol A.

Breckenridge, Sheldon Pollock, and Homi K. Bhabha, eds., *Cosmopolitanism* (Durham, N.C.: Duke University Press, 2002); Jacques Derrida, *On Cosmopolitanism and Forgiveness* (London: Routledge, 2001); and Steven Vertovec and Robin Cohen, eds., *Conceiving Cosmopolitanism: Theory, Context, and Practice* (New York: Oxford University Press, 2003).

92. See Della Pollock, ed., *Exceptional Spaces: Essays in Performance and History* (Chapel Hill: University of North Carolina Press, 1998); Della Pollock, ed., *Remembering : Oral History Performance* (New York: Palgrave Macmillan, 2005); Della Pollock, "Moving Histories: Performance and Oral History," in *The Cambridge Companion to Performance Studies*, ed. Tracy C. Davis (Cambridge and London: Cambridge University Press, 2008), 120–35; Barbara Myerhoff, *Number Our Days: A Triumph of Continuity and Culture among Jewish Old People in an Urban Ghetto* (New York: Simon and Schuster, 1978); and Kamala Visweswaran, *Fictions of Feminist Ethnography* (Minneapolis: University of Minnesota Press, 1994). All of these oral historians position the practice of oral history as a process that is caught in a temporal relationship between the witnesses who tells the stories and the audiences that keeps shifting with time and space. As a consequence, every telling of an oral history with a new audience is a reframing of the story.

93. Straight, "Introduction," in Straight, *Women on the Verge of Home*, 8.

94. See Elif Shafak, "Nomad," in *The Novelist's Lexicon: Writers on the Words that Define Their Work*, ed. Villa Gillet/*Le Monde* (New York: Columbia University Press, 2010), 75; Deleuze and Guattari, *A Thousand Plateaus*; and Pico Iyer, *The Global Soul: Jet Lag, Shopping Malls, and the Search for Home* (New York: Vintage, 2001).

95. Straight, "Introduction," in *Women on the Verge of Home*, 7.

3. A STORY TRAVELS

1. *Musalman* is an Urdu word for Muslim.

2. Jeanette Winterson, *Lighthousekeeping* (New York: Harcourt Books, 2005), 27.

3. Della Pollock, "Moving Histories: Performance and Oral History," in *The Cambridge Companion to Performance Studies*, ed. Tracy C. Davis (Cambridge and London: Cambridge University Press, 2008), 128.

4. *Mohallas* are small ethnically and religiously homogeneous neighborhoods.

5. Ration shops, established by the state, sell basic food essentials to the poor at subsidized rates. Across North India, shops that sell everyday household goods are simply called ration shops.

6. Ian Talbot and Darshan Singh Tatla, eds., *Epicentre of Violence: Partition Voices and Memories from Amritsar* (New Delhi: Orient Longman Ltd., 2006).

7. Ravinder Kaur, *Since 1947: Partition Narratives among Punjabi Migrants of Delhi* (New York: Oxford University Press, 2007), 131.

8. Kaur, *Since 1947*, 142.

9. As is customary for many women of her generation, Labbi Devi does not refer to her husband by any name or title other than the masculine pronoun.

10. A *matric pass* was the equivalent to completing grade 10 in the Cambridge system.

11. An *agency* is a license to open a shop to sell specific branded products.

12. Labbi Devi is referring here to her husband's post-Partition family business in Delhi.

13. Kathryn Anderson and Dana C. Jack, "Learning to Listen: Interview Techniques and Analyses," in *Women's Words: The Feminist Practice of Oral History*, ed. Sherna B. Gluck and Daphne Patai (New York: Routledge, 1991), 11.

14. Kaur, *Since 1947*, 19.

15. Pollock, "Moving Histories," 128.

16. Clifford Geertz, *Works and Lives: The Anthropologist as Author* (Stanford, Calif.: Stanford University Press, 1988), 143–45.

17. Kamala Visweswaran, *Fictions of Feminist Ethnography* (Minneapolis: University of Minnesota Press, 1994), 97–98. I am using just a small portion of Kamala Visweswaran's argument on decentering the subject here. For the purposes of this chapter, I am more interested in addressing ethnography and failure than in addressing the decentering of the field. Decentering of the field, at the same time, remains a necessary thematic for the entire project. Discussions about it emerge in multiple portions of this book.

18. Gayatri C. Spivak, "Can the Subaltern Speak?" in *Marxism and the Interpretation of Culture*, ed. Cary Nelson and Lawrence Grossberg (Urbana and Chicago: University of Illinois Press, 1988), 271–313.

19. Visweswaran, *Fictions of Feminist Ethnography*, 100.

20. Urvashi Butalia's work on Partition provides a discussion about how the state positioned itself as a parent and refugees as children, who needed to be taken care of by the mother country.

21. Ritu Menon and Kamla Bhasin, *Borders and Boundaries: Women in India's Partition*, 2nd ed. (New Delhi: Kali for Women, 1998).

22. Karen Tranberg Hansen, ed., *African Encounters with Domesticity* (Newark, N.J.: Rutgers University Press, 1992), 1.

23. Witold Rybczynski, *Home: A Short History of an Idea* (New York: Penguin, 1986), 75.

24. John Lukacs, "The Bourgeois Interior," *American Scholar* 39 (1970): 616.

25. Rybczynski, *Home*, 75.

26. R. M. George, "Recycling: Long Routes to and from Domestic Fixes," in *Burning Down the House: Recycling Domesticity*, ed. Rosemary Marangoly George (Boulder: Westview Press, 1998), 8. See also Sophie Bowlby, Susan Gregory,

and Linda McKie, "'Doing Home': Patriarchy, Caring, and Space," *Women's Studies International Forum* 20, no. 3 (May 1997): 343–50, and Anne McClintock, *Imperial Leather: Race, Gender, and Sexuality in the Colonial Contest* (London: Routledge, 1995).

27. Hilde Heynen, "Modernity and Domesticity: Tensions and Contradictions," in *Negotiating Domesticity: Spatial Productions of Gender in Modern Architecture*, ed. Hilde Heynen and Gülsüm Baydar (London: Routledge, 2005), 9; McClintock, *Imperial Leather.*

28. Lisa Knopp, "Household Words," *Michigan Quarterly* 40, no. 4 (Fall 2001): 713–25.

29. Knopp, "Household Words," 725.

30. Tonya Davidson, "The Role of Domestic Architecture in the Structuring of Memory," *Space and Culture* 12, no. 3 (August 1, 2009): 340.

31. John Douglas Porteous and Sandra Eileen Smith, *Domicide: The Global Destruction of Home* (Montreal: McGill-Queen's University Press, 2001), 54.

32. Richard Daniels, "Scattered Remarks on the Ideology of Home," *Minnesota Review* 58, no. 1 (2002): 191.

4. HOME OUTSIDE HOME

1. In this "imagined version" of my subject's experiences as a twenty-one-year-old student and as a wife and mother, I call her *Kiran.* The imagined version over, I revert to referring to her—eighty-two years old when I met her—with the honorific *ji.*

2. Paul John Eakin, *Fictions in Autobiography: Studies in the Art of Self-Invention* (Princeton, N.J.: Princeton University Press, 1988); Devika Chawla and Myrdene Anderson, "Stories at the Memory-Imagination Interface," in *Semiotics 2010*, ed. Karen A. Hayworth, Jason Hogue, and Leonard G. Sbrocchi (Ottawa, Ontario: Legas Publishing, 2011), 229–37; Bryant Keith Alexander, "Skin Flint (or, the Garbage Man's Kid): A Generative Autobiographical Performance Based on Tami Spry's Tattoo Stories," *Text and Performance Quarterly* 20, no. 1 (2000): 97–114; Bryant Keith Alexander, "Performance Ethnography: The Reenacting and Inciting of Culture," in *The Sage Handbook of Qualitative Research*, ed. Norman K. Denzin and Yvonna S. Lincoln, 3rd ed. (Thousand Oaks, Calif.: Sage, 2005), 411–41.

3. Michael Taussig, *I Swear I Saw This: Drawings in Fieldwork Notebooks, Namely My Own* (Chicago: University of Chicago Press, 2011), xi.

4. See for example Gloria Anzaldúa, *Borderlands/La Frontera: The New Mestiza* (San Francisco: Aunt Lute Books, 1987); Devika Chawla, "Between Stories and Theories: Embodiments, Disembodiments, and Other Struggles," *Storytelling, Self, Society* 3, no. 1 (2007): 16–30; Kathleen Stewart, *A Space on the Side of the Road* (Princeton, N.J.: Princeton University Press, 1996); and Julie Taylor, *Paper*

Tangos (Durham, N.C.: Duke University Press, 1998). In each of these works, experimental, poetic, fictional, and nonfictional ethnographic accounts merge with each other, and indeed the writers consider the emergent genre to be something that changes the ways in which we come to know our subject matter.

5. Mikhail Bakhtin, *Art and Answerability*, ed. Michael Holquist and Vadim Liapunov, trans. Vadim Liapunov and Kenneth Brostrom (Austin: University of Texas Press, 1990), 9.

6. See Mikhail Bakhtin, *The Dialogic Imagination: Four Essays*, ed. Michael Holquist and Vadim Liapunov, trans. Vadim Liapunov and Kenneth Brostrom (Austin: University of Texas Press, 1981). I would have to relinquish one kind of authorial control in favor of another—to let go of my imagined version, for Kiranji's version of her own story.

7. Della Pollock, ed., *Remembering: Oral History Performance* (New York: Palgrave Macmillan, 2005), 5.

8. Pollock, *Remembering*, 5.

9. Maurice Blanchot and Jacques Derrida, *The Instant of My Death/Demeure: Fiction and Testimony*, trans. Elizabeth Rottenberg (Stanford, Calif.: Stanford University Press, 2000), 29–30. Derrida notes in his essay that if testimony were to become tied to proof, certainty, the archive, and to information, it would lose its imperative.

10. Peter C. van Wyck, *Highway of the Atom* (Montreal and Kingston: McGill-Queen's University Press, 2010), 4. Van Wyck is discussing the relationship between fieldnotes and fiction.

11. See for instance, Henry D. Thoreau, *Walking* (New York: Harper One, 1994).

12. Rebecca Solnit, *Wanderlust: A History of Walking* (New York: Penguin Books, 2000), 5–6.

13. Taussig, *I Swear I Saw This*, 25.

14. Taussig, *I Swear I Saw This*, 50.

15. Norman K. Denzin, *Interpretive Ethnography: Ethnographic Practices for the Twentieth-First Century* (Thousand Oaks, Calif.: Sage, 1997); Clifford Geertz, *The Interpretation of Cultures: Selected Essays* (New York: Basic Books, 1973).

16. Joan Didion, "Why I Write," *New York Times*, 5 December 1976.

17. Taussig, *I Swear I Saw This*, 26.

18. Taussig, *I Swear I Saw This*, 47.

19. A reminder: Following Ohio University Institutional Review Board guidelines, names of persons and institutions are all pseudonyms (save for Labbi Devi in chapter 2, whose name *Labbi* was not her given name in the first place).

20. See Suvir Kaul, ed., *The Partitions of Memory: The Afterlife of the Division of India* (Bloomington: Indiana University Press, 2001).

21. Sara Ahmed, "Home and Away Narratives of Migration and Estrangement," *International Journal of Cultural Studies* 2, no. 3 (December 1, 1999): 343.

22. Chawla, "Between Stories and Theories."

23. The distance from Delhi to Dehradun is roughly 151 miles.

24. Vazira Fazila-Yacoobali Zamindar, *The Long Partition and the Making of Modern South Asia: Refugees, Boundaries, Histories* (New York: Columbia University Press, 2007). Part of Zamindar's work focuses on North Indian Muslim families between Delhi and Karachi. The book juxtaposes the experience of ordinary people and the role of the two states—India and Pakistan—in how "refugees" were managed and how property was administered. My focus here, however, is on family dispersals and separations within India.

25. Gaston Bachelard, *The Poetics of Space* (New York: Beacon Press, 1994), 15.

26. Scott Esposito, "We Are Made of Memories: A Conversation with Mia Couto," *The Paris Review*, 2 May 2013, http://www.theparisreview.org/blog/2013/05/02/we-are-made-of-memories-a-conversation-with-mia-couto/.

27. Ahmed, "Home and Away Narratives," 330.

28. Ahmed, "Home and Away Narratives," 343.

29. Theano S. Terkenli, "Home as a Region," *Geographical Review* 85, no. 3 (1995): 328.

30. Joseph Rykwert, "House and Home," *Social Research* 58, no. 1 (1991): 51.

31. Bachelard, *Poetics of Space*, 14–15.

32. Bachelard, *Poetics of Space*, 6–7.

33. Sigmund Freud, *Civilization and Its Discontents*, ed. and trans. James Strachey (New York: W. W. Norton, 1962), 38.

34. James Clifford, "Traveling Cultures," in *Cultural Studies*, ed. Lawrence Grossberg, Cary Nelson, and Paula Treichler (New York and London: Routledge, 1992), 96–117.

35. Ahmed, "Home and Away Narratives," 335.

36. Caren Kaplan, *Questions of Travel: Postmodern Discourses of Displacement* (Durham, N.C.: Duke University Press, 1996), 106. See also Mary McCarthy, "Exiles, Expatriates, and Internal Émigrés," *The Listener* 86 (November 25, 1971): 705–08.

37. Terkenli, "Home as a Region," 327.

38. Julia Kristeva, *Strangers to Ourselves*, trans. Leon S. Roudiez (New York: Columbia University Press, 1991), 29.

39. Carlos Eire, "Home," *Hedgehog Review* 7, no. 3 (2005): 42.

40. Doreen Massey, *Space, Place, and Gender* (Minneapolis: University of Minnesota Press, 1994).

41. Ahmed, "Home and Away Narratives," 343.

42. Edward Said, *Orientalism* (New York: Vintage, 1979).

43. Avtar Brah, *Cartographies of Diaspora: Contesting Identities* (New York and London: Routledge, 1996), 192.

44. Sara Ahmed et al., eds., *Uprootings/Regroundings: Questions of Home and Migration* (New York: Berg, 2003), 9.

1. Kathleen Stewart, "Atmospheric Attunements," *Environment and Planning D: Society and Space* 29, no. 3 (2010): 1.

2. Stewart, "Atmospheric Attunements," 5.

3. Stewart, "Atmospheric Attunements," 8.

4. Dwight Conquergood, "Rethinking Ethnography: Towards a Critical Cultural Politics," *Communication Monographs* 58, no. 2 (1991): 181. See also Dwight Conquergood, "Performance Studies: Interventions and Radical Research," *Drama Review* 46, no. 2 (2002): 145–56.

5. See, for example, Ruth Behar, *The Vulnerable Observer: Anthropology that Breaks Your Heart* (Boston: Beacon Press, 1996); Conquergood, "Rethinking Ethnography"; and D. Soyini Madison, *Critical Ethnography: Method, Ethics, and Performance* (Thousand Oaks, Calif.: Sage, 2005).

6. Conquergood, "Rethinking Ethnography," 180. See also Gloria Anzaldúa, *Borderlands/La Frontera: The New Mestiza* (San Francisco: Aunt Lute Books, 1987); and Kirin Narayan, *Storytellers, Saints and Scoundrels: Folk Narrative in Hindu Religious Teaching* (Philadelphia: University of Pennsylvania Press, 1989).

7. Clifford Geertz, *After the Fact: Two Countries, Four Decades, One Anthropologist* (Cambridge, Mass.: Harvard University Press, 1995), 44.

8. Trinh T. Minh-ha, *Woman, Native, Other: Writing Postcoloniality and Feminism* (Bloomington: Indiana University Press, 1989), 112.

9. Mieke Bal, "Visual Essentialism and the Object of Visual Culture," *Journal of Visual Culture* 2, no. 1 (2003): 9.

10. Bal, "Visual Essentialism," 9.

11. W. J. T. Mitchell, *Picture Theory: Essays on Visual and Verbal Representation* (Chicago: University of Chicago Press, 1995), 6.

12. Michael Taussig, *I Swear I Saw This: Drawings in Fieldwork Notebooks, Namely My Own* (Chicago: University of Chicago Press, 2011).

13. Taussig, *I Swear I Saw This*, 16.

14. Kenneth Burke, *A Rhetoric of Motives* (Berkeley and Los Angeles: University of California Press, 1969); Conquergood, "Performance Studies"; Taussig, *I Swear I Saw This*.

15. While mobilities theorists present analytical distinctions between motion, movement, and mobility, I am using the words *interchangeably* in this chapter. Timothy Creswell considers movement to be an abstracted mobility that describes the idea of an act of displacement that allows people to move between locations. Movement, says Creswell in *On the Move: Mobility in the Modern Western World* (New York and London: Routledge, 2006), "is the dynamic equivalent of location in abstract space—contentless, apparently natural, and devoid of meaning, history and ideology" (3). Mobility, on the other hand, is the dynamic equivalent of place. Place, in geographical parlance, is a "center of meaning—we

become attached to it, we fight over it and exclude people from it—we experience it. The same cannot be said of location" (3).

16. See Akhil Gupta and James Ferguson, eds., *Anthropological Locations: Boundaries and Grounds of a Field Science* (Berkeley and Los Angeles: University of California Press, 1997).

17. Behar, *The Vulnerable Observer*; Devika Chawla, "Poetic Arrivals and Departures: Bodying the Ethnographic Field in Verse," *Forum Qualitative Sozialforschun /Forum: Qualitative Social Research* 9, no. 2 (2008), http://nbn -resolving.de/urn:nbn:de:0114-fqs0802248; Taussig, *I Swear I Saw This*; Kamala Visweswaran, *Fictions of Feminist Ethnography* (Minneapolis: University of Minnesota Press, 1994); and Margery Wolf, *A Thrice-Told Tale: Feminism, Postmodernism, and Ethnographic Responsibility* (Stanford, Calif.: Stanford University Press, 1992).

18. Yanik Hamel, "Nomad," in *The Novelist's Lexicon: Writers on the Words that Define Their Work*, ed. Villa Gillet/*Le Monde* (New York: Columbia University Press, 2010), 73.

19. Tom Jacobs, "The Strange Energy of Images, and the Humility of Language," *3 Quarks Daily*, 18 June 2012, http://www.3quarksdaily.com/3quarksdaily /2012/06/the-strange-energies-of-images-and-the-humility-of-language.html #more.

20. Thomas A. Sebeok, *Global Semiotics* (Bloomington: Indiana University Press, 2001).

21. The North-West Frontier Province was an area created by the British in their territories in South Asia. The province consisted of three divisions— Peshawar, Dera Ismail Khan, and Malakand.

22. A *tube well* is a type of water well in which a wide stainless steel tube is bored into the ground, to a level that bears water. Such wells often include an open pool into which the water is pumped.

23. Marianne Hirsch, *Family Frames: Photography, Narrative, and Postmemory* (Cambridge, Mass.: Harvard University Press, 1997), 5.

24. Mail service was often interrupted, and the address to which one would send mail was also an issue. People were scattered in camps, and families often did not live together in the first few years.

25. Solan is a small hill station near Shimla, in the Himalayan foothills.

26. Vazira Fazila-Yacoobali Zamindar, *The Long Partition and the Making of Modern South Asia: Refugees, Boundaries, Histories* (New York: Columbia University Press, 2007), 31. Zamindar proposes that it is critical to understand the category of "evacuee," because it was a creation of officialdom produced to describe Muslim citizens of India who were departing or had departed of "their own volition." Of course, there were Muslims who did not depart and often could not depart owing to economic circumstances; these Muslim citizens of India abandoned their homes due to fear of communal violence, and took temporary ref-

uge in the camps, in the hope of eventually returning to their homes. Their property, land, and businesses were defined as "evacuee property" and were to be used in rehabilitating "displaced persons." For the Indian state, Hindus and Sikhs displaced from Pakistan were viewed as higher-priority refugees—those who needed to begin new lives as Indian citizens. In other words, internally displaced Muslim persons were low-priority displaced persons, as compared to Hindus and Sikhs.

27. Zamindar, *The Long Partition*, 31. In her chapter "Economies of Displacement," Zamindar tells the story of Rafi Bhai, whose familial home was lost as a result of its having been declared "evacuee property."

28. Ravinder Kaur, *Since 1947: Partition Narratives among Punjabi Migrants of Delhi* (New York: Oxford University Press, 2007), 194.

29. Kaur, *Since 1947*, 194–95.

30. Kaur, *Since 1947*, 183.

31. Kaur, *Since 1947*, 195.

32. Kaur, *Since 1947*.

33. Gaston Bachelard, *The Poetics of Space* (Boston: Beacon Press, 1994), 5.

34. Paul Basu and Simon Coleman, "Introduction: Migrant Worlds, Material Cultures," *Mobilities* 3, no. 3 (2008): 340.

35. Kaur, *Since 1947*.

36. Hirsch, *Family Frames*.

37. *Soorma* literally means kohl, and is an ancient eye antiseptic and cosmetic made by grinding galena, or lead sulphide. It is commonly used in most parts of South Asia and the Middle East.

38. Yasmin Khan, *The Great Partition: The Making of India and Pakistan* (New Haven, Conn.: Yale University Press, 2007); Zamindar, *The Long Partition*.

39. *Pandit*, learned man, is a title of respect.

40. The Quit India Movement, or the August Movement, was a civil disobedience movement that was launched in August 1942 as a response to Mahatma Gandhi's call for immediate independence through nonviolence. The British response to it was violent, with over 100,000 arrests, mass fines, and public flogging of demonstrators. Many Indian National Congress leaders were arrested and cut off from the world for the next three years.

41. Edward Said, "Reflections on Exile," *Granta 13* (Autumn, 1984): 172

42. Kaur, *Since 1947*, 208.

43. Juhani Pallasmaa, *Architecture in Miniature: Juhani Pallasmaa Finland* (Helsinki: Museum of Finnish Architecture, 1991).

44. Kevin Hannam, Mimi Sheller, and John Urry, "Editorial: Mobilities, Immobilities and Moorings," *Mobilities* 1, no. 1 (2006): 13. See also John Urry, *Global Complexity* (Cambridge: Polity Press, 2003).

45. Tonya Davidson, "The Role of Domestic Architecture in the Structuring of Memory," *Space and Culture* 12, no. 3 (August 1, 2009): 339.

46. Michel de Certeau, Luce Giard, and Pierre Mayol, *The Practice of Everyday Life*, vol. 2: *Living and Cooking*, trans. Timothy J. Tomasik (Minneapolis: University of Minnesota Press, 1998), p. 148.

47. The name of the hotel has been changed in compliance with human subjects research guidelines.

48. Cottage Emporium is a large central government-funded retail store, the size of a small mall, which sells crafts, fabric, jewelry, and furnishings from all states and union territories in India.

49. Amritji is Kiranji's younger cousin, younger by over a decade. While he belongs to the same generation as she, he was only nine when the Partition occurred. His experiences therefore seem almost a generation apart from hers. I consider him to be a participant who spans both the first and second generations.

50. Sara Ahmed et al., "Introduction: Uprootings/Regroundings: Questions of Home and Migration," in *Uprootings/Regroundings: Questions of Home and Migration*, ed. Sara Ahmed et al. (New York: Berg, 2003), 1–22.

51. *Gurmukhi* is the Punjabi script; the *gidda* is a women's folkdance and song from Punjab; *chikki* is akin to an energy bar, made at home from peanuts and jaggery (a kind of unrefined sugar); and *gajak* is a different homemade energy bar, made from jaggery, sesame seeds, and sugar.

52. This Sikh separatist movement, also known as the Khalistan movement, is a global secessionist movement that calls for the creation of a Sikh state (Khalistan) in the Punjab region of South Asia (including the Indian state of Punjabi and the Punjab province in Pakistan).

53. Devika Chawla, "Two Journeys," *Qualitative Inquiry* 9, no. 5 (October 1, 2003): 785–804.

54. Kaur, *Since 1947*, 197.

55. Zamindar, *The Long Partition*, 9.

56. Zamindar, *The Long Partition*, 27–29.

57. Martin Heidegger, "Building, Dwelling, Thinking," in *Poetry, Language, Thought* (New York: Harper and Row, 1971), 148.

58. Hilde Heynen, "Architecture between Modernity and Dwelling: Reflections on Adorno's Aesthetic Theory," *Assemblage* 17 (1992): 80.

59. Quoted in Shelley Mallett, "Understanding Home: A Critical Review of the Literature," *Sociological Review* 52, no. 1 (February 27, 2004): 83; Heynen, "Architecture between Modernity and Dwelling."

60. David Conradson and Deirdre Mckay, "Translocal Subjectivities: Mobility, Connection, Emotion," *Mobilities* 2, no. 2 (2007): 168.

61. Conradson and Mckay, "Translocal Subjectivities," 168.

62. Massimo Cacciari, "Eupalinos or Architecture," *Oppositions* 21 (1980): 107.

63. Heynen, "Architecture between Modernity and Dwelling."

64. Theodor W. Adorno, *Minima Moralia: Reflections from a Damaged Life*, trans. E. F. Jephcott (New York: Verso, 1996).

65. Mallett, "Understanding Home."

66. See James Clifford, "Traveling Cultures," in *Cultural Studies*, ed. Lawrence Grossberg, Cary Nelson, and Paula Treichler (New York and London: Routledge, 1992), 96–117.

67. Kuang-Ming Wu, "The Other Is My Hell; the Other Is My Home," *Human Studies* 16, no. 1 (1993): 193–202.

68. Jens Brockmeier, "Autobiographical Time," *Narrative Inquiry* 10, no. 1 (2000): 61.

69. For similar discussions about fragmentary narratives see, Sidonie Smith and Julia Watson, *Reading Autobiography: A Guide for Interpreting Life Narratives* (Minneapolis: University of Minnesota Press, 2001), 108. See also Joseph Francese, *Narrating Postmodern Time and Space* (Albany: State University of New York Press, 1997).

70. Contemporary scholars interested in the nomad center their discussions on exile in the context of Euro-American modernist literature. I am more interested in the crux of their arguments on exile, displacement, and aesthetic gain.

71. Gilles Deleuze and Felix Guattari, "Treatise on Nomadology," in *A Thousand Plateaus*, trans. Brian Massumi, vol. 2 of *Capitalism and Schizophrenia* (Minneapolis: University of Minnesota Press, 1987), 351–423.

72. Ronald Bogue, "Apology for Nomadology," *Interventions* 6, no. 2 (2004): 169–79.

73. Walter Benjamin, *Charles Baudelaire: A Lyric Poet in the Era of High Capitalism* (London: Verso Classics, 1983). Benjamin describes the *flaneur* as the essential urban spectator, someone who can function as something between an amateur detective and investigator. He is a symbol of the alienation of the city.

74. Caren Kaplan, *Questions of Travel: Postmodern Discourses of Displacement* (Durham, N.C.: Duke University Press), 86.

75. Gilles Deleuze and Felix Guattari, "What is Minor Literature?" in *Kafka: Toward a Minor Literature*, trans. Dana Polan (Minneapolis: University of Minnesota Press, 1986), 17.

76. Kaplan, *Questions of Travel*, 87.

77. Deleuze and Guattari, *A Thousand Plateaus*, 25.

78. Kaplan, *Questions of Travel*, 87.

79. Rosi Braidotti, *Nomadic Subjects: Embodiment and Sexual Difference in Contemporary Feminist Theory*, 2nd ed. (New York: Columbia University Press, 2011), 36.

80. Kaplan, *Questions of Travel*, 88–89.

81. See Peter Adey, *Mobility* (New York and London: Routledge, 2010), and Nick Gill, Javier Caletrío, and Victoria Mason, "Introduction: Mobilities and Forced Migration," *Mobilities* 6, no. 3 (2011): 301–16.

82. Timothy Cresswell, *On the Move: Mobility in the Modern Western World* (New York and London: Routledge, 2006), 56–57.

83. Kaplan, *Questions of Travel*, 28.

84. Kaplan, *Questions of Travel*, 36.

85. Mimi Sheller and John Urry, "The New Mobilities Paradigm," *Environment and Planning A: Society and Space* 38, no. 2 (2006): 207–26.

86. Hannam, Sheller, and Urry, "Editorial," 10. For use of the word *homing* see Avtar Brah, *Cartographies of Diaspora: Contesting Identities* (New York and London: Routledge, 1996) and Anne-Marie Fortier, *Migrant Belongings: Memory, Space, Identity* (New York: Berg Publishers, 2000).

87. Basu and Coleman, "Introduction," 322; Orvar Lofgren, "Motion and Emotion: Learning to Be a Railway Traveller," *Mobilities* 3, no. 3 (2008): 331–51.

88. Peter Adey, "If Mobility Is Everything Then It Is Nothing: Towards a Relational Politics of (Im)mobilities," *Mobilities* 1, no. 1 (2006): 83.

89. Gill, Caletrío, and Mason, "Introduction."

90. Gill, Caletrío, and Mason, "Introduction," 303.

91. Sara Ahmed, "Home and Away Narratives of Migration and Estrangement," *International Journal of Cultural Studies* 2, no. 3 (December 1, 1999): 333; Ahmed et al., "Introduction: Uprootings/Regroundings."

92. Kaplan, *Questions of Travel*, 40; 94.

93. Edward Said, "Reflections on Exile," *Granta* 13 (1984): 170.

94. Said, "Reflections on Exile," 159.

95. Kaplan, *Questions of Travel*, 120.

96. Anita Haya Goldman, "Comparative Identities: Exile in the Writings of Frantz Fanon and W. E. B. Dubois," in *Borders, Boundaries, and Frames*, ed. Mae Henderson (New York and London: Routledge, 1994), 180.

97. Peter van der Veer, "Cosmopolitan Options," in *Worlds on the Move: Globalization, Migration, and Cultural Security*, ed. Jonathan Friedman and Shalini Randeria, 171 (London: I. B. Tauris, 2004).

98. Basu and Coleman, "Introduction," 323.

99. Said, "Reflections on Exile," 166.

100. Eva Hoffman, *Lost in Translation: A Life in a New Language* (New York, Penguin, 1990), 44.

101. Clifford, "Traveling Cultures," 110.

102. Said, "Reflections on Exile," 159.

103. John Noyes, "Nomadism, Nomadology, Postcolonialism: By Way of Introduction," *Interventions* 6, no. 2 (2004): 159–60.

104. Gill, Caletrío, and Mason, "Introduction," 304.

6. HEARTH CROSSINGS

1. Ritu Menon and Kamla Bhasin, *Borders and Boundaries: Women in India's Partition*, 2nd ed. (New Delhi: Kali for Women, 1998), 41.

2. Menon and Bhasin, *Borders and Boundaries*, 42–45.

3. Urvashi Butalia, *The Other Side of Silence: Voices from the Partition of India* (Durham, N.C.: Duke University Press, 2000).

4. Butalia, *The Other Side of Silence*.

5. K. H. Adler, "Gendering Histories of Homes and Homecomings," *Gender and History* 21, no. 3 (November 1, 2009): 455–64; Hilde Heynen, "Modernity and Domesticity: Tensions and Contradictions," in *Negotiating Domesticity: Spatial Productions of Gender in Modern Architecture*, ed. Hilde Heynen and Gülsüm Baydar (New York and London: Routledge, 2005), 1–29; Bilinda Straight, ed., *Women on the Verge of Home* (Albany: State University of New York Press, 2005).

6. Straight, *Women on the Verge of Home*, 8.

7. A *joint family* is a multiplicity of genealogically related nuclear families living under the same roof, sharing worship, food, and property. A *semi-joint family* could be one in which a son and his family live together with his parents, while his siblings (sisters and perhaps younger brothers) live elsewhere.

8. *Love marriages* are marriages wherein marital partners choose each other unaided by family or kin. According to recent estimates, 90 percent of marriages in India are arranged.

9. Under the Indian constitution and Indian penal code, *Hindu* is very broadly defined. Persons who are Hindu, Jain, Sikh, or Buddhist—by birth, upbringing, or conversion—are considered Hindu for legal purposes. See Patricia Uberoi, ed., *Social Reform, Sexuality, and the State*, Contributions to Indian Sociology: Occasional Studies, 7 (New Delhi: Sage, 1996), 327.

10. Uberoi, *Social Reform, Sexuality, and the State.*

11. Prabhati Mukherjee, *Hindu Women: Normative Models* (Calcutta: Orient Longman Ltd., 1994), 57.

12. Devika Chawla, "Arranged Selves: Role, Identity, and Social Transformations Among Indian Women in Hindu Arranged Marriages," Ph.D. diss., Purdue University, 2004.

13. Joshua M. Price, "The Apotheosis of Home and the Maintanence of Spaces of Violence," *Hypathia* 17, no. 4 (2002): 60; 40. In the essay Price argues that the ideological construction of home as a place of safety and refuge cloaks violence against women. Home is produced, cleaned, and organized by the very people—women—who might find neither solace nor respite in it.

14. Price, "Apotheosis of Home," 40–41.

15. Price, "Apotheosis of Home," 41.

16. Edward Said, *Orientalism* (New York: Vintage, 1979), 55.

17. Julia Wardhaugh, "The Unaccommodated Woman: Home, Homelessness and Identity," *Sociological Review* 47, no. 1 (1999): 96–97. See also Doreen Massey, *Space, Place, and Gender* (Minneapolis: University of Minnesota Press, 1994); Sara Ahmed, Claudia Castaneda, Anne-Marie Fortier, and Mimi Sheller, eds., *Uprootings/Regroundings: Questions of Home and Migration* (New York: Berg,

2003); and bell hooks, *Yearning: Race, Gender and Cultural Politics* (Boston: South End Press, 1999).

18. Roberta Rubenstein, *Home Matters: Longing and Belonging, Nostalgia and Mourning in Women's Fiction* (New York: Palgrave Macmillan, 2001).

19. Ahmed, Castaneda, Fortier, and Sheller, *Uprootings/Regroundings*, 5; see also Massey, *Space, Place, and Gender.*

20. Price, "The Apotheosis of Home," 58. See also Maria C. Lugones and Joshua M. Price, "Dominant Culture: El Deseo por un Pobre," in *Multiculturalism from the Margins*, ed. Dean A. Harris (Westport, Conn.: Bergin and Garvey Press, 1995), 216; and Marilyn Frye, *Politics of Reality* (Trumansburg, N.Y.: Crossing Press, 1983).

21. David Sibley, Geographies of Exclusion: Society and Difference in the West (London: Routledge, 1995), 94.

22. Shelley Mallett, "Understanding Home: A Critical Review of the Literature," *Sociological Review* 52, no. 1 (February 27, 2004): 62–89.

23. Uberoi, *Social Reform, Sexuality, and the State.*

24. Female foeticide continues to be a problem in India, although sex-selective abortion based on ultrasound scans is illegal. Sons continue to be seen (by many) as wage-earners and breadwinners. Statistics show that fewer girls than boys are being born or surviving. The gender imbalance has widened every decade since independence in 1947. According to the 2011 Census, 914 girls were born for every 1,000 boys under the age of six, compared with 927 for every 1,000 boys in the 2001 Census. For more details see Ministry of Home Affairs, Government of India, Census of India, 2011, http://censusindia.gov.in/.

25. Menon and Bhasin, *Borders and Boundaries*, 14.

26. Shirley Ardener, *Perceiving Women* (New York: John Wiley, 1982), xi–xxiii.

27. Butalia, *The Other Side of Silence*, 12.

28. Kathryn Anderson and Dana C. Jack, "Learning to Listen: Interview Techniques and Analyses," in *Women's Words: The Feminist Practice of Oral History*, ed. Sherna B. Gluck and Daphne Patai (New York: Routledge, 1991), 11.

29. See Mieke Bal, "Visual Essentialism and the Object of Visual Culture," *Journal of Visual Culture* 2, no. 1 (2003): 5–32.

30. Mallett, "Understanding Home," 79.

31. In the entire numbered section on how home is performed by women, I use italics for commentary and roman font for interview quotes with the goal of offsetting the section.

32. The Arya Samaj is a progressive Hindu reform movement that was spearheaded by Swami Dayanand in 1875. The Vedas are considered the most important texts for the followers of this movement. The movement condemns iconolatry, polytheism, animal sacrifice, pilgrimage, the caste system, ancestor worship, untouchability, and child marriage.

33. Ian Talbot and Darshan Singh Tatla, eds., *Epicentre of Violence: Partition Voices and Memories from Amritsar* (New Delhi: Orient Longman Ltd., 2006).

34. The Red Fort, Jama Masjid, and Qutab Minar are historic monuments in Delhi that were built by Moghul rulers. Poonamji also mentions Delhi's Birla Mandir, also known as the Laxminarayan Temple, a magnificent Hindu temple built by the wealthy Birla family.

35. Mallett, "Understanding Home," 72.

36. *Paan* is an edible preparation of betel leaves with areca nut and/or cured tobacco. It is eaten in many parts of Asia as a stimulant.

37. Julia Kristeva, *Strangers to Ourselves*, trans. Leon S. Roudiez (Columbia University Press, 1991), 3.

38. Massey, *Space, Place and Gender*.

39. Sigmund Freud, *The Uncanny*, trans. David McLintock (New York: Penguin Classics, 2003).

40. Tyson Lewis and Daniel Cho, "Home Is Where the Neurosis Is: A Topography of the Spatial Unconscious," *Cultural Critique* 64, no. 1 (2006): 69.

41. Kathy Mezei and Chiara Briganti, "Reading the House: A Literary Perspective," *Signs* 27, no. 3 (2002): 841.

42. Straight, *Women on the Verge of Home*, 2. See also Arjun Appadurai, *Modernity at Large: Cultural Dimensions of Globalization* (Minneapolis: University of Minnesota Press, 1996); Homi Bhabha, "The World and the Home," *Social Text* 31/32 (1992): 141–53; Danielle Sears Vignes, "'Hang It Out to Dry': Performing Ethnography, Cultural Memory, and Hurricane Katrina in Chalmette, Louisiana," *Text and Performance Quarterly* 28, no. 3 (2008): 344–50; and Danielle Sears Vignes, "Hang It Out to Dry: A Performance Script," *Text and Performance Quarterly* 28, no. 3 (2008): 351–65.

43. Theodor W. Adorno, *Minima Moralia: Reflections from a Damaged Life* (New York: Verso Books, 1996).

44. See also Frederic Jameson, *The Seeds of Time* (New York: Columbia University Press, 1996); and Michael Hardt and Antonio Negri, *Empire* (Cambridge: Harvard University Press, 2001).

45. See Gilles Deleuze and Felix Guattari, *A Thousand Plateaus*, trans. Brian Massumi, vol. 2 of *Capitalism and Schizophrenia* (Minneapolis: University of Minnesota Press, 1987).

46. Homi K. Bhabha, *The Location of Culture* (New York and London: Routledge, 1994), 11.

47. Homi Bhabha, "The World and the Home," 141.

48. Mezei and Briganti, "Reading the House," 842.

49. Alison Light, *Forever England: Femininity, Literature, and Conservatism between the Wars* (London and New York: Routledge, 1991), 219; Mezei and Briganti, "Reading the House."

50. Veena Das, Jonathan M. Ellen, and Lori Leonard, "On the Modalities of the Domestic," *Home Cultures* 5, no. 3 (2008): 352.

51. Michael Jackson, *At Home in the World* (Durham, N.C.: Duke University Press, 1995), 80.

7. REMNANTS

1. *Ghee* is clarified butter and *paranthas* are buttered and warm homemade flatbreads eaten as breakfast in many homes in northern India. They are often stuffed with cheese, meats, and different vegetables.

2. Rebecca Solnit, *A Field Guide to Getting Lost* (New York: Penguin, 2005), 38.

3. Paul John Eakin, *Fictions in Autobiography: Studies in the Art of Self-Invention* (Princeton, N.J.: Princeton University Press, 1988), 5.

4. Marianne Hirsch, *Family Frames: Photography, Narrative, and Postmemory* (Cambridge, Mass.: Harvard University Press, 1997), 245.

5. *Zardozi* is an ornate style of Persian embroidery that has existed in India ever since the period of the Rig Veda (1700–1100 B.C.). It prospered during Mughal rule. In Persian, *zardozi* literally means sewing with gold.

6. Priya Kumar, *Limiting Secularism: The Ethics of Coexistence in Indian Literature and Film* (Minneapolis: University of Minnesota Press, 2008); Vazira Fazila-Yacoobali Zamindar, *The Long Partition and the Making of Modern South Asia: Refugees, Boundaries, Histories* (New York: Columbia University Press, 2007).

7. The *ghazal* is a poetic form in rhyming couplets and refrains.

8. The *sherwani*, traditionally associated with the Muslim aristocracy, is a long coat-like garment worn in South Asia; *chooridar pyjamas* are tight-fitting trousers. The sherwani, which is Pakistan's national dress, is very similar to an *achkan*, or doublet, but is often made from heavier suiting fabrics and is lined. It is worn over a *kurta* (a loose-fitting, often collarless shirt) and chooridar pyjamas, *khara* pyjamas (looser-fitting trousers), or salwar (loose-fitting trousers tapering to the ankle).

9. Hirsch, *Family Frames*, 242.

10. Alok Bhalla, *Partition Dialogues: Memories of a Lost Home* (New Delhi: Oxford University Press, 2006).

11. I take this phrase from Pablo Neruda's poem entitled "Poetry": ". . . Poetry arrived / in search of me."

12. Khushwant Singh, *Train to Pakistan* (New York: Grove Press, 1956).

13. Suvir Kaul, ed., *The Partitions of Memory: The Afterlife of the Division of India* (Bloomington: Indiana University Press, 2002), 14.

14. Kaul, *Partitions of Memory*, 14.

15. Zamindar, *The Long Partition*.

16. Kaul, *Partitions of Memory*, 12.

17. Bapsi Sidhwa, *Ice Candy Man* (India: Penguin, 1989).

18. *Earth* is the film based on *Ice Candy Man* directed by Deepa Mehta and released in 1998.

19. Both are Partition-themed films released in 2003. *Khamosh Pani* was directed by Sabiha Sumar (Vidhi Films, Karachi, 2003); *Pinjar* was directed by Chander Prakash Dwivedi (Lucky Star Entertainment, Mumbai, 2003).

20. Hirsch, *Family Frames*, 242–43.

8. MY FATHER, MY INTERLOCUTOR

1. Bryant Keith Alexander, "Skin Flint (or, the Garbage Man's Kid): A Generative Autobiographical Performance Based on Tami Spry's Tattoo Stories," *Text and Performance Quarterly* 20, no. 1 (2000): 97–114.

2. Victor Turner, *The Anthropology of Performance* (New York: Paj Publications, 1988), 24.

3. Alexander, "Skin Flint (or, the Garbage Man's Kid)," 101.

4. Della Pollock, ed., *Remembering: Oral History Performance* (New York: Palgrave Macmillan, 2005); Della Pollock, ed., *Exceptional Spaces: Essays in Performance and History* (Chapel Hill, N.C.: University of North Carolina Press, 1998).

5. Della Pollock, "Moving Histories: Performance and Oral History," in *The Cambridge Companion to Performance Studies*, ed. Tracy C. Davis (Cambridge: Cambridge University Press, 2008), 124.

6. Urvashi Butalia, *The Other Side of Silence: Voices from the Partition of India* (Durham, N.C.: Duke University Press, 2000), 29.

7. Krishna Pokharel, "Are New Delhi's Trees a British Legacy?" *India Real Time*, 26 January 2012, http://blogs.wsj.com/indiarealtime/2012/01/26/are-new-delhis-trees-a-british-legacy/.

Adey, Peter. "If Mobility Is Everything Then It Is Nothing: Towards a Relational Politics of (Im)mobilities." *Mobilities* 1, no. 1 (2006): 75–94.
———. *Mobility*. London: Routledge, 2010.
Adler, K. H. "Gendering Histories of Homes and Homecomings." *Gender and History* 21, no. 3 (November 1, 2009): 455–64.
Adorno, Theodor W. *Minima Moralia: Reflections from a Damaged Life.* Translated by E. F. Jephcott. New York: Verso Books, 1996.
Agee, James, and Walker Evans. *Let Us Now Praise Famous Men.* Boston: Houghton Mifflin, 1941, 2001.
Ahmed, Sara. "Home and Away Narratives of Migration and Estrangement." *International Journal of Cultural Studies* 2, no. 3 (December 1, 1999): 329–47.
Ahmed, Sara, Claudia Castaneda, Anne-Marie Fortier, and Mimi Sheller. "Introduction: Uprootings/Regroundings: Questions of Home and Migration." In Ahmed, Castaneda, Fortier, and Sheller, *Uprootings/Regroundings*, 1–22.
Ahmed, Sara, Claudia Castaneda, Anne-Marie Fortier, and Mimi Sheller, eds. *Uprootings/Regroundings: Questions of Home and Migration.* New York: Berg, 2003.
Alexander, Bryant Keith. "Performance Ethnography: The Reenacting and Inciting of Culture." In *The Sage Handbook of Qualitative Research*, edited by Norman K. Denzin and Yvonna S. Lincoln, 411–41. 3rd ed. Thousand Oaks, Calif.: Sage, 2005.
———. "Skin Flint (or, the Garbage Man's Kid): A Generative Autobiographical Performance Based on Tami Spry's Tattoo Stories." *Text and Performance Quarterly* 20, no. 1 (2000): 97–114.
Anderson, Kathryn, and Dana C. Jack. "Learning to Listen: Interview Techniques and Analyses." In *Women's Words: The Feminist Practice of Oral History*, edited by Sherna B. Gluck and Daphne Patai. New York: Routledge, 1991.
Anzaldúa, Gloria. *Borderlands/La Frontera: The New Mestiza.* San Francisco: Aunt Lute Books, 1987.

Appadurai, Arjun. *Globalization*. Durham, N.C.: Duke University Press, 2001.

———. *Modernity at Large: Cultural Dimensions of Globalization*. Minneapolis: University of Minnesota Press, 1996.

———. "Place and Voice in Anthropological Theory." *Comparative Studies in Society and History* 30, no. 1 (1988): 3–24.

Appiah, Kwame Anthony. *Cosmopolitanism: Ethics in a World of Strangers*. Issues of Our Time series, edited by Henry Louis Gates Jr. Annotated ed. New York: W. W. Norton, 2006.

Ardener, Shirley. *Perceiving Women*. New York: John Wiley and Sons, 1982.

Azad, Maulana Abdul Kalam. *India Wins Freedom*. Delhi: Orient Longman Ltd., 1988.

Bachelard, Gaston. *The Poetics of Space*. Translated by Maria Jolas. Boston: Beacon Press, 1994.

Bakhtin, Mikhail. M. *Art and Answerability*. Edited by Michael Holquist and Vadim Liapunov. Translated by Vadim Liapunov and Kenneth Brostrom. Austin: University of Texas Press, 1990.

———. *The Dialogic Imagination: Four Essays*. Edited by Michael Holquist and Vadim Liapunov. Translated by Vadim Liapunov and Kenneth Brostrom. Austin: University of Texas Press, 1981.

Bal, Mieke. "Visual Essentialism and the Object of Visual Culture." *Journal of Visual Culture* 2, no. 1 (2003): 5–32.

Basu, Paul, and Simon Coleman. "Introduction: Migrant Worlds, Material Cultures." *Mobilities* 3, no. 3 (2008): 313–30.

Behar, Ruth. "Foreword." In Straight, *Women on the Verge of Home*, ix–xi.

———. *The Vulnerable Observer: Anthropology that Breaks Your Heart*. Boston: Beacon Press, 1996.

Benjamin, Walter. *Charles Baudelaire: A Lyric Poet in the Era of High Capitalism*. London: Verso Classics, 1983.

Bhabha, Homi K. *The Location of Culture*. London: Routledge, 1994.

———. "The World and the Home." *Social Text* 31/32 (1992): 141–53.

Bhalla, Alok. *Partition Dialogues: Memories of a Lost Home*. New York: Oxford University Press, 2006.

Bhasin, Kamla, Ritu Menon, and Nighat Said Khan, eds. *Against All Odds*. New Delhi: Kali for Women, 1994.

Bhattacharjea, Ajit. *Countdown to Partition: The Final Days*. New York: HarperCollins Publishers India, 1997.

Blanchot, Maurice, and Jacques Derrida. *The Instant of My Death/Demeure: Fiction and Testimony*. Translated by Elizabeth Rottenberg. Stanford, Calif.: Stanford University Press, 2000.

Bogue, Ronald. "Apology for Nomadology." *Interventions* 6, no. 2 (2004): 169–79.

Bowlby, Sophie, Susan Gregory, and Linda McKie. "'Doing Home': Patriarchy, Caring, and Space." *Women's Studies International Forum* 20, no. 3 (May 1997): 343–50.

Brah, Avtar. *Cartographies of Diaspora: Contesting Identities*. New York and London: Routledge, 1996.

Braidotti, Rosi. *Nomadic Subjects: Embodiment and Sexual Difference in Contemporary Feminist Theory*. 2nd. ed. New York: Columbia University Press, 2011.

Breckenridge, Carol A., Sheldon Pollock, and Homi K. Bhabha, eds. *Cosmopolitanism*. Durham, N.C.: Duke University Press, 2002.

Brockmeier, Jens. "Autobiographical Time." *Narrative Inquiry* 10, no. 1 (2000): 51–73.

Burke, Kenneth. *A Rhetoric of Motives*. Berkeley and Los Angeles: University of California Press, 1969.

Butalia, Urvashi. *The Other Side of Silence: Voices from the Partition of India*. Durham, N.C.: Duke University Press, 2000.

Carr, David. *Time, Narrative, and History*. Bloomington: Indiana University Press, 1986.

Cacciari, Massimo. "Eupalinos or Architecture." *Oppositions* 21 (1980): 106–16.

Certeau, Michel de, Luce Giard, and Pierre Mayol. *The Practice of Everyday Life*, vol. 2: *Living and Cooking*. Translated by Timothy J. Tomasik. Minneapolis: University of Minnesota Press, 1998.

Chakrabarty, Dipesh. "Reviews: History and Historicality." *Postcolonial Studies* 7, no. 1 (2004): 125–30.

Chawla, Devika. "Arranged Selves: Role, Identity, and Social Transformations among Indian Women in Hindu Arranged Marriages." Ph.D. diss., Purdue University, 2004.

———. "Between Stories and Theories: Embodiments, Disembodiments, and Other Struggles." *Storytelling, Self, Society* 3, no. 1 (2007): 16–30.

———. "Performing Home/Storying Selves: Home and/as Identity in Oral Histories of Refugees in India's Partition." In *Identity Research and Communication*, edited by Nilanjana Bardhan and Mark P. Orbe, 103–18. Lanham, Md.: Lexington Books, 2012.

———. "Poetic Arrivals and Departures: Bodying the Ethnographic Field in Verse." *Forum Qualitative Sozialforschung/Forum: Qualitative Social Research* 9, no. 2 (2008). http://nbn-resolving.de/urn:nbn:de:0114-fqs0802248.

———. "Two Journeys." *Qualitative Inquiry* 9, no. 5 (October 1, 2003): 785–804.

———. "Walk, Walking, Talking Home." In *Handbook of Autoethnography*, edited by Stacy Holman Jones, Tony E. Adams, and Carolyn Ellis, 162–72. Walnut Creek, Calif.: Left Coast Press, 2013.

Chawla, Devika, and Myrdene Anderson. "Stories at the Memory-Imagination Interface." In *Semiotics 2010*, edited by Karen A. Hayworth, Jason Hogue, and Leonard G. Sbrocchi, 229–37. Ottawa, Ontario: Legas Publishing, 2011.

Chopra, P. N., ed. *Experiment with Provincial Authority, 1 January–31 December 1937*. Vol. 1 of *Towards Freedom: Documents on the Movement for Independence in India, 1937–47*, general ed. P. N. Chopra. New Delhi: Indian Council of Historical Research and Oxford University Press, 1985.

Clifford, James. "Introduction: Partial Truths." In *Writing Culture: The Poetics and Politics of Ethnography*, edited by James Clifford and George E. Marcus, 305. Berkeley and Los Angeles: University of California Press, 1986.

———. "Traveling Cultures." In *Cultural Studies*, edited by Lawrence Grossberg, Cary Nelson, and Paula Treichler, 96–117. New York and London: Routledge, 1992.

Conquergood, Dwight. "Performance Studies: Interventions and Radical Research." *The Drama Review* 46, no. 2 (2002): 145–56.

———. "Rethinking Ethnography: Towards a Critical Cultural Politics." *Communication Monographs* 58, no. 2 (1991): 179–94.

Conradson, David, and Deirdre Mckay. "Translocal Subjectivities: Mobility, Connection, Emotion." *Mobilities* 2, no. 2 (2007): 167–74.

Cresswell, Timothy. *On the Move: Mobility in the Modern Western World*. London: Routledge, 2006.

Daniels, Richard. "Scattered Remarks on the Ideology of Home." *Minnesota Review* 58, no. 1 (2002): 187–95.

Das, Veena, Jonathan M. Ellen, and Lori Leonard. "On the Modalities of the Domestic." *Home Cultures* 5, no. 3 (2008): 348–72.

Davidson, Tonya. "The Role of Domestic Architecture in the Structuring of Memory." *Space and Culture* 12, no. 3 (August 1, 2009): 332–42.

Deleuze, Gilles, and Felix Guattari. *Anti-Oedipus: Capitalism and Schizophrenia*. Translated by Robert Hurley, Mark Seem, and Helen Lane. Penguin Classics deluxe edition. New York: Penguin, 2009.

———. *A Thousand Plateaus*. Translated by Brian Massumi. Vol. 2 of *Capitalism and Schizophrenia*. Minneapolis: University of Minnesota Press, 1987.

———. "What is Minor Literature?" In *Kafka: Toward a Minor Literature*, translated by Dana Polan. Minneapolis: University of Minnesota Press, 1986.

Denzin, Norman K. *Interpretive Ethnography: Ethnographic Practices for the Twenty-First Century*. Thousand Oaks, Calif.: Sage, 1997.

Derrida, Jacques. *On Cosmopolitanism and Forgiveness*. New York and London: Routledge, 2001.

Desai, Anita. *Clear Light of Day*. New York: Harper and Row, 1980.

Despres, C. "The Meaning of Home: Literature Review and Directions for Future Research and Theoretical Development." *Journal of Architectural and Planning Research* 8, no. 2 (1991): 96–115.

Didion, Joan. "Why I Write." *New York Times*, 5 December 1976.

Eakin, Paul John. *Fictions in Autobiography: Studies in the Art of Self-Invention*. Princeton, N.J.: Princeton University Press, 1988.

Earth. DVD. Directed by Deepa Mehta. Toronto: Cracking the Earth Films, 1998.

Eire, Carlos. "Home." *Hedgehog Review* 7, no. 3 (2005): 37–45.

Esposito, Scott. "We Are Made of Memories: A Conversation with Mia Couto." *The Paris Review,* 2 May 2013. http://www.theparisreview.org/blog/2013/05 /02/we-are-made-of-memories-a-conversation-with-mia-couto/.

Fortier, Anne-Marie. *Migrant Belongings: Memory, Space, Identity.* New York: Berg Publishers, 2000.

Fox, Richard G. "Introduction: Working in the Present." In *Recapturing Anthropology: Working in the Present,* edited by Richard G. Fox, 1–16. Santa Fe, N.M.: School of Advanced Research Press, 1991.

Francese, Joseph. *Narrating Postmodern Time and Space.* Albany: State University of New York Press, 1997.

Freeman, M. "Charting the Narrative Unconscious: Cultural Memory and the Challenge of Autobiography." *Narrative Inquiry* 12, no. 1 (2002): 193–211.

Freeman, Mark. "Mythical Time, Historical Time, and the Narrative Fabric of the Self." *Narrative Inquiry* 8, no. 1 (1998): 27–50.

Friedan, Betty. *The Feminine Mystique.* New York: W. W. Norton, 1963.

Friedman, Jonathan, and Shalini Randeria. *Worlds on the Move: Globalization, Migration, and Cultural Security.* London and New York: I. B. Tauris, 2004.

Freud, Sigmund. *Civilization and Its Discontents.* Edited and translated by James Strachey. New York: W.W. Norton, 1962.

———. *The Uncanny.* Translated by David McLintock. New York: Penguin Classics, 2003.

Frye, Marilyn. *Politics of Reality.* Trumansburg, N.Y.: Crossing Press, 1983.

Geertz, Clifford. *After the Fact: Two Countries, Four Decades, One Anthropologist.* Cambridge, Mass.: Harvard University Press, 1995.

———. *The Interpretation of Cultures: Selected Essays.* New York: Basic Books, 1973.

———. *Works and Lives: The Anthropologist as Author.* Stanford, Calif.: Stanford University Press, 1988.

George, R. M. "Recycling: Long Routes to and from Domestic Fixes." In *Burning Down the House: Recycling Domesticity,* edited by Rosemary Marangoly George, 1–22. Boulder: Westview Press, 1998.

Gill, Nick, Javier Caletrío, and Victoria Mason. "Introduction: Mobilities and Forced Migration." *Mobilities* 6, no. 3 (2011): 301–16.

Goldman, Anita Haya. "Comparative Identities: Exile in the Writings of Frantz Fanon and W. E. B. Dubois." In *Borders, Boundaries, and Frames,* edited by Mae Henderson, 107–208. New York and London: Routledge, 1994.

Goswami, Manu. *Producing India: From Colonial Economy to National Space.* Chicago: University of Chicago Press, 2004.

Guha, Ranajit. *History at the Limit of World-History.* New York: Columbia University Press, 2002.

———. "The Small Voice of History." In *Subaltern Studies: Writings on South Asian History and Society,* vol. 9, edited by Shahid Amin and Dipesh Chakrabarty, 1–13. New Delhi: Oxford University Press, 1996.

Gupta, Akhil, and James Ferguson, eds. *Anthropological Locations: Boundaries and Grounds of a Field Science.* Berkeley and Los Angeles: University of California Press, 1997.

Gupta, P. S., ed. *1943–44.* Vol. 5 of *Towards Freedom: Documents on the Movement for Independence in India, 1937–47,* general ed. P. N. Chopra. New Delhi: Indian Council of Historical Research and Oxford University Press, 1997.

Hannam, Kevin, Mimi Sheller, and John Urry. "Editorial: Mobilities, Immobilities, and Moorings." *Mobilities* 1, no. 1 (2006): 1–22.

Hansen, Karen Tranberg, ed. *African Encounters with Domesticity.* Newark, N.J.: Rutgers University Press, 1992.

Hardt, Michael, and Antonio Negri. *Empire.* Cambridge, Mass.: Harvard University Press, 2001.

Hasan, Mushirul. *India's Partition: Process, Strategy, and Mobilization.* New Delhi: Oxford University Press, 1993.

———. *Legacy of a Divided Nation: India's Muslims since Independence.* New Delhi: Oxford University Press, 1997.

Heidegger, Martin. "Building, Dwelling, Thinking." In *Poetry, Language, Thought,* translated by Alfred Hofstadter, 143–61. New York: Harper and Row, 1971.

Heynen, Hilde. "Architecture between Modernity and Dwelling: Reflections on Adorno's Aesthetic Theory." *Assemblage* 17 (1992): 78–91.

———. "Modernity and Domesticity: Tensions and Contradictions." In *Negotiating Domesticity: Spatial Productions of Gender in Modern Architecture,* edited by Hilde Heynen and Gülsüm Baydar, 1–29. New York and London: Routledge, 2005.

Hirsch, Marianne. *Family Frames: Photography, Narrative, and Postmemory.* Cambridge, Mass.: Harvard University Press, 1997.

Hoffman, Eva. *Lost in Translation: A Life in a New Language.* New York: Penguin, 1990.

Holquist, Michael. *Dialogism: Bakhtin and His World.* London and New York: Routledge, 1990.

hooks, bell. *Yearning: Race, Gender, and Cultural Politics.* Boston: South End Press, 1999.

Iyer, Pico. *The Global Soul: Jet Lag, Shopping Malls, and the Search for Home.* New York: Vintage, 2001.

Jackson, Michael. *At Home in the World.* Durham, N.C.: Duke University Press, 1995.

Jacobs, Tom. "The Strange Energy of Images, and the Humility of Language." *3 Quarks Daily*, 18 June 2012. http://www.3quarksdaily.com/3quarksdaily /2012/06/the-strange-energies-of-images-and-the-humility-of-language .html#more.

Jalal, Ayesha. *The Sole Spokesman: Jinnah, the Muslim League and the Demand for Pakistan*. Cambridge: Cambridge University Press, 1985.

Jameson, Frederic. *The Seeds of Time*. New York: Columbia University Press, 1996.

Kaplan, Caren. "Deterritorializations: The Rewriting of Home and Exile in Western Feminist Discourse." *Cultural Critique* 6 (1987): 187–98.

———. *Questions of Travel: Postmodern Discourses of Displacement*. Durham, N.C.: Duke University Press, 1996.

Kaul, Suvir, ed. *The Partitions of Memory: The Afterlife of the Division of India*. Bloomington: Indiana University Press, 2001.

Kaur, Ravinder. *Since 1947: Partition Narratives among Punjabi Migrants of Delhi*. New York: Oxford University Press, 2007.

Khamosh Pani. Directed by Sabiha Sumar. 99 min. Karachi: Vidhi Films, 2003.

Khan, Furrukh A. "Speaking Violence: Pakistani Women's Narratives of Partition." In *Gender, Conflict and Migration*, edited by Navneets Chadha Behera, 97–115. New Delhi: Sage, 2006.

Khan, Yasmin. *The Great Partition: The Making of India and Pakistan*. New Haven, Conn.: Yale University Press, 2007.

Knopp, Lisa. "Household Words." *Michigan Quarterly* 40, no. 4 (Fall 2001): 713–25.

Kondo, Dorinne. "The Narrative Production of 'Home,' Community, and Political Identity in Asian American Theater." In Lavie and Swedenburg, *Displacement, Diaspora, and Geographies of Identity*, 97–119.

Kristeva, Julia. *Strangers to Ourselves*. Translated by Leon S. Roudiez. New York: Columbia University Press, 1991.

Kumar, Priya. *Limiting Secularism: The Ethics of Coexistence in Indian Literature and Film*. Minneapolis: University of Minnesota Press, 2008.

Lavie, Smadar, and Ted Swedenburg, eds. *Displacement, Diaspora, and Geographies of Identity*. Durham, N.C.: Duke University Press, 1996.

———. "Introduction: Displacement, Diaspora, and Geographies of Identity." In Lavie and Swedenburg, *Displacement, Diaspora, and Geographies of Identity*, 1–25.

Lewis, Tyson, and Daniel Cho. "Home Is Where the Neurosis Is: A Topography of the Spatial Unconscious." *Cultural Critique* 64, no. 1 (2006): 69–91.

Light, Alison. *Forever England: Femininity, Literature, and Conservatism between the Wars*. London and New York: Routledge, 1991.

Lofgren, Orvar. "Motion and Emotion: Learning to Be a Railway Traveller." *Mobilities* 3, no. 3 (2008): 331–51.

López, Daniel, and Tomás Sánchez-Criado. "Dwelling the Telecare Home Place, Location and Habitability." *Space and Culture* 12, no. 3 (August 1, 2009): 343–58.

Lugones, Maria C., and Joshua M. Price. "Dominant Culture: *El Deseo por un Alma Pobre* (The Desire for an Impoverished Soul.)" In *Multiculturalism from the Margins: Non-Dominant Voices on Difference and Diversity*, edited by Dean A. Harris, 103–28. Westport, Conn.: Bergin and Garvey Press, 1995.

Lukacs, John. "The Bourgeois Interior." *American Scholar* 39 (1970): 616–30.

Madison, D. Soyini. *Critical Ethnography: Method, Ethics, and Performance*. New York: Sage, 2005.

Majumdar, Amit. *Partitions*. New York: Metropolitan Books, 2011.

Mallett, Shelley. "Understanding Home: A Critical Review of the Literature." *Sociological Review* 52, no. 1 (February 27, 2004): 62–89.

Martin, Biddy, and Mohanty, Chandra T. "Feminist Politics: What's Home Got to Do with It?" In *Feminist Studies, Critical Studies*, edited by Teresa de Lauretis, 191–212. Urbana and Chicago: University of Illinois Press, 1986.

Massey, Doreen. *Space, Place, and Gender*. Minneapolis: University of Minnesota Press, 1994.

McCarthy, Mary. "Exiles, Expatriates, and Internal Emigrés." *The Listener* (November 25, 1971): 705–08.

McClintock, Anne. *Imperial Leather: Race, Gender, and Sexuality in the Colonial Contest*. London and New York: Routledge, 1995.

Menon, Ritu, and Kamla Bhasin. *Borders and Boundaries: Women in India's Partition*. 2nd ed. New Delhi: Kali for Women, 1998.

Mezei, Kathy, and Chiara Briganti. "Reading the House: A Literary Perspective." *Signs* 27, no. 3 (2002): 837–46.

Mitchell, W. J. T. *Picture Theory: Essays on Visual and Verbal Representation*. Chicago: University of Chicago Press, 1995.

Minh-ha, Trinh T. *Woman, Native, Other: Writing Postcoloniality and Feminism*. Bloomington: Indiana University Press, 1989.

Ministry of Home Affairs, Government of India. Census of India, 2011. http://censusindia.gov.in/.

Mukherjee, Prabhati. *Hindu Women: Normative Models*. Calcutta: Orient Longman Ltd., 1994.

Myerhoff, Barbara. *Number Our Days: A Triumph of Continuity and Culture among Jewish Old People in an Urban Ghetto*. New York: Simon and Schuster, 1978.

Narayan, Kirin. "How Native Is the 'Native' Anthropologist?" *American Anthropologist* 95, no. 3 (1993).

———. *Storytellers, Saints, and Scoundrels: Folk Narrative in Hindu Religious Teaching*. Philadelphia: University of Pennsylvania Press, 1989.

Noyes, John. "Nomadism, Nomadology, Postcolonialism: By Way of Introduction." *Interventions* 6, no. 2 (2004): 159–68.

Oakley, Ann. *Housewife*. London: Allen Lane, 1974.

Pallasmaa, Juhani. *Architecture in Miniature: Juhani Pallasmaa Finland*. Helsinki: Museum of Finnish Architecture, 1991.

Pandey, Gyanendra. *Remembering Partition: Violence, Nationalism and History in India*. Cambridge: Cambridge University Press, 2002.

Philips, C. H., and M. D. Wainwright, eds. *The Partition of India: Policies and Perspectives*. London: Allen and Unwin, 1970.

Pinjar. Directed by Chander Prakash Dwivedi. 188 min. Mumbai: Lucky Star Entertainment, 2003.

Pokharel, Krishna. "Are New Delhi's Trees a British Legacy?" *India Real Time*, 26 January 2012. http://blogs.wsj.com/indiarealtime/2012/01/26/are-new-delhis-trees-a-british-legacy/.

Pollock, Della, ed. *Exceptional Spaces: Essays in Performance and History*. Chapel Hill: University of North Carolina Press, 1998.

———. "Moving Histories: Performance and Oral History." In *The Cambridge Companion to Performance Studies*, edited by Tracy C. Davis, 120–35. Cambridge: Cambridge University Press, 2008.

———. *Remembering: Oral History Performance*. New York: Palgrave Macmillan, 2005.

Porteous, John Douglas, and Sandra Eileen Smith. *Domicide: The Global Destruction of Home*. Montreal: McGill-Queen's University Press, 2001.

Prakash, Gyan, ed. *After Colonialism: Imperial Histories and Postcolonial Displacements*. Princeton, N.J.: Princeton University Press, 1995.

Price, Joshua M. "The Apotheosis of Home and the Maintenance of Spaces of Violence." *Hypathia* 17, no. 4 (2002): 39–70.

Rao, H. Bhaskar. *The Story of Rehabilitation*. Delhi: Department of Rehabilitation, 1967.

Rich, Adrienne. "The Tourist and the Town." In *The Fact of a Door Frame*, 368. New York: W. W. Norton, 2002.

Ricoeur, Paul. *Oneself as Another*. Translated by Kathleen Blamey. Chicago and London: University of Chicago Press, 1992.

Rubenstein, Roberta. *Home Matters: Longing and Belonging, Nostalgia and Mourning in Women's Fiction*. New York: Palgrave Macmillan, 2001.

Rushdie, Salman. *Midnight's Children: A Novel*. New York: Knopf, 1980.

Rybczynski, Witold. *Home: A Short History of an Idea*. New York: Penguin, 1986.

Rykwert, Joseph. "House and Home." *Social Research* 58, no. 1 (1991): 51–62.

Said, Edward. *Orientalism*. New York: Vintage, 1979.

———. "Reflections on Exile." *Granta 13: After the Revolution* (1984): 159–72.

Sarkar, Sumit. *Modern India, 1885–1947*. Madras: Macmillan India Ltd., 1983.

Scarry, Elaine. *The Body in Pain: The Making and Unmaking of the World*. New York: Oxford University Press, 1985.

Sebeok, Thomas A. *Global Semiotics*. Bloomington: Indiana University Press, 2001.

Shafak, Elif. "Nomad." In *The Novelist's Lexicon: Writers on the Words that Define Their Work*, edited by Villa Gillet/*Le Monde*, 74–76. New York: Columbia University Press, 2010.

Sheller, Mimi, and John Urry. "The New Mobilities Paradigm." *Environment and Planning A: Society and Space* 38, no. 2 (2006): 207–26.

Sibley, David, *Geographies of Exclusion: Society and Difference in the West*. London: Routledge, 1995.

Sidhwa, Bapsi. *Cracking India: A Novel*. Minneapolis, Minn.: Milkweed Editions, 1991.

———. *Ice Candy Man*. London: Heinemann, 1988; New Delhi: Penguin, 1989.

Singh, Khushwant. *Train to Pakistan*. Bombay: India Book House, 1956; New York: Grove Press, 1956.

———. *Train to Pakistan*. With photographs by Margaret Bourke-White. 50th anniversary edition. Delhi: Roli Books, 2006.

Sinha-Kerkhoff, Kathinka. "Partition, Memory and Multiple Identities in the Champaran District of Bihar, India." In *The Memory of Catastrophe*, edited by Peter Gray and Kendrick Oliver, 147–57. Manchester: Manchester University Press, 2004.

Smith, Sidonie, and Julia Watson. *Reading Autobiography: A Guide for Interpreting Life Narratives*. Minneapolis: University of Minnesota Press, 2001.

Solnit, Rebecca. *A Field Guide to Getting Lost*. New York: Penguin, 2005.

———. *Wanderlust: A History of Walking*. New York: Penguin Books, 2000.

Somerville, P. "The Social Construction of Home." *Journal of Architectural and Planning Research* 14, no. 3 (1997): 226–45.

Spelman, Elizabeth V. "Repair and the Scaffold of Memory." In *What Is a City? Rethinking the Urban after Hurricane Katrina*, edited by Rob Shields and Phil Steinberg, 140–53. Athens: University of Georgia Press, 2008.

Spivak, Gayatri Chakravorty. "Can the Subaltern Speak?" In *Marxism and the Interpretation of Culture*, edited by Cary Nelson and Lawrence Grossberg, 271–313. Urbana and Chicago: University of Illinois Press, 1988.

———. "Subaltern Studies: Deconstructing Historiography." In *Deconstruction: Critical Concepts in Literary and Cultural Studies*, edited by Jonathan D. Culler, 4:220–44. London: Routledge, 2003.

Stewart, Kathleen. "Atmospheric Attunements." *Environment and Planning D: Society and Space* 29, no. 3 (2010): 445–53.

———. *Ordinary Affects*. Durham, N.C.: Duke University Press, 2007.

———. *A Space on the Side of the Road*. Princeton, N.J.: Princeton University Press, 1996.

Straight, Bilinda, ed. *Women on the Verge of Home*. Albany: State University of New York Press, 2005.

Talbot, Ian, and Darshan Singh Tatla, eds. *Epicentre of Violence: Partition Voices and Memories from Amritsar.* New Delhi: Orient Longman Ltd., 2006.

Tan, Tai Yong, and Gyanesh Kudaiysa. *The Aftermath of Partition in South Asia.* London and New York: Routledge, 2000.

Taussig, Michael. *I Swear I Saw This: Drawings in Fieldwork Notebooks, Namely My Own.* Chicago: University of Chicago Press, 2011.

Taylor, Julie. *Paper Tangos.* Durham, N.C.: Duke University Press, 1998.

Tedlock, Dennis, and Bruce Mannheim. "Introduction." In *The Dialogic Emergence of Culture,* edited by Dennis Tedlock and Bruce Mannheim, 1–32. Bloomington: University of Illinois Press, 1995.

Terkenli, Theano S. "Home as a Region." *Geographical Review* 85, no. 3 (1995): 324–34.

Thoreau, Henry D. *Walking.* New York: Harper One, 1994.

Trouillot, M. "Anthropology and the Savage Slot: The Poetics and Politics of Otherness." In Fox, *Recapturing Anthropology,* 17–44.

Tuan, Yi-Fu. *Cosmos and Hearth: A Cosmopolite's View.* Minneapolis: University of Minnesota Press, 1996.

Uberoi, Patricia, ed. *Social Reform, Sexuality, and the State.* Contributions to Indian Sociology: Occasional Studies, 7. New Delhi: Sage, 1996.

Urry, John. *Global Complexity.* Cambridge: Polity, 2003.

Van Wyck, Peter C. *Highway of the Atom.* Montreal and Kingston: McGill-Queen's University Press, 2010.

Veer, Peter van der. "Cosmopolitan Options." In *Worlds on the Move: Globalization, Migration, and Cultural Security,* edited by Jonathan Friedman and Shalini Randeria, 167–78. London: I. B. Tauris, 2004.

Vertovec, Steven, and Robin Cohen, eds. *Conceiving Cosmopolitanism: Theory, Context, and Practice.* New York: Oxford University Press, 2003.

Vignes, Danielle Sears. "Hang It Out to Dry: A Performance Script." *Text and Performance Quarterly* 28, no. 3 (2008): 351–65.

———. "'Hang It Out to Dry': Performing Ethnography, Cultural Memory, and Hurricane Katrina in Chalmette, Louisiana." *Text and Performance Quarterly* 28, no. 3 (2008): 344–50.

Visweswaran, Kamala. *Fictions of Feminist Ethnography.* Minneapolis: University of Minnesota Press, 1994.

Walsh, Katie. "British Expatriate Belongings: Mobile Homes and Transnational Homing." *Home Cultures* 3, no. 2 (2006): 123–44.

Wardhaugh, Julia. "The Unaccommodated Woman: Home, Homelessness, and Identity." *Sociological Review* 47, no. 1 (1999): 91–109.

Winterson, Jeanette. *Lighthousekeeping.* New York: Harcourt Books, 2005.

Wolf, Margery. *A Thrice-Told Tale: Feminism, Postmodernism, and Ethnographic Responsibility.* Stanford, Calif.: Stanford University Press, 1992.

Wu, Kuang-Ming. "The Other Is My Hell; The Other Is My Home." *Human Studies* 16, no. 1 (1993): 193–202.

Zamindar, Vazira Fazila-Yacoobali. *The Long Partition and the Making of Modern South Asia: Refugees, Boundaries, Histories.* New York: Columbia University Press, 2007.

Zirbel, Katherine E. "My Shafiqa: Concerning the Travels and Transgressions of a Southern Egyptian Woman." In *Women on the Verge of Home*, edited by Bilinda Straight, 71–88. Albany: State University of New York Press, 2005.